D0207904

Identities in Talk

Identities in Talk

edited by

Charles Antaki and Sue Widdicombe

SAGE Publications
London • Thousand Oaks • New Delhi

First published 1998

SAGE Publications Ltd
6 Bonhill Street
London EC2A 4PU

SAGE Publications Inc.
2455 Teller Road
Thousand Oaks, California 91320

SAGE Publications India Pvt Ltd
32, M-Block Market
Greater Kailash – I
New Delhi 110 048

British Library Cataloguing in Publication data

A catalogue record for this book is available
from the British Library

ISBN 0 7619 5060 5
ISBN 0 7619 5061 3 (pbk)

Library of Congress catalog card number 98–060740

Typeset by Mayhew Typesetting, Rhayader, Powys
Printed in Great Britain by Redwood Books, Trowbridge, Wiltshire

Contents

Contributors

Charles Antaki is at the Department of Social Sciences, Loughborough University, England. Email: c.antaki@lboro.ac.uk

Colin Clark is at the Surrey European Management School, Surrey University, England. Email: C.S.Clark@surrey.ac.uk

Dennis Day is at the Centre for Cultural Contact and International Migration (RIM), Göteborg University, Sweden. Email: dennis@ios.chalmers.se

Robert Dingwall is at the Department of Sociology and Social Policy, Nottingham University, England. Email: robert.dingwall@nottingham.ac.uk

Anne Dunnett is at the Moray House Institute, Heriot-Watt University, Edinburgh, Scotland.

Derek Edwards is at the Department of Social Sciences, Loughborough University, England. Email: D.Edwards@lboro.ac.uk

David Greatbatch is at the Department of Sociology and Social Policy, Nottingham University, England. Email: david.greatbatch@nottingham.ac.uk

Stephen Hester is at the School of Sociology and Social Policy, University of Wales, Bangor, Wales. Email: s.k.hester@bangor.ac.uk

Andy McKinlay is at the Department of Psychology, University of Edinburgh, Scotland. Email: MCKINLAY@afbl.ssc.ed.ac.uk

Isabella Paoletti is at the Social and Economic Research Department, INRCA, Ancona, Italy. Email: IPAOLETT@unipg.it

Sue Widdicombe is at the Department of Psychology, University of Edinburgh, Scotland. Email: s.widdicombe@ed.ac.uk

Robin Wooffitt is at the Department of Sociology, University of Surrey, England. Email: rcw@soc.surrey.ac.uk

Don H. Zimmerman is at the Department of Sociology, University of California, Santa Barbara, USA. Email: dzimmerman@descartes.ucsb.edu

Transcription Notation

The transcription symbols used in this book are an attempt to capture something of the sound of the talk as it was originally spoken. There is some variety among contributors, both in the fine-grainedness of their transcription, and in the notation symbols they use. All symbols, however, derive from those developed by Gail Jefferson (see Atkinson and Heritage, 1984: ix–xvi).

(.)	The shortest hearable pause, less than about 0.2 of a second
(..) (...)	Approximately timed pauses: half a second and one second respectively
(0.3) (2 secs)	Examples of exactly timed pauses
˙hh, hh	Speaker's in-breath and out-breath respectively
hehh, hahh	Laughter syllables with some attempt to capture 'colour'
wo(h)rd	(h) denotes 'laughter' within words
((sniff))	A description enclosed in double brackets indicates a non-speech sound
cu-	A dash denotes a sharp cut-off of a prior word or sound
lo:ng	Colons show that the speaker has stretched the preceding letter or sound. The more colons the greater the extent of the stretching
(word)	Material within brackets represents the transcriber's guess at an unclear part of the tape
(syll syll)	Unclear speech rendered as approximations to number of syllables
( )	Unclear speech or noise to which no approximation is made
run=	'Equals' signs link material that runs on
=on	
↑word	Arrows indicate the onset of a rising or falling intona-
↓word	tional shift
?	Indicates a rising tone
.	Indicates a 'natural' ending
,	Indicates a comma-like pause
under	Underlining indicates emphasis
CAPITALS	Capital letters indicate speech noticeably louder than that surrounding it
°soft°	Degree signs indicate speech spoken noticeably more quietly than the surrounding talk. Double degree signs indicate greater softness

>fast<	'Greater than' and 'less than' signs indicate that the talk
<slow>	they encompass was produced noticeably quicker or slower than the surrounding talk
over⌈lap	Square brackets between adjacent lines of concurrent
⌊overlap	speech denote the start of overlapping talk
→	Side arrow indicates point of special interest in the extract, addressed in the text
[...]	Indicates that material has been left out of the extract
[high pitch]	Material in square brackets indicates transcriber's commentary

1 Identity as an Achievement and as a Tool

Charles Antaki and Sue Widdicombe

This book is about identity, of course, but browsing readers who flip through its pages might wonder at the presence of so many lines of transcribed talk, often laced around with a filigree of curious symbols. What has talk got to offer us, they will ask, in trying to understand identity? Are the contributors recommending that we ask people to tell us who they are, and treat them as informants about what identities they have, and about what those identities lead them to think and do? No, it is not that. The contributors to this book do not want to treat people as informants, nor do they want to interpret what people say, still less speculate on the hidden forces that make them say it. Rather, they want to see how identity is something that is *used* in talk: something that is part and parcel of the routines of everyday life, brought off in the fine detail of everyday interaction.

An Ethnomethodological and Conversation Analytic Perspective on Identity

The chapters of the book are informed by the general ethnomethodological spirit of treating social life as the business that people conduct with each other, displayed in their everyday practices. We use the permissive phrase 'ethnomethodological spirit' (and the rather vague term 'everyday practices') because to do so tolerantly allows common ground in people's increasingly various recommendations as to just how to go about doing this sort of analysis. What is common to all the contributors to this book, at least, is the early ethnomethodology of Harold Garfinkel (1967) – to distil it brutally, his notion that social life is a continuous display of people's local understandings of what is going on – and its conversation analytic crystallization in Harvey Sacks's insight that people accomplish such local understanding by elegantly exploiting the features of ordinary talk. Every contributor takes those pioneers' anti-mentalist and anti-cognitivist view of how analysis should proceed, and what analysis will reveal. Identity, in this view, and to use an ethnomethodological contrast, ought not be treated as an explanatory 'resource' that we as analysts haul with us to a scene where people are interacting, but as a 'topic' that requires investigation and sweat once we get there.

Identities in Practice

Once we are at a scene, the ethnomethodological argument runs, we shall see a person's identity as his or her display of, or ascription to, membership of some feature-rich category. Analysis starts when one realizes that any individual can, of course, sensibly be described under a multitude of categories. You might say that that is hardly a good point of departure, since, obviously, most possible descriptions of a person simply are not true (neither of the book's editors is Portuguese, very fat, has more than two lungs, and so on). But as the ethnographer-turned-conversation-analyst Michael Moerman put it, 'the "truth" or "objective correctness" of an identification is never sufficient to explain its use' (1974: 61; first published 1968). Something else – many other things – comes into play.

The interest for analysts is to see which of those identifications folk actually use, what features those identifications seem to carry, and to what end they are put. The ethnomethodological spirit is to take it that the identity category, the characteristics it affords, and what consequences follow, are all knowable to the analyst only through the understandings displayed by the interactants themselves. Membership of a category is ascribed (and rejected), avowed (and disavowed), displayed (and ignored) in local places and at certain times, and it does these things as part of the interactional work that constitutes people's lives. In other words, the contributors to this book take it not that people passively or latently have this or that identity which then causes feelings and actions, but that they work up and work to this or that identity, for themselves and others, there and then, either as an end in itself or towards some other end.

The earliest explicit appearance of this programme is in Harvey Sacks's very early work on the fundamental importance of people's use of categories – of which an 'identity' category is a peculiarly protean sort – as a practical matter of transacting their business with the world. His lectures in the mid-1960s to early 1970s (as reproduced in Sacks, 1992) returned time and time again to the way people organized their world into categories, and used those categories – and the features that they implied – to conduct their daily business. Once Sacks had put these notions in the air, ethnomethodologists and conversation analysts went out to see how people use categorical work (which might be ascription, display, hinting, leakage and so on), with no commitment to any position on whether someone truly 'had' this or that identity category, or what 'having' that identity made them do or feel.

Five General Principles

All this is still rather up in the air, and wants bringing down to earth. Let us make a list of five things, gathered up from the literature since Sacks, which seem to be central to an ethnomethodological, and more specifically a conversation analytic, attitude to analysing identity. The list looks like this (and we shall explain the more abstruse-sounding expressions in a moment):

- for a person to 'have an identity' – whether he or she is the person speaking, being spoken to, or being spoken about – is to be cast into a *category with associated characteristics or features*;
- such casting is *indexical and occasioned*;
- it *makes relevant* the identity to the interactional business going on;
- the force of 'having an identity' is in its *consequentiality* in the inter- action; and
- all this is visible in people's exploitation of the *structures of conver- sation*.

We do not want to say that every analyst will favour all five principles equally, and all of the time. There is variety in, and sometimes outright warfare over, what can reasonably be called ethnomethodology or conver- sation analysis (see, for example, Graham Watson's (1992) admirably non- partisan overview); but, trying to be ecumenical, we do want to say that getting a sense of how these five principles are used is to get a good flavour of the general ethnomethodological analytic attitude (as it is expressed, in varying strengths, by the contributions to this book). Now let us see if we can make a bit more sense of the unfamiliar terms above.

Categories with associated characteristics or features   Certainly all contributors to the book would want to respect Sacks's foundational work on membership categorization devices. Sacks made a great deal of what he saw as the absolute centrality, in human affairs, of people's use of language to arrange and rearrange the objects of the world into *collections* of things. These collections ('membership categorization devices') – 'the family', say, or 'middle-class occupations' – would order together what would otherwise be disparate objects, or objects knowable under some other description. So casting person A, B, C and D as (say) 'cabin crew' unites them into a team and imposes on them a range of features which come along with that team- label (in Sacks's term, they would now have 'category-bound features'). They would now be flight attendant, bursar, first-class steward and so on, with cabin-crew attributes of being polite, knowledgeable about aircraft safety, well-travelled, and so on. But if you cast the very same people as 'white-collar union members', you dissolve any such job-specific implica- tions and replace them with what is conventionally knowable about people who have joined a staff association; if you cast them as 'British', you allow them to pass through British immigration checks, without caring about whether they are in a union or not, and so on. A person, then, can be a member of an infinity of categories, and each category will imply that she or he has this or that range of characteristics. There is an important corollary to this: not only do categories imply features, but features imply categories. That is to say, someone who displays, or can be attributed with a certain set of features, is treatable as a member of the category with which those features are conventionally associated. If you look and act a certain way, you might get taken to be a flight attendant; if you have certain legal documents with certain appropriate authorizations, you can be taken to be British.

Indexicality and occasionedness   The notion here, borrowed from linguistics, is that there is a class of expressions which make different sense in different places and times – 'here', 'I', 'this', and so on. What Sacks wanted to do with it was to extend its use to expressions of category membership – to say that they make different sense according to the company they keep. It is hard, he argues, to read a report that, say, 'a thousand teenagers died in traffic accidents last year' without taking it that the people referred to 'are' teenagers, even that they died in that way *because* they were teenagers, that teenager was the relevant category under which to describe them in those circumstances (as opposed, say, to 'cyclists', 'pedestrians', and so on, or – though this is tellingly hard to see – 'people of various heights' or 'people who tend to watch a lot of television' and other characteristics made irrelevant by the indexical context). Once we have that under our belt, we see also what he means by occasionedness: that any utterance (and its constituent parts) comes up indexically, in a here and now, and is to be understood so. In other words, a good part of the meaning of an utterance (including, of course, one that ascribes or displays an identity) is to be found in the occasion of its production – in the local state of affairs that was operative at that exact moment of interactional time. It might be, for example, that the classification of person Z as a 'teenager' is occasioned by the local environment of the interaction being a survey count of road-accident victims, with the participants looking for age information as they work their way through a series of dossiers full of information of all kinds.

Making relevant and orienting to   It is probably true to say that a majority of the contributors would endorse some form of Schegloff's (1991) powerful development of the Sacksian case that one should take for analysis only those categories that people make relevant (or orient to) and which are procedurally consequential in their interactions. Let us just unpack that a little. *Make relevant* and *orient to* are two bits of conversation analytic terminology which look rather off-putting, but their oddity makes memorable the notion that identity work is in the hands of the participants, not us. It is they who propose that such-and-such an identity is at hand, under discussion, obvious, lurking or 'relevant to' the action in whatever other way. It is they who 'orient to' something as live or operative, without necessarily naming it out loud – thus, I can 'orient to' what you just said as if it were a question, or as a statement, or as a joke, and so on; I can 'orient to' you as my father, an ex-public schoolboy, a successful business-man, and so on.

Procedural consequentiality   That too looks rather fearsome, but again its very awkwardness is a useful signal that something is being marked off from more comfortably literal ways of describing who people 'are'. Schegloff (1992) makes explicit (and vivid) the recommendation that we should take identities for analysis only when they seem to have some visible effect on how the interaction pans out. Put this together with relevance, and what you have is the discipline of holding off from saying that such and such a person is doing whatever it is he or she is doing because he or she is this or that supposed identity. It is, for example, holding off from saying 'this person is a quantity surveyor' until and unless there is some evidence in the interaction that his or her behaviour was, in fact, conse-quential *as* the behaviour of a quantity surveyor. It might well not be, if the scene we are looking in on is treated by the participants as being something where such information is entirely irrelevant: a religious service, say, or a hobbyists' weekend. It is as well to realize the radicality of this move, as critics have pointed out and against which Schegloff defends himself (in, for example, Schegloff, 1997): it does mean holding off from using all sorts of identities which one might want to use in, say, a political or cultural frame of analysis (the fact that this participant is a man, or a Jew, or Dutch, and so on) until and unless such an identity is visibly consequential in what happens.

Conversational structures   Once you are in another person's sensory orbit, anything either of you does is up for interpretation as being meaningful for the other. What you do is a signal. But it is not like a lighthouse beacon, which simply shines at a given brightness and revolves at a given speed. Your demeanour – your talk – changes to fit something the other person does, and vice versa. The things which determine whether something fits, Sacks spotted, are tremendously powerful structural regularities in the way that talk is organized. A summons calls up a response, a question wants an answer, and so on. In his words, '"Conversation" is a series of *invariably relevant* parts' (Sacks, 1992, Vol. I: 308; emphasis added). If you like, the point that Sacks is making is that these regularities hold sway whether the participants like it or not. Around a bridge table, once North has made a bid, East must follow, and what East says is understandable only given what North has just said. North's bid 'makes relevant' East's bid in a regular conversational structure that all the players play to. Indeed, once a bid has been made (or a question has been asked, a summons issued, and so on, to make the more general point), the regularity of what happens next is so powerful – so normative – that it is impossible for East *not* to declare a position, in some way or another. Even a grunt will be taken to mean something (presumably a rather ungracious 'No bid').

The point of this for our purposes is that such structures are generally there and available for anyone who speaks the language. Conversation is made up of regular structures of the bid-making and the question–answer sort (and those of overlap, interruption, repair, topic shift and the many more, both simple and complex, that you will meet in the body of the chapters of the book), all of which do some business or other. Indeed, conversation is so thick with such things that many people now follow Schegloff's (1987) very useful recommendation and try to say 'talk-in-interaction' rather than 'conversation', if only to avoid the casual sense of talk as vague and inconsequential. The structures of talk-in-interaction are powerfully usable by anyone, at any time, so as to set a scene for the next turn at talk. Indeed they *must* be used; it is not the case that talk-in-interaction is a stream of largely inert gas with only the occasional surprise to wake people up. Every turn at talk is part of some structure, plays against some sort of expectation, and in its turn will set up something for the next speaker to be alive to.

A Worked Example

Let us try to illustrate the application of these five principles. Consider this strip of talk, and what Schenkein, in a classic of the conversation analysis (CA) literature on identity (Schenkein, 1978), has to say about it:

(1) (From Schenkein, 1978: 60. [Transcription notation for this, and all the extracts in the book, can be found on pp. viii–ix.])

		[. . .]
67	→ Pete:	I gather you also wanna try t'sell me
68		some insurance.
69		(2.0)
70	Alan:	Now- that doesn't sound like a bad
71		idea- no, ih- it would be nice. But
72		what I'd like to do,
73		(3.0)
74	Alan:	Uhh, do you have any insurance.

Pete's utterance at line 67 is, according to Schenkein, an identity-rich characterization of Alan: it is an utterance which 'draws upon a generally available description of the interests and practices of an abstract identity category like "salesmen" generally' (Schenkein, 1978: 63.) This is a nice illustration of the very pervasive notion, originating with Sacks and visible in all the chapters in this book, that we mentioned above – that things can be shepherded together into collections, or *categories*, and that once there they take on the *features associated with those categories*. Here, that Pete is pigeonholing Alan as one of that set of people who are 'salesmen'. It is worth labouring the point that it is not we analysts who are unilaterally saying either that 'Alan is a salesman' nor even that 'Pete thinks that Alan is a salesman' – it is a matter of us recognizing that Pete is *treating* Alan as a salesman, that Pete is 'making relevant' (or 'orienting to') this identity for Alan and for the interaction. The importance of the expression 'treats Alan as' (over 'thinks Alan is'), let alone the unilateral 'Alan is' is that it keeps our eyes open to the possibility that what Pete is doing is not simply showing us what he thinks (whatever that means), but that his utterance might be designed actually to do something.

Now, what has gone on in the episode so far that will help us see what it might be that this making-relevant might be doing? To answer that is to show how Pete's utterance is 'occasioned' – that is to say, fostered by the local business at hand. We pull back a little and see how the just-previous lines went:

(2)   (From Schenkein, 1978: 59–60; a stretch just before extract (1) above.)

```
50        Alan:       Mm hmm. It just tells you some of the
51                    basic concepts. And, I give a memobook,
52     →             out. And also let me put my magic card
53     →             innit.
54     → Pete:       Your magic card?
55     → Alan:       My magic card, this makes the whole
56                    thing a s- sort of a kaleida-scopic
57                    experience – not really it's just,
58                    y'know, uh two dimensional a(hh)c-
59                    tually hehh hehh hehh hehh hehh heh ih- it
60                    all depends on y'know, what you've
61                    been doing right before you, look at
62                    the card I guess if it's two dimen-
63                    sional.
64        Pete:       Righ(h)t
65                    (2.0)
66        Alan:       Uhh,
67        Pete:       I gather you also wanna try t'sell me some insurance
```

Pete eventually gets to the familiar line (67) about Alan, but first look at the business of the 'magic card', because this is an excellent illustration of the principle that *conversational regularities* are wonderfully subtle resources to be exploited for identity work. Schenkein shows how Pete (in line 54) treats what Alan says as a puzzle, that is to say, something that in the circumstances wants some account. Indeed, Schenkein spots this as an example of a very general conversational sequence, which he calls the 'puzzle-pass-solution' sequence. You can see it in any stretch of talk where the first speaker's turn includes something which the second speaker treats as a puzzle, obliging the first speaker to make intelligible what they originally said.

Alan might have used the sequence by putting the curious reference to a 'magic card' into the conversation – as a 'puzzle' – so as to elicit just that 'pass' reaction from Pete ('your magic card?'), because that allows Alan to come up – in the 'solution' – with a turn's worth of further material. Alan then can introduce new material, and that can be at any distance he likes from the ostensible business at hand. Now look at what Alan does come up with as an explanation of what is magical about this card, and think of it in terms of category-bound activities: it is quite possible to read his laughing reference to 'what you've been doing right before' as implying doing something about which one could take a jocular attitude, possibly because it is in some way naughty, and which, more certainly, is about doing something which interferes with your perceptual abilities such that you get a 'kaleidoscopic experience'. It is surely not too interpretative to see this as a rather conspiratorial reference to taking drugs. If so, and if Pete ratified it, it would put Alan on a very different identity in the interaction: not now a salesman, or, at least, not a 'straight' salesman, but one who can happily and conspiratorially own up to the pleasures of taking perception-altering drugs. In parenthesis, of course, this is the sort of identity that Alan on other occasions might well want *not* to promote: a reminder that identity displays are *indexical* in the sense that they mean different things at different times and places, and that admission to taking drugs will do Alan different business in a courtroom than here. Here the identity it promotes – that is to say, the category label that seems to be implied by these features – is something like 'fellow recreational drug user', which suggests a social, non-business link with Pete and disarms the possible 'default' identity of someone who hands out (back in lines 51–2) 'memobooks' about insurance – namely, of course, insurance salesmen.

That is the environment which *occasions* Pete saying what he says in line 67. See how it gives the lie to the notion that he is merely 'saying what he thinks': to bring up Alan's persona as a salesman just *now*, when Alan has floated the alternative of being a fellow recreational drug user, is sharply to bring things back to business, and for Pete to resist the blandishments of someone who is only, after all, there to 'try t'sell me some insurance'.

What of *procedural consequentiality*? The opening words of Schenkein's original article are these: 'The transcript below represents the opening few moments of an eventually lengthy conversation between a life insurance salesman and a prospective client' (1978: 57). Now you could say that this was exactly what Schegloff is warning against, since it seems to be an analyst's gloss on who these people are, rather than see what is consequential in the data. But we quickly see that it is just a shorthand – that Schenkein is going to show us, in the body of the data, just how it is that these two people work up these identities (and others) for themselves, with visible effects in the way the interaction goes. Indeed, we have seen plenty of that already. But here is one more example.

Pete has, in line 67, made visible his understanding that Alan is to be treated as a salesman. See how it proves consequential in the way Alan reacts to it in lines 70–4:

(3)   Repeat of extract (1)

```
67        Pete:        I gather you also wanna try t'sell me
68                     some insurance.
69                     (2.0)
70     → Alan:        Now- that doesn't sound like a bad
71     →              idea- no, ih- it would be nice. But
72     →              what I'd like to do,
73     →              (3.0)
74     →              Uhh, do you have any insurance.
```

One might simply say that Alan doesn't reject the ascription of insurance salesman outright, but that would be to gloss some much more subtle work that his talk manages to do. Rather than say 'yes, that is my business', he treats Pete as having made the *novel suggestion* that Alan sell insurance (that would be a good idea, he teases). This has the elegant effect of managing to turn Pete's rejection of the alternative identity Alan had just been promoting into an affirmation of it. It cannot be a 'not a bad idea' for an *insurance salesman* to try to sell insurance, but it might be for someone who was not. You do not say 'it wouldn't be a bad idea to have a cup of tea' while the cup is at your lips. In other words, Alan treats what Pete says as consequential: by dealing neatly with it as a joke, he orients to it as a threat to the alternative identity that it is in his interest to promote. Once the threat is defused, he moves smoothly into a more serious register ('But what I'd like to do . . .') and ends up asking exactly the sort of question that displays an interest in Pete's current insurance arrangements, which is, of course, a classic ingredient in the salesman's make-up.

The Upcoming Chapters

Those five principles – telegraphically: category name and features; indexicality; relevance; consequentiality; use of conversational regularities – capture a good part of the sort of analytic sentiments that you will come across in this book. But before we turn to introducing the upcoming chapters, it is worth just going back to the top of the list to pick over something that troubles ethnomethodologists and conversation analysts, or, it might be better said, is used by friendly critics to encourage them to be troubled. The worry is over categories and their features. The critic will say: how do you know that such-and-such a thing (a word, an expression, an adjective that someone in the interaction has used) is indeed an identity category, or the associated characteristic of an identity category? How do you know that 'being interested in whether someone already has insurance' is indeed a classical feature of the category 'salesman', as we blithely asserted in the paragraph above?

Some analysts would argue that they know it is because they are members of the culture that produces the talk, and to try to ignore that would be as useless as it would be counterproductive. They are entirely happy to work with the margin of cultural familiarity that Sacks allowed himself in a good deal of his early writing, and, in analysing identity, to call upon what they know is conventionally associated with membership of various categories, and to distinguish among what ordinary folk treat as different categories with different sorts of features. Such work very explicitly bases itself on Sacks's foundational work on categories, membership categorization devices and category-bound attributes, and indeed is sometimes referred to as 'membership categorization analysis' (e.g., Eglin and Hester, 1992; Hester and Eglin, 1997a). We shall return to it below, when we come to introducing the chapters of Part III.

But some analysts would fight shy of that. Rather than deal in the structural properties of various sorts of category, they prefer to cleave strictly to the sort of analysis exemplified by Schegloff's (1991) recommendations (as we described above) to abide only by what is patent in the development of the interaction. Of course, analysts cannot switch off their cultural knowledge, just as they cannot switch off their ability to speak the language spoken by the people they are studying. They might even go out and explicitly learn the language and the culture, as Moerman (1988) does, by carefully set-out-able ethnography. But what they will want to be absolutely clear about is that if they *do* see something culturally familiar in the data, that is an at-first, preliminary, in-principle sighting, and they would be obliged to say how it is there for the participants. Such analysts might want to work with what their cultural competence identifies roughly as this or that category, but then they will want to see how that category gets used by the participants themselves. Schenkein (1978) is happy to approach Pete and Alan's talk with what he knows about their (and his) culture – that, in America in the late 1970s (and so on), the category 'salesman' has this or that feature – but he is concerned to show us how that was patent in their talk, and how both parties batted those identities around.

That is exactly the point of departure for all the chapters in Part I. Derek Edwards in Chapter 2 wants to work with categories in the Sacksian sense, and show the business that is transacted with them by participants: how some category-attribute of a person is, in the phrase that Edwards uses in his title, 'the relevant thing about her'. Edwards shows how it is, in a stretch of action where a married couple is talking to a counsellor about their troubles, that things which a culturally competent reader can 'understand' – references to 'obvious' words like 'girls' and 'married women' – are mobilized to promote people's interests in ways which are *not* so obvious at first sight, or on a literal reading. So it is that, for example, the husband can get in a dig about his wife by drawing attention to her behaviour when she is out with what he calls 'the girls'; and that the wife can attend to the range of implications of 'the girls' by respecifying them as 'married women'. As Edwards says, 'The category "married woman" does not get used here merely because that is *what they are*, or *how they think of themselves*. [. . .] Its use attends to local, rhetorically potent business in [the] talk' (p. 30). It suits the wife's rhetorical purpose that 'the relevant thing about her' – just at that moment – is her status as a member of a sober group of people with mature responsibilities: married women, not 'girls'.

The theme is continued by Andy McKinlay and Anne Dunnett (Chapter 3) who look at the way that, in the course of a radio interview, somebody who self-identifies as a 'gun-owner' orients to the socially questionable aspects of such a category membership. What they see is the speaker working up for him- or herself a curiously hybrid identity – that of someone who is at the same time a responsible 'average citizen' and yet, not very averagely, one who might resort to lethal violence. In doing so they mobilize a set of contrasts with, on the one hand, other groups who are hearably *not* 'average' ('criminals' and 'gang-bangers') who do carry guns; and, on the other, irresponsible or thoughtless ordinary people who are not prepared to repel predators – unlike them, the gun-owner can say 'whoever gets into [ ] my bedroom [ ] is gonna be in for a big surprise' (McKinlay and Dunnett, p. 44). This notion of recasting, or disavowing, a given identity is also a strong thread in Chapter 4, where Sue Widdicombe looks at the delicate business of warranting and rejecting category affiliation in the course of informal interviews with people who look as though they could be punks or gothics.

A theme common to these chapters is the notion of the salience of identities, or how different identities are occasioned. This is certainly a strong element in the final chapter of the section, where Antaki (Chapter 5) analyses how jocular ascription (of the apparently cryptic identities 'Fagin' and 'the terminally dim') is not a matter of bald pigeonholing for cognitively private imperatives, but rather for interactionally occasioned, public, interactional business. Like the others, he is wary of the cognitivist enterprise and critical of the way that this is dealt with in the psychological accounts of categorization which rely on pre-given, often simply demographic or 'objective' categories, and trade in abstractions of categorization as an automatized, interactionally neutral feature of a brain in limbo.

In Part II we turn to rather more purely formal aspects of talk – that is, to what the contributors here call the elements of 'discourse identities': features like whether one is addressing someone or being addressed; asking or answering; summoning or being summoned, and so on. 'Participants assume discourse identities' Zimmerman explains in Chapter 6, 'as they engage in various sequentially organized activities: current speaker, listener, story teller, story recipient, questioner, answerer, repair initiator, and so on' (p. 90). These discourse identities are the materials out of which larger, more recognizably 'social' or 'institutional' identities are built. So it is, for example, that two participants incarnate the social identities of 'emergency services call-taker' and 'legitimate caller' only by, first, successfully managing the discursive obligations of soliciting information, giving it, responding to requests from the other, and so on. When it goes wrong – as when, in one of his examples, Zimmerman shows us a caller trying to tell the call-taker a blue joke – it goes spectacularly wrong.

Wooffitt and Clark's analysis of equally vivid data (from the stage performance of a person claiming to be a medium) has the same logic: how is it that the speaker can mobilize the 'managerial' aspects of talk – of being a questioner, interrupter, and so on – to manifest a social identity? They show how the stage performer (as we might sceptically gloss her identity) very elegantly and precisely exploits the properties of such apparently mechanical aspects of talk, such as overlap and occlusion, to accomplish the formal discourse identity 'knowing recipient'. For example, she asks an informant a question, starts to get an answer, then cuts her off, claiming already to have known what she was about to say. The trick is, of course, that the informant has already given the performer a good amount of information before getting cut off – quite enough to be spun out into a supposedly clairvoyant message from the other side. Greatbatch and Dingwall's data (in Chapter 8) come from divorce mediation sessions (which echo some of the concerns of the participants in Edwards's data from relationship counselling sessions). They show how the participants in that scene continuously and continually refresh their own and each others' identities. For example, one of the set of formal features of talk is that a speaker may design his or her talk in such a way as to cast anyone in the room (or anywhere else) as a direct addressee, and the others as either intended or unintended overhearers. This feature is, like any other feature of the management of talk, open for use, and Greatbatch and Dingwall make a persuasive case that their divorce mediation participants use it to set up larger, institutional and other social identities for each other.

As for the chapters in Part III, here we return to the thread of categorical analysis which we mentioned earlier: the notion that one need not attend quite so minutely to the moment-by-moment manoeuvring of talk, and might profitably concentrate instead on the way people deploy *any* props under their control: words in talk, certainly, but also text, signs, documents, and so on. Identity categories can be invoked in any medium, the argument goes, and are recognizable through the cultural vocabulary the analyst shares. If you like, this is more respectful – less ironic – about what speakers are up to: the analysts' accounts will be concerned with how people's descriptions of each other (in all sorts of texts) work, but will not be trying to finesse them or translate them into another language. Indeed, D.R. Watson (1997) makes a very strong bid for the propriety of this way of working by complaining that even the apparently clean technology of conversation analysts – with all its hygienic-looking typographical conventions – is actually rather contaminated. It smuggles a prior reading into the analysis simply by labelling their lines in their transcripts as issuing from 'Doctor' or 'Counsel', and so on. A more strictly categorical analysis will not want to do that. In any case, the interest is in identity category work done as it were directly in the speakers' manipulation of conventionally known category-rich sorts of talk: either category labels themselves, or descriptions of features that conventionally imply category labels.

In Chapter 9, Hester very specifically uses such 'membership categorization analysis' to show how it is that such an institutional category as 'deviant' is constructed – in his words, how it 'is identified, described, explained, understood, made sense of, and treated as the grounds for various kinds of remedial intervention' (p. 136). In his transcript of discussions between teachers and educational psychologists he shows how both use structural properties of Sacks's membership categorization devices – especially the property of category contrast – to manage the description of children as being either within, or outwith, the boundaries of the category 'deviant' (with the consequence of then being referable to the educational psychologist, or not). Day, in Chapter 10, shows how it is that a speaker can use category-bound features to hint at, or otherwise indirectly make relevant, another speaker's ethnic categorization. One of the features of Day's chapter is the subtlety he teases out in the way a speaker can cast another person as 'ethnic' without actually doing anything so bald as to say so outright; how that casting can have the effect of disqualifying the person from a certain range of activities and, putting the shoe on the other foot, the delicacy by which the person can work to mitigate or resist such ascription and its consequences. In Chapter 11, Paoletti draws on the idea of category-bound activities of the category 'old', and shows how being senile is a collaborative construction which may be produced by the interviewer avoiding asking for clarification even when that would be quite reasonable – in her case, when confronted with what are, conventionally, 'incoherent' answers. In all these chapters, indexicality, relevance and consequentiality are all certainly there, but they take something of a back seat to the prime importance of the analyst recognizing the sorts of categories used by the speakers, and seeing relationships and contrasts among their implied, if not always spoken, associated features.

All this attention to the specifics of talk in interaction might make one forget that this sort of treatment of identity is at odds with what happens elsewhere in the social sciences. So it is appropriate that, at the end of the book, Widdicombe, in Chapter 12, looks to see what the distinction between identity as an analysts' and a participants' category will yield in a survey of other approaches. She uses the sort of analyses seen in the body of the book to reflect on identity in traditional sociology and psychology, and in new directions in social constructionism, poststructuralism and postmodernism.

Concluding Comments

What we guess is now obvious is that the chapters in the book are not going to be matters of interviewing informants to see what they say about themselves, nor are they going to be investigations into what contributors simply assert (for whatever reason) are interesting or important identities. The contributors do not start with a traditional list of identities that might want looking into, headed by the usual demographic categories like age and sex, or categories of political interest like nationality or ethnicity. That would be a poor guide to the banal yet consequential identity categories that crop up in the routineness of life. People work up and resist identities in indexical, creative and unpredictable ways. They deploy such identities as fellow recreational drug user (to take the example from Schenkein, above); hotrodder, hairstylist (to take two canonical examples from Sacks, 1979, 1992); or (to take examples from the chapters of this book) the average citizen, the affectionate father, the terminally dim, the-caller-with-a-legitimate-complaint-and-not-a-time-waster, and so endlessly on. Of course, people *do* have recourse to the more classic kinds of identity, such as 'girl' versus 'married woman', or 'normal' versus 'deviant', which many would take to be proper sorts of 'identities' that require our attention. They *are* indeed identities that require attention – on occasion – but only when made so by participants in interactions, and not, as we shall see, always in predictable ways, with literal meanings.

The variety of uses of identity categories is given by the permutations of the resources that conversational interaction provides. We shall see that people use a whole range of things, most of which, like the puzzle-pass-solution sequence that we spent some time on above, simply would not appear on our radar if we did not pay pretty close attention to how people organized their lives with each other. It is in the fine grain of that organization, as it happens in moment-to-moment interaction, that the contributors to the book will be inspecting identity in use.

PART I

SALIENCE AND THE BUSINESS OF IDENTITY

2   The Relevant Thing about Her: Social Identity Categories in Use

Derek Edwards

One of the central themes in this book, from the introduction onwards, is how social identity categories are handled *in use*. The classical treatment of this is Harvey Sacks's (1979, 1992) 'hotrodder' study, together with related bits of analysis and his remarks on 'membership categorization devices' (see also Hester and Eglin, 1997a; Jayyusi, 1984; Widdicombe and Wooffitt, 1995). Sacks examined how a group of 1960s 'teenagers' (the label is contentious), in group therapy sessions, talked around issues of who they were and what they did. 'Hotrodder' was a term they used for themselves, a word derived from ownership and activities with customized cars (hotrods). But the deployment of the term 'hotrodder', as a description of people, was effectively a way of drawing boundaries around who did and did not count (for a current speaker, in the current talk) as legitimate members of that category. Among the features of the uses of this word, were how it was aligned with various other terms (e.g., descriptions of cars and activities), and how it contrasted with alternatives (e.g., 'teenager', which was an adult's, outsider's, description).

Sacks's general concern was with how conversational participants *use* descriptive categories of this kind, and apply membership criteria, as a way of performing various kinds of discursive actions. His approach contrasts with how such categories figure in other kinds of social science, as *analysts' categories* of people, according to which the analyst offers explanations of what they do, what they say, and how they think. This shift, towards treating categorizations of that kind as topics under investigation (participants' resources for doing descriptions and explanations) rather than as analysts' explanatory resources, is a key feature of ethnomethodological work (Wieder, 1988) that figures also in discourse analytic studies of group identity (Wetherell and Potter, 1992). So Sacks's focus on *members' categories* was part of an empirical investigation of how verbal categories are actually used in conversation, and those uses included defining and policing group membership. For example, the notion that 'hotrodder' could be considered 'a revolutionary category' (Sacks, 1979, 1992) depends on this notion of *members' categories*. They can be part of 'doing rebellion, the first feature of which is that one sets up a category you administer yourself' (Sacks, 1992, Vol. I: 174). More obvious examples of that include the promotion of racial (Sacks's example) and gender politics. According to Sacks, 'we could say that what dominant groups basically own is how it is that we see reality, and that there's an order of revolution which is an attempt to change how it is that persons see reality' (ibid.: 398).

Of course, category usage is an endemic feature of discourse, and whereas rebellion is not always the thing at issue, there is generally *something* at issue. Discourse is pervasively rhetorical (Billig, 1987; Edwards and Potter, 1992), which is to say, oriented to alternative possible ways of describing things – to argument, contention, and agreement (see Heritage, 1984a). So Sacks's work on *social* categories was part of a larger concern with the conversational business done by *all* words, and as such it can be contrasted with currently popular cognitive and social psychological approaches to categorization. For example, the cognitive psychology of categories and metaphors (Gibbs, 1994; Lakoff, 1987; Rosch, 1978) is dominated by perceptual-cognitive assumptions about the prelinguistic origins of language and mind, rather than seeking to discover the kinds of discursive actions that verbal categories may be designed and deployed for. For various discourse-based critiques and alternatives to those cognitivist assumptions, with regard to categorization and social psychological theories of it, see Billig (1985), Condor (1988), Edwards (1991, 1995a, 1997), Jayyusi (1984), Potter and Wetherell (1987), and Widdicombe and Wooffitt (1995).

In social psychology the major approaches to social and personal identity categories are 'social identity theory' (Tajfel, 1982a) and its more cognitivist derivative, 'self categorization theory' or 'SCT' (Turner, 1987). These are extensions of basic cognitive category theory (Wetherell, 1996), with origins in Bruner's (1957) early work on perceptual categorization (see Tajfel, 1980), and drawing more recently on Rosch's (1978) perceptual approach to 'natural' and 'basic' categories. Rather than discussing SCT in detail here (let alone the more historically situated social identity theory of Tajfel – see Billig, 1996), I intend to pursue the nature of identity categories empirically, using conversational materials. But some features of SCT are worth highlighting, to provide a critical edge to the discursive approach I shall take (and to trail a theme that re-emerges in the chapters by McKinlay and Dunnett, Widdicombe, and Wooffitt and Clark).

Like Sacks and conversation analysis, SCT is concerned with group membership as a members' concern, a matter of how people categorize *themselves* (thus, 'self categorization'), rather than something imposed on them by other people's definitions:

> a psychological group is defined as one that is psychologically significant for the members, to which they relate themselves subjectively . . . that they privately accept membership in, and which influences their attitudes and behaviour . . . it is not simply a group one is *in,* but one which is subjectively important in determining one's behaviour. (Turner et al., 1987: 1–2; original emphasis)

Despite the shared concern with people's own categorizations of themselves and of others, SCT and conversation analysis (CA) immediately part company in their analytical stances towards it. The quotation from Turner signals some immediate differences. For Turner, self categorizations, however they may be expressed, are in the first place essentially psychological, subjective, private mental processes, that exert a determining influence on thought and behaviour. They are therefore amenable to, and approachable in terms of, experimental variables and their effects. On the other hand, for Sacks, self categorizations, like categorizations of other people and of everything else, are discursive actions done in talk, and performative of talk's current business. So the best way to examine them is to find how they are used, and what kinds of discursive business they do, on and for the occasions when they are deployed. Further, there is no explanatory primacy given to *self* categorizations, as a psychological starting point for how everyone sees the world.

The difference between CA and its discourse analytic (DA) relatives on the one hand, and SCT on the other, is not merely a matter of catering for variability (Potter and Wetherell, 1987). Both approaches recognize that a person may categorize him- or herself (or other people or things) differently, from one situation to another. The difference lies in how this variability is conceived and investigated, and the difference is, once again, a profound one. According to Turner,

> the functioning of the social self-concept is situation-specific: particular self-concepts tend to be activated ('switched on') in specific situations producing specific self-images . . . as a function of an interaction between the characteristics of the perceiver and the situation. (Turner et al., 1987: 44)

Note the terms 'activated', 'switched on', 'producing', and the mechanical, rather than social, sense of 'interaction'. This causes-and-variables kind of terminology locates SCT firmly within the theoretical and methodological traditions of experimental psychology, and sends us in pursuit of factors and circumstances, mental mechanisms and situational variables. Although Sacks (1992) also used terms such as 'machinery' and 'device' as metaphors for conversational interaction, his analyses of talk were ethnomethodological rather than cognitivist and causal, and far from mechanical: see Edwards (1995a) on this, and Coulter (1990) for some uses of ethnomethodology and conversation analysis in generating a critique of standard psychological theory and method. In contrast to SCT, CA and (related kinds of) DA approach 'situational variability' as an *intrinsic feature* of talk and social action, in the sense that talk is always action-performative, designed for its occasions, reflexively constituting the sense of those occasions (Garfinkel and Sacks, 1970; Heritage, 1984a), and rhetorically oriented. Rather than categorizations being switched into activity by situations, discourse works to define events, and make relevant its situations, by the kinds of categorizations it deploys. If this sounds rather abstruse, and the switchboard model easier to grasp, the cure is to set theory aside for a while and start dealing with some conversational materials, and examine how they work. I shall return briefly to contrasts with SCT later.

The title of this chapter, 'the relevant thing about her', is inspired by a discussion by Harvey Sacks (1992) of a fragment of data from the same group therapy sessions as produced the 'hotrodder' talk. We can use it as a point of departure before looking at some other data. 'Dan' is the therapist.

(1)   (Sacks, 1992, Vol. I: 597, line numbers added)

1	Ken:	So did Louise call or anything this morning?
2	Dan:	Why, didju expect her t'call?
3	Ken:	No, I was just kinda hoping that she might be able to figure
4		out some way t-to come to the meetings and still be able
5		t'work. C'z she did seem like she d-wanted to come back, but
6		uh she didn't think she could.
7	Dan:	D'you miss her?
8	Ken:	Well in some ways yes, it's- it was uh nice having- having
9		the opposite sex in-in the room, you know, havin' a chick in
10		here.

Sacks focuses on Ken's switch from a named person ('Louise') to a generalized gender category (line 9: 'the opposite sex . . . *a chick*') to account for his concern for her absence, and to specify in what restricted sense he might 'miss her' (lines 7–8). 'Chick' is one of a variety of colloquial gender categorizations available to this group (1960s California teenagers), such that its choice signals something further about what the speaker is doing than merely his choice of a gender category. Sacks does not pursue that issue, and its possibly sexist implications; indeed, he understands the remark as, locally and for them, part of a compliment.

The feature that Sacks highlights is that, by using the generalized gender categories 'opposite sex' and 'chick', Ken effectively forestalls any inference that his concern might have been personal. As Sacks puts it, 'he wasn't going to say he likes her or anything like that' (1992, Vol. I: 60). The gender categorizations work on the basis that Louise, as the only girl in the group, is uniquely, if impersonally, identifiable by gender, and that gender is picked out by Ken as the *relevant thing about her*. Further, Sacks examines how it functions as a 'safe compliment' categorization, in that it attends to the possible perceptions of other group members, who are all male. He imagines how something like 'it was nice having someone smart in the room' might invoke unfavourable implications for the rest of the group, smartness being one of 'a whole range of categories which also *can* apply to any other person in the room' (ibid.; 60; original emphasis).

We might add that 'in the room' and 'in here' (line 9) further specify the range of that relevance, to the meetings they are taking part in, rather than any more general, context-independent, sexual, or personal interest Ken might have had in Louise. So the way in which 'identity' categories work, at least in this example, is that by selecting one rather than another, speakers can perform and manage various kinds of interactionally sensitive business, including their motives and reasons for doing things and saying things. Further, the nature of relevant contexts or 'situations' is also talk's business, being categorized, specified, or invoked, as a way of defining and restricting the range of that relevance. As always, for both persons and situations, if they did not *have to be* described that way (or described at all), then the way they *are* described can be examined for what it might specifically be doing.

Married with Kids

Picking up from Sacks's example, I shall explore some ways in which person and situation categories work in discourse. My data are also a series of therapy-oriented talk sessions, but involving a married couple taking part in relationship counselling. 'Connie' and 'Jimmy' are a working-class Irish couple living in England, both aged 35 and with three children. The audio-taped data are taken from the first two sessions which they attended. Their counsellor is a middle-class Englishman. Conventionally, in intro-ducing a data set of this kind, I have started to specify various 'identity' categories for these people. The assumption behind doing that is that information of this kind is relevant in some way to our understanding of what is going on, that it is the kind of thing we need to know, the kind of explanation-relevant demographic information routinely provided in ethnographies, surveys, interview studies, experiments, and so on. They are also the kinds of categories that SCT generally deals with: 'the self defined as male, European, a Londoner, etc.' (Turner, 1987: 29).

But before we go along with these conventions, and give this kind of information some kind of explanatory relevance, two cautions are in order. The first is that, in the analysis of discourse, what we are interested in is the possible relevance of categories of this kind *for them*. As with Sacks's 'Ken' and 'Louise', we are interested in whether, and how, categories of this kind may figure as resources that *they* use in producing accounts and descriptions. Secondly, we should be wary of calling even this rather neutral and routine-looking stuff 'information' (see also Edwards, 1997). Given that they are potentially available for doing discursive 'business', categories such as gender, age, parental and marital status, nationality, etc., are not merely factual, or even value-laden observations that have an automatic relevance to people's conversational activities. The analytic task is to find if, when, and for what, they may have such relevance (Schegloff, 1992b). Indeed, rather than starting with a pre-defined or conventional list of such items, what we need to do is find whatever it is that participants do invoke, and how they use it.

In the body of the chapter I am going to offer some analyses of data that come from counselling sessions, and a word is in order about their provenance. The sessions were audio-recorded by the counsellor, with the knowledge and consent of his clients, whose permission to use the recordings for research purposes was rewarded by having to pay only half the usual fee for counselling. Each session lasted about an hour and runs to around 35 single-spaced pages of transcript. I know nothing of any of the three participants (and have never met them) outside of what is said on tape. Person and place names have been altered. As for notation, the general CA conventions are listed on pages viii–ix in this volume, and in addition I use asterisks to denote a high, 'squeaky' tone of voice.

In the data extracts that follow, I examine how a variety of kinds of 'identity' arise and are made relevant in, and to, the interaction. Following that, picking up the 'relevant thing about her' theme, I focus more specifically on various contrastive uses of the categories 'girls', 'married women', and other related descriptions. First, let us examine a sequence (extract 2) early in Jimmy and Connie's first counselling session, in which the counsellor, having obtained from Connie and Jimmy some initial descriptions of their marital problems, elicits various identity categorizations that presumably have some relevance to the business at hand, such as (generally speaking) relationship troubles and counselling.

(2) (DE–JF:C2:S1:p.4. Note that each extract is prefaced by a code specifying the data set and the place of the extract within it. Here 'DE–JF:C2:S1:p.4' specifies data transcribed by D. Edwards and J. Fong, couple 2, session 1, page 4.)

```
177    Counsellor:  ↑Oka↓y so, (0.5) for me̲ list↓enin:g, (.) you̲'ve
178                 got (0.5) ri̲ch an:d, (.) complicated lives, I̲
179                 nee:d to get some histo⌈ry to put-      ⌉
180    Connie:                              ⌊Yyeh mmm,=⌋
181    Jimmy:       ⌈Mmm. (.) Ye̲:h. (.) O̲h ye:h.   ⌉
182    Connie:      ⌊=Yeh (.) that's (.) exactly wha⌋t ⌈ih °um° ⌉
183    Counsellor:                                    ⌊i- i-    ⌋ uh
```

184		(.) to begin ↓to make some sense of it. ˙hhh so:,
185		(0.2) hh↑how old ↓are you no:w?
186		(.)
187	Connie:	I'm thirty fi:ve,
188		(0.6)
189	Jimmy:	Thirty five.
190		(0.4)
191	Counsellor:	Right. And you::'ve >been married< how many years:,
192	Connie:	Just °twelve years now.°=
193	Jimmy:	=Thirteen years [in September.]
194	Connie:	⌊Thirteen years⌋ in September.=
195	Counsellor:	=°Okay.° ˙hhh And you have how many children.
196	Connie:	Three children.
197		(0.7)
198	Counsellor:	And they are::
199		(0.7)
200	Connie:	[One iss]
201	Jimmy:	⌊twelve ⌋
202		(0.3)
203	Jimmy:	[Eight]
204	Connie:	⌊just ⌋ eleven, (0.3) one is (0.2) just seven, (.)
205		and the other eight.
206	Counsellor:	El- eleven:, ei[ght, (.) and seven.]
207	Connie:	⌊eight and seven.⌋ Yeh.=
208	Counsellor:	=Fine.
209		(.)
210		The eldest i:s ↑boy gir:l,=
211	Jimmy:	Bo[y.
212	Connie:	⌊Boy.
213	Counsellor:	Boy:,
214	Connie:	°David.°
215	Jimmy:	>Boy girl boy.<
216		(0.4)
217	Counsellor:	>Boy girl boy. So the< eight year old's the girl.
218		(0.8)
219		°Okay.° ˙hh Married tw↑elve yea::::rs, (0.3) an::d-

Note how the counsellor sets up the provision of various kinds of identity categories. First, there are some relevant identities for the current interaction, as a counsellor–client encounter, and in fact these have been partly established well before this point. The session starts (in line 1, not given here) with the counsellor switching on the tape recorder and checking whether his clients have 'been to Relate before'. And of course, my own labels for them identify them as 'Connie' and 'Jimmy', and the other participant as 'counsellor'. It is worth dwelling on this for a moment before looking at the transcribed details. The names 'Connie' and Jimmy' identify the couple personally and informally, whereas the 'counsellor' appears merely in role. So the couple's personal identities are implicationally relevant to the analysis, whereas the counsellor's personal identity, as someone with a life history and set of personal concerns, is irrelevant. His role says (according to my transcript) all we need to know about him. These are not arbitrary choices of description, but rather, they reflect the materials under analysis, the bases on which the participants talk to each other.

In the recorded sessions the counsellor is not named, and nor are details of his personal life discussed; he talks as counsellor, and constitutes himself in that role, relative to them, each time he speaks (e.g., 'for me listening' and 'I need to get some history', lines 177–9, as well as in how he generally addresses them, informs them about his methods of counselling, asks questions, directs the flow of discussion, tells them about payment, and so on). In contrast, Connie and Jimmy are referred to by those names, by each other and by the counsellor, and it is their personal lives, not his, which are opened up for examination. In fact, 'Connie' and 'Jimmy' are pseudonyms, and other specific identifying information has been altered. Not only does that protect their lives from unethical intrusion, but it also says something about our analytic interests. We are interested in how persons talk about themselves, often in intimate detail. But it does not matter to us who they actually are. The names 'Connie', 'Jimmy', and 'counsellor', reflect our analytic interests and also something of theirs, preserving both how they address each other (in these recorded sessions), and also the asymmetry of their social interaction.

With regard to the talk itself, note that it is the counsellor, as an interactional participant, who specifies the categories of interest and also their explanatory relevance: he accounts for his requiring these details of their marital status and history, in order for him to 'make some sense' (line 184) of their 'rich and complicated lives' (line 178). Their complicated lives, and his making sense (rather than *his* complicated life and their sense of that), are descriptive orientations to the business of counselling, to what they are all doing here, talking to each other in the way that they do. It is the counsellor who introduces the various categories (length of marriage, age of children, etc.) as a resource for his understanding (line 184), for putting what they have already begun telling him (prior to extract (2)) into some kind of narrative, and possibly explanatory context ('history', 'make sense' – lines 179–84). The details that he asks for appear to be of a routine kind, and not much is made of them in extract (2). But things *do* get made of them, and we shall look at a few.

Before we do that, consider what *kinds* of 'sense' they *may* provide. This is quite easy to imagine. Being married or not, for example, might provide grounds for claims, stories, and complaints, based on marriage vows and responsibilities, commitments, expectations of fidelity, and so on. Their ages, both absolute and relative to each other, are potential bases for explaining shared or differential interests, expectations, and kinds of relationships. Length of marriage provides possible grounds for narrating circumstances prior to troubles, a relationship's history, causes and consequences, such as maybe having married at a young and inexperienced age, or not yet having given it enough time, and so on. Children and their ages provide for adducing additional kinds of commitment, neglect, differential responsibilities, household divisions of labour, extra strains on the marriage, reasons for staying together, and so on. We can invent all kinds of possibilities and, of course, it is our understanding of such possibilities that make these kinds of materials coherent and analysable, for participants as much as for analysts. But the analytic task is not to produce idealized and presumptive stories of this kind, nor to use them as a 'given' basis for analysts' explanations, or psychological models, of what people do or say. Our task is to examine what it is, if anything, that people do with these kinds of categorizations.

Consider a few details from extract (2): the fact that Connie and Jimmy have children, the way Connie corrects Jimmy with regard to the children's ages (lines 201–5), the fact that the counsellor picks up Connie's corrected version as the one to go with (lines 206–8), and again how the counsellor picks up and repeats the fact that they have been 'married tw↑elve yea::::rs,' (line 219), with emphatic and drawn-out emphasis. First, Connie's correction of Jimmy and its uptake by the counsellor: these start to identify her (for them and us) as the one who owns best knowledge of the children. This is therefore, however minimally, a way in which demographic details such as having children, their ages, and parental identities, can start to be specified in particular ways and made discursively relevant.

There are other, more explicit ways. A few moments prior to extract (2) Connie had been providing, at the counsellor's prompting, a sketch of the troubles that brought them to seek counselling. Her story includes extract (3), concerning a time when Jimmy had 'walked out on' her.

(3)   (DE–JF:C2:S1:p.2)

```
67      Connie:     An:d that'ss (.) when I RANG I actually ra:ng
68                  because I was on my ow:n.
69                  (1.0)
70      →           coping with my children ↑y'know?
71                  (0.7)
```

So the children here are Connie's (emphatically 'my children', line 70), and being left to cope with them 'on my ow:n' (line 68) features as part of a specification of her troubles with Jimmy, of his part in those troubles, and of her need for help.

Marital status, and length of time married, also figure as rhetorical resources, and not merely as background factual information. An example of this occurs in the talk that continues after extract (2). The counsellor picks up the notion that they have been married twelve years, and immediately uses that to locate an event they had mentioned earlier, concerning a 'pub incident' involving a big argument and Jimmy eventually 'walking out'.

(4)   (continuing from (2))

```
219        Counsellor:  °Okay.°  ˙hh Married tw↑elve yea::::rs, (0.3) an::d-
220                     ˙hhh the time of the first walk out, after the pub
221                     incident?  ˙h wa::s t↑wo years ago did you sa↑:y?
222        Connie:      Two years but now we:'ve had (.) problems,
223                                 ⌈(   )⌉
224        Jimmy:       ⌊Well⌋ LONG before that we've had things where I've (.)
225                     uh I'm going. I'd get in the car- an' ⌈go.  ⌉
226        Counsellor:                                       ⌊Ten ⌋ years.
227                     You've been walking out. ((sniffs))
228        Connie:      No⌈:. No        ⌉
229        Jimmy:         ⌊YEH yeh- ⌋
```

The topic of what counts as a fully fledged 'walking out', and how long Jimmy has been doing it, becomes a hotly contended one in their talk, and we see only the start of it in (4). The counsellor sums it up: twelve years marriage (line 219), two years since the first walk-out (line 221), corrected to perhaps ten (line 226). We can imagine that this first formulation, that their troubles may be of only two years' duration, starts to generate possibilities for when and therefore how their troubles may have started, for what caused them, and who was to blame. Additionally, the notion that there may therefore have been many years of marriage before their troubles started, provides further possibilities for narrative accounts and potential bases for solutions; such as, it was okay once, so it can be again. But any such line of reasoning is quickly cut short, first by Connie (line 222) and then by Jimmy (line 224), who upgrades Connie's 'problems' to the status of earlier instances of 'walking out'. In fact, this develops into a major bone of contention between them, with Connie defining the marriage as basically good, solid, and just what she wanted (prior to his 'affair'), while Jimmy emphasizes the constant rows and (verbal) 'fights' they have had since the beginning, and how he has been walking out, or on the verge of it, all along (see Edwards, 1995b). Extract (4) includes the start of that contention (lines 228 and 229) within the counselling sessions. We can see from these materials how even the most ostensibly obvious, factual, trivial, demographic kinds of person-identifying categories can be invoked, worked up, played down, and otherwise used by participants as part of the discursive business at hand.

Girls and (Married) Women

In order to explore some of the rhetorical subtleties of identity category usage in the couple counselling materials, I shall focus on various uses of the terms *girl* and *woman*. Logically and semantically, these words might be thought to refer to distinct categories of people, younger versus older, although where exactly the boundary is drawn may vary. One such boundary is marriage. The *Oxford English Dictionary* (on CD-ROM, 1992) defines *girl* as 'a female child; commonly applied to all young unmarried women', and lists various related and combined senses glossed as 'sweetheart' and 'prostitute'. *Woman* is given as 'an adult female human being'. I am not proposing that dictionaries tell us what people mean by the words they use, on any particular occasion. But we can start with the idea that *girl* and *woman* are separate categories with fuzzy and permeable boundaries, carrying potentially useful conventional associations with age, marital status, and potential sexual availability. The thing of interest here is some specific instances of how they were applied to the same individuals, and how such applications performed and managed discursive, rhetorical business, in signalling, in some bit of talk about someone, what I have called 'the relevant thing about her'.

Prior to extract (5) below, Connie has been telling of how Jimmy had left her on her own, 'coping with my children' (see extract (3)), and how she had subsequently found him 'living with someone else', another woman. Connie attributes Jimmy's walking out to his relationship with this other woman. For his part, Jimmy blames the walking out on various aspects of Connie's long-term behaviour. In extract (5), Connie cites Jimmy's affair as the prior and true cause (line 83) of his leaving.

(5)   (DE–JF:C2:S1:p.2)

```
75        Connie:     (. . .) So (.) I'm here really to- (1.0) I dunno:
76                    I just want to ta:lk to somebody, 'n (0.8) see:
77                    why it happened, 'n (0.5) ↑things like that y'know?
78                    (0.8)
79        Counsellor: To explore what happened.=
80        Connie:     =To explore: what happened exactly y'know, because
81                    I can't accept (1.0) I can't accept (1.0) y'know: (.)
82                    what he's telling me, (0.5) y'know?= =I just belie:ve
83   →               that this girl was here all alo:ng, (0.2) and that's why.
84                    (0.5)
```

Again we can see how some of the married-with-children kinds of identity categories, that were introduced in extract (2), can start to be used as discursive resources in the production of narrative accounts. The specific item of interest here, in extract (5), is 'this girl' in line 83. Whereas Connie might well have said 'this woman', the expression 'this girl' serves to downgrade her status, if not her threat, as an unattached, unmarried, available, possibly young, female. I do not want to make too much of those connotations at this point, nor to hinge an analysis on a single word: it is not possible to nail down precise meanings of that kind. Indeed, that is part of the functionality of such fuzzy categories, that they can invoke various indexical possibilities without making explicit claims that might be easier to rebut.

Nevertheless we can follow the descriptions *woman* and *girl* in how Jimmy deals with Connie's claims. Following Connie's account of her problems, the counsellor invites Jimmy to say something.

(6)   (following shortly after (5))

```
98        Jimmy:      (. . .) U::m (0.8) it's >not right< to sa:y that (0.5)
99                    >I didn't leave Connie for another woman.<
100                   (0.6)
101                   But (0.4) I was liv- sleepin' away for (0.5) 'bout
102                   three- three weeks (.) ↓four weeks three weeks (0.4)
103   →               whatever, (0.6) when I moved in: (.) with a wo- girl,
104                   which I did have (1.0) uh: a bit of a fling with (.)
105                   when Connie went on holiday last year.
106                   (1.2)
107                   U::m
108                   (2.0)
109                   a:nd moved in with her, (0.6) (uh, what, three weeks?)
110                   (2.8)
111                   uhh (0.8) then moved back ↑out.
112                   (2.0)
```

Jimmy denies leaving Connie 'for another woman' (line 99), which is consistent with his general story of long-term marital strife, and Connie's outrageous flirtatiousness, as the cause of his leaving (see Edwards, 1995b). Leaving someone 'for another woman' is a recognizable cultural idiom for this kind of activity. But note Jimmy's repair in line 103, where he apparently starts to say 'woman' and corrects it to 'girl'. The category he uses switches from the denied and generalized one ('another woman'), to the particular person with whom he admits he 'moved in'. Aligning himself with Connie's description, 'girl', enables Jimmy to make his own use of any downgrading of her status that the switch allows. Note how this fits with other features of his talk: what Connie had previously called an 'affair', Jimmy refers to as 'a bit of a fling' (line 104), specifically located during a holiday (line 105) rather than something long-term. He also softens Connie's prior description 'living with' into 'moved in with' (line 103), a more locative rather than sexual kind of expression, reinforced by how he shortly 'then moved back out' (line 111). So Jimmy's adoption of the term *girl* manages to align with Connie's, while helping to downgrade the status of his relationship with the 'girl', and counter Connie's claim that something more serious, long-term, and marriage-threatening had been going on 'all along' (extract (5), line 83).

Contrasts between the expressions *girl* and *woman* are not driven by objective category membership, nor a slavish adherence to semantics, nor even to invoke the specific kinds of implications we have seen in extracts (5) and (6) with regard to Jimmy's 'other woman'. Connie also uses both terms *girl* and *woman* when talking about herself and her friends. The instances I shall examine centre around Connie's complaint about Jimmy's attitude to her having nights out with her female friends. Connie complains that Jimmy unreasonably disapproves, and gets extremely and irrationally jealous, of what she might be getting up to with other men, thus severely restricting her freedom in going out. Jimmy defends his suspicions as rational and based on his knowledge of what she is like after a few drinks. At least, this crude summary must suffice, given the lack of space to show here how these concerns are worked up and managed, with marvellous rhetorical intricacy, in their talk.

In extract (7) (from session 2) the counsellor invites Connie to spell out 'quietly to Jimmy' her desire for more 'freedom of choice' in what she does. I should say that in this extract you will see quotation marks within speakers' turns, but they don't signal actual quotations. Rather, they show the speaker overtly 'doing quotation' as a presentational feature of talk, speaking 'in the voice' of another (see Wooffitt, 1992), usually with a shift in tone of voice, rate of speech, or a kind of acted-out lilting quality to the delivery (e.g., Edwards, 1995b), sometimes imitative of another speaker, and often, as below, separated off by pauses.

(7)   (DE–JF:C2:S2:p.22)

1375	Connie:	>What I would like to be able to do is,< when my friend
1376		rings me up, (0.5) every six weeks, or: when they're
1377 →		having a ↑girls' night out, >to be able to say,< (.)
1378		"yeh I'd love to go." (0.7) Without (0.2) THAT meaning,
1379		(.) going out with my frie:nds (.) doesn't have anything
1380		to do: (0.2) with not wanting to sit in with you.
1381		(0.8)
1382		That's what I mean.
1383		(.)
1384		I just (.) want (0.8) you know how o:ften it happens,
1385		(.) an' I just like to go out with you, (0.8) sitting
1386		there saying, (.) "th*a- y*eh th*at's f*ine," (0.8)
1387		no:t (.) with sitting there with a fa:ce that's (.)
1388		I kno:w I've (.) touched on a sore spot.
1389		(1.0)
1390		I just- that's what I would like. (.) And (.) as I said,
1391		(.) you know (.) how often that that happens.
1392		(0.6)
1393		When my frie:nd rings me up (.) "I have a pro:blem,"
1394		(1.3)
1395		y'know: "d'y'fa:ncy comin out, an hav'n a chat?" (.)
1396		"Ye:h I'd love to go:, no: problem, (.) I'll see you
1397		such and such a time,"= but I don't feel that I have
1398		to (0.3) say, (.) "would you ↑mi:nd Jimmy? (0.9) if I
1399		go out," (0.7) or::, (0.9) whatever.

The thing of interest again here is how relevant identities are formulated, concerning Connie and her friends, and how those formulations work in company with other descriptive categories – activities, places, circumstances, narrative details. The focal details here, for the analytic points I want to make, are 'friend(s)' and 'girls' night out' (lines 1375 and 1377 respectively). The people Connie wants to go out with are her friends (not some unknown quantity, some anonymous bunch of women, say), and rather than this being an activity she is especially looking to do, Connie's role is reactive (lines 1376, 1393) to an occasional telephone call from one of them. The burden upon Jimmy of such events is played down: it happens only 'every six weeks' or so (line 1376), and 'you know how often it happens' (line 1384). The activity and purpose of such nights out is the kind of thing friends do, having a 'chat' about some 'problem' (lines 1393–5). The categories 'friend(s)' and 'girls' work together with these and other details (e.g., the 'just' in line 1385) to define these nights out as entirely unthreatening and harmless to Jimmy, such that his objections and suspicions are unfounded.

If I may again gloss the content of some intervening talk, Jimmy responds that Connie is asking him to 'trust' her, but he cannot do that, knowing how she 'behaves' when 'out with company'. The category 'company' nicely works to widen the social scope of Connie's nights out with her women friends, without being explicit enough to require a denial. He also attends to the objection that he is not there to see what she does on girls' nights out:

(8)   (DE–JF:C2:S2:p.23)

```
1427     Jimmy:      Well (.) I never kn↑ew what you're like (.) on- when
1428                 you're out with the girls. (.) But I know what you're
1429                 like when you're out with me: with a load of ↑people.=
1430     Connie:     =Yye:h, well I've been ma⌈rried for-      ⌉
1431     Jimmy:                                ⌊a:nd the:n-⌋
1432                 (0.5)
1433                 ⌈(              )⌉
1434     Connie:     ⌊I:'ve been⌋ married for twe:lve ↑years Jimmy,=
1435                 I:'ve never had an affai:r or: an atta-
1436                 invo:lve⌈ment   with   anybody   else.      ⌉
1437     Jimmy:             ⌊↑That's ↓what you're tellin' ↑me,⌋
1438                 ⌈y- you're a:lways tellin' me that.  ⌉
1439     Connie:     ⌊ That's the truth. And you kno:w ⌋ that's the truth.
```

Jimmy claims to be extrapolating from what he knows Connie to be like, on occasions that he *has* directly witnessed. Note again here Connie's rhetorical use of their twelve years of marriage (see the discussion of extract (2)), as a basis for her claim to long-term fidelity and trustworthiness, a nice counter to Jimmy's mistrust of her which, with perfect symmetry, invokes which of them *has* had an affair. Jimmy 'ironizes' her claim as mere words (line 1437). But let us stay with the 'girls' Connie wants to go out with. Jimmy's formulation, 'when you're out with the girls' (lines 1427–8) echoes Connie's prior description, 'a girls' night out', though significantly omitting Connie's account of how such events are triggered by 'a friend' wanting to talk about a 'problem'. Jimmy uses the categories 'girls' and going 'out', compares that to occasions he has witnessed (line 1429), and goes on (in further talk) to build it all as problematic, a socializing, pub-based kind of event in which Connie has a few drinks and becomes flirtatious. Jimmy concurs with the counsellor's suggestion, that he fears Connie 'might end up in bed with someone else'.

Now, the category 'girls', as we saw earlier with regard to Jimmy's affair, is nicely appropriate for any such sexual developments – nicely, that is, for Jimmy's version of things. Jimmy tells of an evening when Connie came home late from such a girls' night out, and Connie disputes his story and re-tells it in her own words. The counsellor then sets up 'a little experiment' for them. This is a counselling-oriented exercise in mutual understandings, in which Connie will tell her side of things, and Jimmy has to repeat what Connie says, and then vice versa. I shall restrict the analysis to Connie's re-telling, omitting (again for brevity's sake) the way Jimmy, in repeating it, manages also to parody it. So Connie proceeds to talk again of her 'girls' nights out', but now (in extract (9)) *reformulates their relevant identities*, as 'married women'.

(9) (DE–JF:C2:S2:p.30)

```
1846   Connie:      (. . .) when I go out with the gir:ls, it's a:ll married
1847                women talking about our ki:ds or somebody rin:gs (.)
1848                ˙hh they have a pro:blem, y'know (.) "d'you fancy go-"
1849                (.) that's uh- (.) the gir:ls night out
1850                (. . .)((several turns omitted here))
1851                When I go out with people it's normally a crow:d of
1852                married women, (.) which Jimmy knows each and every
1853                one of them.
1854                (0.8)
1855                Ri:ght? It's normally to a pub, that's nor:mally quiet,
1856                (0.5) you kno:w that there's (.) ↑no:body in it (.)
1857                because it's normally on a Wednesday or a Thursday night
1858                that we would go out, (.) there's ve:ry few people out,
1859                (0.2) an' it's a:lways a quiet pub. (.) Ni:ne out of ten
1860                times it would be that type of pla:ce because (.)
1861   Counsellor:  But what about the ti:me that it isn't?=
1862   Connie:      =The on:ce (.) it would be: I actually remember once
1863                now, (.) an' that's why I said ni:ne out of ten times
1864                'cos I KNO:W Jimmy is going to say it, ˙h
1865   Jimmy:       [th- the- ]
1866   Connie:      [the one ] night we went was to (.) the- m- (.) this
1867                Manhattan Rock Cafe:, (.) which was (.) no wa:y you
1868                could possibly ta:lk in because it's lou:d its music
```

1869	but (.) <u>full</u> o' women on a Thursday night which I will
1870	state <u>again</u>. ˙hhh <u>But</u> (.) ˙hh th<u>i</u>s isn't <u>nor:</u>mally the
1871	pub (.) that we go to, (.) <u>nor:</u>mally as I sai:d it's (.)
1872	either (.) maybe somebody's <u>bir</u>thday? (0.2) That's (.)
1873	a reason we go out an' have a few drinks, ˙h an<u>other</u>
1874	it could be: somebody has a problem like <u>re</u>cently a
1875	<u>fri</u>end of mine had a pro:blem that wanted to talk, ˙hh
1876	<u>the:se</u> are the ni:ghts out, (.) <u>these</u> are the (.)
1877	thi:ngs we sit around ↑<u>one</u> table (.) <u>full</u> of <u>mar</u>ried
1878	<u>wo</u>men, (0.2) an' that's (.) <u>nor</u>mally our nights out.

Connie takes this re-telling opportunity to attend to Jimmy's objections to 'girls' nights out', and to define the specific occasion he complained of, both as harmless and as exceptional (the pervasive and emphatic 'normally', and 'nine times out of ten', and lines 1861–71). The 'girls' are respecified as 'all married women' (lines 1846, 1852, 1877), and all known to Jimmy (line 1852). Their activities consist of recognizably harmless category-relevant things for 'married women' to do, such as talking about their children, talking about personal problems, or celebrating a birthday (lines 1847, 1872, 1874). Rather than looking for any kind of additional male company, they routinely choose a quiet pub and a quiet night (lines 1855–60) so they can chat about personal and family matters. Note how the details work, how relevant identities (married women) are built not only by naming folk as such, but by combining those descriptions with category-relevant activities (talking about their children and problems) and places (quiet, empty pubs, not noisy night clubs), including how they 'sit around one table' together, as a group and exclusively ('full of' married women, line 1877), rather than, say, looking to pair off with any men who might be around. The category 'married women' does not get used here merely because that is *what they are*, or *how they think* of themselves. It was not used when Connie first described her nights out. Its use attends to local, rhetorically potent business in their talk. Further, it occurs in narrative combination with descriptions of places and circumstances that, rather than serving as situational variables, are as much talk's business to define and make relevant as are the descriptions of persons.

Concluding Comments

In contrast to the cognitions-in-context model of social categorizations offered by a psychological account such as self categorization theory (SCT), the analysis of how categorizations of self and others arise in discourse emphasizes their locally constructed, occasioned, and rhetorically oriented nature. In SCT there is scant interest in discovering empirically what the categories are that people use, nor how they use them. Rather, given that we know what the categories pretty obviously are, the aim is to explain how people will place themselves and others into them, according to the situations they find themselves in. In discursive psychology, that kind of mechanical variables-and-effects model is replaced by one in which categorizations are studied as empirical phenomena occurring in talk and text. Rather than fitting into a causal matrix, categorizations feature in actively worked-up versions, that constitute the sense of the very circumstances in which they are used. Indeed, 'the situations they find themselves in' are ordinarily no less subject to the vagaries of categorization and description than the people themselves. The situational flexibility found, in how discourse categories are used, is not triggered or 'switched on' by situations so much as defining and making them relevant, providing for their interpretation, countering alternative versions, generating some kind of narrative and explanatory sense of things. Those definitions are things people do in their talk, rather than things that experimenters do for them by providing conditions and variables within which to record their responses.

One of the virtues of SCT is that it has partially dissolved the distinction between 'social' and 'personal' identity that was used in social identity theory. Rather than denoting distinct psychological entities, these are now conceived as products of the same kinds of cognitive categorizations (Oakes et al., 1994). According to SCT, 'self-concepts are categories and like all categories are based on the perception of intra-class similarities and inter-class differences between stimuli' (Turner, 1987: 44). Social identities will predominate over personal ones, for example, where between-group differences are perceived as more salient than within-group differences between persons. It is as if, when Connie and Jimmy shift between the inter-class alternatives 'girls' and '(married) women', they do so having first 'processed' intra-class similarities, as if checking, for instance, which category was the best designator of people's perceptually salient properties.

It is an extraordinary psychology of mental processes that we are driven to (see Edwards, 1997, and what Button et al., 1995, call 'spectatorism') when we ignore how discourse and social interaction work. Despite SCT's vocabulary of perception and 'stimuli', the groups and categories to which people may belong, that they identify with, aspire to, or count themselves members of ('the self defined as male, European, a Londoner, etc.', Turner, 1987: 29) are also *verbal categories* (Wetherell and Potter, 1992). Discursive psychology's point of departure is the observation that, being verbal categories that folk may apply, these are indeed categories like any other, that is, *descriptions* that can be analysed in the same way as other descriptions, as discourse phenomena. The task is to analyse what people do with the words they use.

Such analysis – of what people *do* with categorical descriptions – gets us away from idealizations such as what Turner (1987) defines as three hierarchically nested 'levels' of the self concept. These are derived from Rosch's (1978) work on 'natural' categories, where there are superordinate levels (e.g., furniture), that include intermediate levels (e.g., chair), that in turn include subordinate levels (e.g., dining chair). Thus, according to Turner, self concepts can be divided into at least three levels of abstraction: the superordinate level of the self as human being, in contrast to other forms of life; the intermediate level of ingroup-outgroup categorizations such as 'American', 'female', and so on; and the subordinate level of personal self-categorization in terms of one's personality or other kinds of individual differences. These levels can be said to define one's 'human', 'social' and 'personal' identity respectively (Turner, 1987: 45).

Again, the trouble is how permeable these rather idealized 'levels' are. Differentiations between members of social groups (men and women, Scots and Maoris, etc.), are likely to deploy the same kinds of 'personality' categories as distinguish individuals (laziness, meanness, aggressiveness, cruelty, efficiency, etc.). And even the distinctions between what (or who) is 'human' or not, or to be *treated as* human or not (e.g., the Great Apes Project, artificial intelligence, human infants, see Edwards, 1994), deploy the same kinds of descriptions and attributions as folk do for each other (intelligence, rationality, empathy, communicative competence, etc.).

It is not just a matter of recognizing group versus personal categorizations *on sight*. Conventional demographic identities such as male and female, working man and housewife, married woman and girl, parent and child, and so on, are quite capable of being used for doing very personal kinds of category work with regard to narrated events and accountability in them, as we saw with Connie and Jimmy. Similarly, ostensibly personal or dispositional kinds of categories, such as being jealous or flirtatious, sociable or morose, can be worked up as some kind of group membership, just as Connie and Jimmy did with regard to Connie's taking part in 'girls' nights out', and how they categorize themselves and each other as being one *kind* of person rather than another (Edwards, 1995b).

Again, ostensibly obvious 'group membership' categories, such as the fact that the couple are Irish and the counsellor English (national identities), fail to materialize as anything they treat as relevant. England and Ireland do crop up plenty of times. They figure as *locations* in narratives of marital separation, having to seek work, going home for holidays, needing to visit friends and relations, opportunities for affairs, distinctions between one kind of separation (holiday, work) and another (walking out, splitting up). But these are the kind of thing that living in town versus countryside, small town versus city, north versus south, etc., can be used for. But Jimmy and Connie here make nothing at all of *being Irish*, which of course is not to say that they may not do so sometimes. The point is that virtually any categorization can function as a way of locating someone as a member of some group or another, and that group membership can be invoked and deployed for local, 'personal' business; that is the kind of thing people do, and attend to, and counter, in their talk. This is, of course, one of the central themes of this book as a whole, as is the recommendation that the best way of seeing how they do that, and what they do with it, is to study their talk.

Asking what people are *doing*, when their talk reveals that they assign descriptions (i.e., categories) to themselves and to each other, requires a theory and methodology for dealing with descriptions, with discourse approached as a species of social action. Social cognition theories essentially lack a theory of language, and a way of dealing with it empirically as a social phenomenon. Harvey Sacks (1979, 1992) started to show us how 'identity' categories can be approached empirically, how insider–outsider issues are worked up and attended to in talk, how descriptions can perform 'membership' business, and how that can perform further, local, interactional business in the current talk. Categorization is approachable discursively as something we actively do, and do things with (Edwards, 1991), rather than some piece of perceptual machinery that gets switched on by 'stimulus' events. Social categorizations are interaction's business, its matters in hand, not its causal effects or conditions.

Note

Thanks are due to Margaret Wetherell, Jonathan Potter, and Michael Billig for useful comments on an earlier draft of this chapter.

3 How Gun-owners Accomplish Being Deadly Average

Andy McKinlay and Anne Dunnett

The search for a proper understanding of self and identity has provided a rich vein of research in the social sciences. The present chapter, like the others in this collection, is part of that disparate set of writings whose roots lie in fields as diverse as ethnomethodology, literary studies and the writings of the 'new' continental philosophers. The style of this book, of course, is towards the discourse – and conversation – analysis part of the terrain. We offer an example of this approach by showing how self and identity can be analysed by attending to the fine-grain detail of conversational interactions. At the end of the chapter, we shall also try to show how the conversation-analytic perspective can handle problems – like the 'salience' of identity categories – which other traditions find hard to cope with.

The particular identity issue at stake in this chapter – what it means to someone to view himself or herself as a gun-owner – is, unfortunately, all too socially relevant, given the gun-related outrages which occurred while this chapter was being prepared, and in countries as far apart as Scotland, the United States and Australia. In the light of this, the following analysis may be read, on a practical level, as an attempt by social science to help us understand more clearly the nature of the debate between those who oppose gun-ownership and those who support it. It is sometimes suggested that the conversation-analytic approach is problematic if for no other reason than that it has no real-world application. One of the ways in which this complaint can be countered is for those interested in conversation analytic research to tackle, head-on, substantive issues which concern people in their daily lives.

Selves in Discourse

The suggestion that an understanding of one's self and others as social beings may be regarded as a constructive outcome of discursive interactions is made by several different discourse theorists, whose work ranges from the 'discourse-as-rhetoric' end of the analytic spectrum to the conversation analytic end. From a rhetorical perspective, Billig (1987) claims that traditional social psychology has overestimated the power of explanatory devices such as stereotypes by concentrating solely on the generalization of thought which they provide. His suggestion is that alongside any social generalization, it is possible to discover discrete particularizations which can be seen to challenge or modify the claim made by means of the generalization. In the case of generalizations which apply to people, this would mean that when researchers find generalizations about self and others to be in use, they are also likely to find people making exceptions to those generalizations, viewed as general rules, by formulating particular cases which stand outside those rules.

In this sense, social interaction involving depictions of (or understandings about) oneself and others can be thought of in terms of debate, where the general consequences of stereotypical generalization are opposed by specific instances of particularization which seek to challenge, or make exception to, that generalization. Central to this notion of debate is what Billig (1987) terms 'witcraft'. Billig is careful to point out that not all forms of communication involve witcraft. However, this leaves open the possibility that in cases of self- or other-generalization perceived by participants to be 'difficult', 'problematic' or 'open to argument', the processes of ordinary talk which Billig identifies as witcraft will come into play.

Wetherell and Potter have suggested that rhetorical studies of this sort can benefit from applying more detailed analyses at the level of specific discourses or interpretative repertoires (Wetherell and Potter, 1992) or from the more fine-grain analysis typified by conversation analysis (Potter and Wetherell, 1988a). In one set of interviews (Potter and Wetherell, 1988b), they questioned people who had witnessed riots involving anti-apartheid campaigners protesting about the South African rugby team's tour of New Zealand in 1981. Interviewees had the task of accounting for the violence and conflict they observed. Wetherell and Potter describe in these accounts a number of different versions of 'the other' which respondents drew on. They isolated three: the idea of 'the ordinary person' (applicable to the police); the idea of the 'genuine' demonstrator; and the idea of the protester whose motives are 'not genuine' (an example of an accounting device which Wetherell and Potter call 'the stirrer'). Wetherell and Potter's conclusion was that their interviewees constructed these various versions of others' identities in order to achieve an explanation of the riots which avoided large-scale condemnation of fellow New Zealanders. The conclusion which can be drawn from this is that the social characterizations which underpin ascriptions of social identity are always open to reformulation by participants in those cases where the characterization leads to apparent identity problems.

Widdicombe and Wooffitt's conversation analytic study of youth subcultures (Widdicombe, 1993; Widdicombe and Wooffitt, 1995) is another example of the discursive opportunities offered by social identification. In their study of how young people accounted for the way they became 'goths', Widdicombe and Wooffitt interviewed a number of people at rock concerts, asking them about how they came to belong to this specific subculture. Their interest was in the following dilemma which questions about identity posed for such individuals. It would be relatively straightforward for respondents to construe their own social identity in terms of the social group which their clothing seems to make salient – the goths. But simple identification with that group raises an interesting problem for those identified: the potential problem of being thought to be the sort of person who merely copies a trend. Widdicombe and Wooffitt showed that accounts people offered of themselves *qua* goths were designed specifically to avoid any inference that they became goths to copy others. Respondents achieved this by emphasizing that their own dressing as goths occurred before meeting others who dressed in that way, and that their own choice of dress arose in ignorance of the existence of such others.

What this suggests is that in providing accounts of oneself, one can be seen to use such accounts to construct a 'version' of oneself just as Wetherell and Potter's interviewees provided identities for others. Moreover, as was the case with Wetherell and Potter, Widdicombe and Wooffitt show that these accounts can be specially tailored to provide solutions to problems which someone may perceive in his or her account of self. In the Widdicombe and Wooffitt example, the respondents' problem is one of maintaining a sense of individuality, of avoiding been seen as 'part of the herd'. The respondents' discursive solution was to establish in their accounts differences, as well as similarities, between self and relevant others. This shows that there is a sense in which people can self-ascribe social characterizations while, at the same time, avoiding the implications which go with those characterizations.

Analyses of everyday discourse have, then, begun to demonstrate that issues of self and identity can be fruitfully explored by close attention to the sorts of accounts which people offer in response to a variety of topics. What is revealed is that people employ a variety of discursive mechanisms in order to solve identity-related problems which arise in interaction with others.

To this extent, contemporary studies of self and discourse develop the ethnomethodological concern with understanding how everyday 'practical reason' can be seen to guide social interactions. For example, Sacks (1974) has suggested that conversational participants often draw upon 'membership categorization devices'. Sack's claim was that people construe others and their activities by identifying sets of categories ('devices') which can be used in participants' explanation of themselves, or others, and their actions. The value of categorization for social actors is that certain activities can be treated as 'bound' to certain categories and this bounded-ness provides a common-sense understanding of the world. In this way, everyday knowledge about categories which 'fit' together into devices (e.g., baby/mummy, boss/worker) and the activities bound to those categories represent a shared basis on which social actors can demonstrate their common grasp of 'what is going on' in an interaction. The conversation analytic perspective on the self develops this idea with its emphasis on conversational work. For the conversation analyst, what is important about 'the self' is the way in which a given person can constructively deploy discourse, for example by manipulating categorization devices, in a way that both speaker and hearer demonstrably recognize as 'appropriate' or 'acceptable'.

The following sections, which present data taken from interviews with gun-owners, demonstrate some of these phenomena. As the analysis reveals, the participants display no difficulties in establishing two apparently inconsistent versions of themselves within the context of the same interview. Some of the consequences of this finding are discussed in the final section.

'Inconsistent' Identities

These data are taken from interviews with members of an American gun club. Edited versions of these conversations were broadcast as part of Radio Scotland's *Kane Over America* series which presented a variety of views of contemporary American life and culture. The transcriptions presented here are taken from original, unedited tapes. 'Bob' is the radio interviewer, 'Ted' is the gun club's representative for the National Rifle Association of America (NRA), and 'Carol' is a member of the gun club. The structure of the extracts can be classified in common-sense terms as a series of questions and answers. However, as Schegloff (1984) has argued, everyday syntactical categories are as likely to hide as to reveal the actual nature of what goes on in a conversation. One of the outcomes of the following analyses will be the discovery that when Ted and Carol respond to previous utterances made by Bob, their conversational contributions achieve far more than accomplishing an 'answer' to Bob's 'question'.

In the USA, as in the UK, the prevalence of gun ownership is a matter of social and political debate. As a result, both gun-owners and proponents of gun-control laws recognize gun ownership as a contentious issue. Gun-control proponents view gun ownership as something which makes society less safe and more violent. Gun ownership proponents view gun ownership as something which makes 'normal' citizens safer from the violence perpetrated by criminals. However, it is questionable whether an understanding of this wider social debate is required in order to provide an adequate analysis of the sort of interactions which occur between Bob and Carol and Bob and Ted (Antaki, 1994). Following Schegloff's understanding of the distinction between syntactic and conversational structure, a number of implications can be drawn just from the fact that Ted and

Carol can be seen to treat 'answers' to Bob's 'questions' as a resource for achieving quite different aims other than answering a question in an appropriate manner.

For example, in an early part of the interview with Ted, Bob asks Ted to describe the history and purpose of the NRA, and Ted's response begins with a review of the development of the NRA:

(1)

1	Bob:	give me an idea of when the NRA started and what are
2		its aims
3	Ted:	well the NRA was started back in the 1800's (em) (.) it
4		was originally started basically as a group for
5		competition shooters and it has grown from that into
6		the main protector of gun rights in the United States
7		(ah) they do lobbying they work with the legislatures
8		both state and national (.) (em) to try to protect the rights
9		that are guaranteed under the Constitution of the
10		United States for the the <u>average</u> citizen to be able to
11		own a handgun or a rifle

To begin with, it can be noted that Ted's account of the purpose of the NRA employs a three-part list structure (lines 6–9) of the sort identified by Atkinson (1984) as a rhetorical device. The NRA: (a) do lobbying; (b) work with the legislatures; and (c) try to protect rights. One feature of this rhetorical device is that it allows the speaker to indicate that all three parts of the list exemplify some common feature (Jefferson, 1991). Thus Ted is able to demonstrate right away that the NRA is associated with law-abiding political processes. At the end of his response (lines 9–10), Ted identifies the NRA's purpose as providing protection of the right for the 'average' citizen to own guns. Moreover, this right is characterized by means of the semi-legalistic formulation 'guaranteed under the Constitution of the United States' (lines 8–9). One feature of this appeal is that it lends some apparent backing (Antaki, 1994) to Ted's claim that gun-owners are not to be seen as out of the ordinary. So irrespective of knowledge of wider social issues, the analyst is already able to regard as noteworthy this particular formulation of those whose rights the NRA seeks to 'protect': they are average people whose wishes have legal status.

What happens to this version of the gun-owner as a legally endowed, average citizen can be seen by following through the conversational turns that occur immediately after Ted's first response.

(2)

12	Bob:	that's one of the great bedrocks of the NRA isn't it that
13		in the Constitution there is the right to bear arms (.) for
14		every American

15	Ted:	well that's (.) the whole <u>basis</u> of the NRA without the
16		(eh) constitutional right to bear arms we wouldn't have
17		a fight on our hands in the first place (em) (.) the
18		founding fathers saw fit to put a piece in the
19		Constitution that guaranteed the people the right to bear
20		and carry <u>arms</u> (.) (em) we were a pioneering nation (eh)
21		we started out with guns not only to defend ourselves
22		but (.) we had to hunt and bring down food for the table
23		(emm) we had to (.) each man had to defend his home in
24		the wilderness (uh) it was just a a piece of the furniture
25		(.) (uh) every man had a rifle at least in the house
26	Bob:	so who are you fighting against at the moment (and) at
27		this time (.) who are your opponents
28	Ted:	well really I don't like to consider 'em opponents (eh)
29		everybody has a different <u>opinion</u> on gun rights (emm)
30		even within our own groups we have our own dis (eh)
31		differences of opinion some people (.) have a much
32		stronger opinion where they don't want to give up any
33		type of rights (.) others are more willing to <u>compromise</u>
34		to (uh) (.) to try to work with the particular situation that
35		they are in (ahh)the biggest (.) proportion of people in
36		the United States that own weapons (.) they use them in
37		a shooting range like we're here for competition or for
38		relaxation they use it for <u>hunting</u> or they keep a gun at
39		home for defence (.) and they're not out on the streets
40		committing <u>crimes</u> and (.) they're not out on the streets
41		doing vigilante justice (emm) so the average person – is
42		just there (.) to have the weapon for their use and not to
43		disturb anybody else

It is clear that the pace of events picks up in the turns which follow the initial contributions of Bob and Ted. Bob picks up on Ted's characterization of gun-owners by talking of those whose 'rights' the NRA protect as 'every American'. In response, Ted elaborates on his appeal to the legality of gun ownership by backing it with an appeal to the authority figure of 'the founding fathers'. Moreover, he then goes on to provide a narrative account of the way in which gun-owners came to have this legally and authoritatively sanctioned status (lines 18–21). One of the conversational functions of narrative is that the plausibility of a claim can be increased by locating it within a narrative structure (Edwards and Potter, 1992). In this instance, Ted's historical story of the hardy pioneer can be read as a means of further establishing the everyday status of guns: 'just a piece of furniture'.

Ted's description of the gun-owner as someone doing nothing out of the ordinary and whose action in owning a gun has well established legal and authoritative status allows Ted to continue by concluding that the gun-owner is just 'the average person'. It is in this context that Ted's assertion on lines 16–17 that the NRA had a fight on its hands comes into especially sharp focus. If Ted as a gun-owner and member of the NRA is the sort of unexceptionable person he himself makes out, the idea that the NRA is nevertheless fighting someone or something raises difficulties. Bob's subsequent query of 'who are your opponents' sharpens this point by highlighting Ted's historical account as an inadequate rationale for the NRA of today. In the light of this, Ted's next contribution can be seen to be a masterpiece of group category formulation work. He begins (lines 28–31) by issuing a 'conversational repair' (Heritage, 1984a) questioning Bob's formulation which apparently follows on from his own earlier 'fight' claim. First, the people the NRA are fighting are not 'opponents'. This has the immediate effect of helping bolster the earlier notion of the gun-owner as an average citizen. Instead of a 'them and us' situation in which the NRA fight against clearly defined others, it transpires that 'everybody has a different opinion'. The implication which can be taken from this is that opinion about gun ownership does not separate out two classes of people. Rather, this opinion represents something which is *unique to each individual*. Having blurred the possible distinction between gun-owners and those they fight against, Ted amplifies this by fragmenting the idea of gun-owners as a group (lines 30–2).

Having negotiated the potential threat raised by his own 'fight' claim to the view of the gun-owner as an average citizen, Ted returns to his original theme. The end of his response to Bob's 'who are you fighting' query consists of the development of a contrastive pair (again, a powerful rhetorical structure; see Atkinson, 1984). One of the functions of contrasting oneself with another is to cast one's own side in a favourable light. Here, Ted contrasts the 'biggest proportion' of gun-owners with criminals and vigilantes. The actions of criminals and vigilantes can be understood to be unacceptable. In Sacks's terms, unacceptable behaviour is 'bound' to those categories and this binding forms part of the 'practical reasoning' which Ted and Bob bring to bear on their interaction. Ted then contrasts the criminal and vigilante categories with those who are 'the biggest proportion'. By contrasting gun-owners with criminals and vigilantes, the implication is that while the activities of the latter are unacceptable, the activities of the former are not. This contrast leads Ted naturally into a restatement of his theme that the gun-owner is just an 'average person'. We are seeing someone 'normalizing a stigmatized practice', as Lawrence calls it in his analysis of an interviewee handling the accusation of 'operating a house of prostitution' (Lawrence, 1996: 189).

This initial analysis already points towards some theoretically interesting conclusions. In the first place, it is clear that Ted is accomplishing a rich portrayal of the gun-owner as a particular sort of person who is an 'average joe' and whose activities have legal and authoritative sanction. In relation to the earlier theoretical discussion of self and other categorizations, it is especially interesting to note that Ted relies upon two quite different categorization devices. On the one hand, the gun-owner as average citizen is no different from anyone else. The apparent distinction between those who support gun ownership and those who do not is illusory. Opinion on gun ownership turns out to be unique to each individual. On the other hand, the averageness of the gun-owner clearly differentiates him or her from some other class of people who might use guns with criminal intent.

The force of these constructive achievements can be seen to appear later in the same conversation. When, a little later, Bob turns to recent newspaper coverage of gun-related events, he frames his comment in a particular way such that the whole notion of gun-owners as an easily identifiable group is cast into doubt.

(3)

131	Bob:	I was hearing some reports in some (.) recent local
132		newspapers about some citizens' militia organization in
133		Oklahoma starting up I mean (.) are these rumours
134		conspiracy theories (.) the wilder fringes of the anti-gun
135		movement
136	Ted:	(ahh) the idea of militias and whatnot they're they're
137		the <u>fringe</u> groups they're the minority (emm) (.) you're
138		gonna have wild folks in any group that you put
139		together and we don't condone or (.) agree with what
140		they believe in (.) (emmm) -((1 syl)) as I said the average
141		citizen believes in realistic laws and obeys 'em (.) and
142		we're not out there trying to overthrow the government

Bob's comment relies on a now-agreed notion that gun-owners do not constitute an easily identifiable group. Instead of having clearly identifiable boundaries, the group has 'fringes' (lines 133–4). Moreover, the same contrastive device which Ted had earlier employed appears again, in that these 'fringes' are depicted as 'wild', with the implication that they are wilder than the average gun-owner (lines 136–40). Ted returns to his earlier theme of blurring potential group categorization by stating that any group has 'wild folks' in it. Here, the contrast pair of 'wild' versus 'average' is used to demonstrate that group ascriptions are inherently dangerous, since they might result in aggregating people who disagree. This lends support to Ted's earlier accomplishment in demonstrating that there is no easy way to group people in terms of their opinion on gun-ownership. Moreover, Ted's characterization of 'the average citizen' implies that this category is bound to behaviour such as believing in realistic laws. This contrasts with the case of the 'wild folks' whose beliefs are not condoned. Thus, Ted not only develops a contrast between the 'wild' and 'average' categories, he also treats believing in laws as a category-bound activity associated with people in the 'average' category.

So one of Ted's achievements in the conversation is to provide a complex account of gun-owners which identifies them as average, law-abiding citizens. Now since many average, law-abiding citizens in the United States do not own guns, it is clear that there is at least one distinction between gun-owners and non-gun-owners: a gun-owner has the capacity to shoot someone. This represents a potential problem to the depiction of gun-owners as average citizens. Specifically, it raises the problem that the gun-owner has to choose between two apparently inconsistent identities: the average citizen who is like everyone else (though not like criminals) and the gun-toting defender of self and others who may use deadly force when confronted with an antagonist. However, as the following extracts show, this potential difficulty of inconsistent identities can be resolved.

(4)

341	Bob:	do you think that guns make people safer –
342	Ted:	((1 syl)) (that's) a personal opinion (hh) (.) (amm) (.) I
343		know that I feel safer in my home knowing that I have a
344		self defense weapon there (um) it <u>is</u> my home (.) I (.) will
345		do anything I can to keep from having to pull a weapon
346		on somebody but if they come back in the bedroom with
347		me and it comes down to between me and them (hh) (.)
348		then yeah I am gonna try to make it them instead of me
349	Bob:	mm because a lot of opponents of gun control would say
350		that that one of the reasons why gun deaths <u>happen</u> is
351		because that guns are in the <u>home</u> I think that the largest
352		proportion isn't through criminal activities but through
353		things like suicides and through (.) the escalation of
354		domestic disputes and someone reaches for a gun in the
355		drawer (.) is that perhaps a problem maybe not a
356		problem in Oklahoma but maybe a problem generally –
357	Ted:	no I really don't think the gun is the problem (emm)
358		maybe part of the American society is the problem that
359		we have those (.) those situ<u>ations</u> but it's been my
360		experience with people in flash anger if they can't reach
361		a gun they're gonna reach for a knife and they can't find
362		a knife they'll reach for a club and if they can't find that
363		they'll use their fists and (.) (emm) I really don't think
364		it's the weapon that is the cause of the death it's the
366		situation in the <u>household</u> or the (.) the breakdown in
367		the society that we have which definitely is nothing to
368		do with the handgun itself

Ted's initial response to Bob's question is to query the extent to which the question admits of a simple answer, as opposed to being 'a personal opinion'. He then follows this by switching from talk of general cases such as 'the average citizen' to a description of himself, stating that owning a gun makes him feel safe (lines 342–4). The implication, that Ted feels safe because he has the capacity to shoot someone else, is softened by his description of his gun as a 'self defense weapon' and the limitation of the generality of its use to the legitimate boundaries of 'home'. Moreover, one reading of Ted's subsequent statement (lines 347–9) is that it is a response to the possible implication that Ted is only able to feel safer as a result of gun ownership because his gun represents a danger to someone else.

His claim takes a specific form which might be regarded as a mixture of extreme case formulation (Pomerantz, 1986) and narrative construction involving an implicit contrast between facing an antagonist in the home and elsewhere. The effect of this is to allow Ted to demonstrate that while he might shoot someone, this would only be the outcome of a particularly extreme set of circumstances. Ted would only shoot someone if the person was 'back in the bedroom'. It is noteworthy that Ted refrains from explicitly mentioning shooting: in such extreme cases as someone being back in the bedroom, the outcome is described as a case of 'if it comes down to me or them . . . I am gonna try to make it them'. What this identity formulation achieves is safely to dissolve the apparent inconsistency of the deadly force user and the non-violent citizen.

This helps to reinforce the notion that Ted would 'do anything I can to keep from having to pull a weapon'. That is, it underlines Ted's identity as a user of deadly force as arising only in extreme circumstances – circumstances, indeed, that he would do everything he could to avoid or mitigate. There is, therefore, no difficulty for Ted in characterizing himself both as a non-violent person and as someone who might shoot someone else.

Neverthless, the inconsistency is kept live by Bob's questioning Ted's claim that the gun is used for self defense in his home. What Ted now does is develop a further implicit contrast between 'people in flash anger' and other sorts of people (line 360). Here, he redeploys the three-part list device which was noted at the start of the analysis in depicting the difficulty with people in flash anger. If they cannot 'reach a gun' then they (a) reach for a knife or (b) reach for a club or (c) use their fists. This highlights the violent impulse, common across all three parts of the list, which is what characterizes the difference between 'flash anger' people and other people. The effectiveness of this strategy of providing a concrete description of people in flash anger is heightened by the fact that Ted offers this description within the context of a much more general idea of societal breakdown. One of the functions of systematically vague expressions such as 'American society is the problem' and 'breakdown in society' is that, in virtue of the vagueness of the claim, it can be difficult to find a precise rebuttal (Edwards and Potter, 1992). The embedding of a specific three-part listing of the actions of people in flash anger within this systematically vague construction of societal problems thereby allows Ted to work up, then emphasize the differences between the categories 'people in flash anger' and 'other people'.

Average, Normal Citizens

What the conversation between Bob and Ted reveals is that Ted is able to generate a picture of gun-owners as average or normal citizens who both are and are not just like everybody else. Their very averageness means that they are not different from others; even their opinions on gun ownership cannot be used to categorize them as different from other groups. On the other hand, their averageness or normality also means that they can be easily categorized as different from groups such as criminals and vigilantes, fringe groups, wild folks or people in flash anger. Of course gun ownership might result in the gun-owner shooting someone, but this consideration only arises within the context of extreme circumstances. In this way, the apparent inconsistency of depicting gun-owners as both average or normal and yet willing to use deadly force is safely negotiated.

The same notion of the gun-owner as average or normal (in so far as he or she is not a member of some problematic social category) and yet, in extreme circumstances, deadly, also appears in Bob's conversation with Carol.

(5)

111	Bob:	Because obviously one of the things about (.) <u>wo</u>men
112		and guns in America now (.)
113	Carol:	Mmm
114	Bob:	is pre<u>cisely</u> to do with the climate of rape of misogyny
115		⌈of sexual harassment
116	Carol:	⌊well yeah a lot of women a lot of women are (.) more
117		and more women are finding the <u>need</u> to (.) protect
118		themselves because – (amm) the gun laws being what
119		they are – the <u>criminals</u> are the ones that are going to
120		disregard any kind of licensing laws and the criminals
121		and the gang-bangers are the ones that are gonna be
122		<u>carrying</u> (.) (ahhh) I'll tell you the truth I have a I keep a
123		12 gauge shotgun in my apartment as well *((laughs))*
124	Bob:	wow
125	Carol:	(ahh) (.) and whoever gets into my apartment into my
126		bedroom who doesn't belong there is gonna be in for a
127		<u>big</u> surprise – because ( ) if someone gets in there to rob
128		I mean if if all they wanted was <u>stuff</u>, my stereo my TV
129		they could have whatever stuff they wanted wouldn't
130		bother me they could have the stuff (.) (hh) but you
131		know and I know what's gonna happen and (.) that is
132		<u>not</u> gonna happen to me it's happened to my friends
133		(amm) happened to a friend of mine (.) she was raped
134		got the guy went to trial they crucified <u>her</u> (.) on the
135		stand (snaps fingers) the guy walked that is <u>not</u> going to
136		happen to me there is no way that is going to happen to
137		me and it's as simple as that and I made that decision a
138		long long time ago

Bob's initial statement, with its emphasis on '<u>wo</u>men' (line 111) sets the scene for a potential contrast of the sort which was seen earlier in Ted's

conversation. The nature of the contrast is hinted at by Bob's identification, by means of a three-part listing, of what the important issue is in
respect of women and guns: (a) rape; (b) misogyny; and (c) sexual
harassment. One commonality among these three features isolated by Bob
is the notion of women as the victims of crime. Carol picks up on this
characterization as people dealing with problems who 'need' to protect
themselves from criminals (lines 117–19). The vagueness of her original
formulation 'a lot of women' is developed by her reformulation of this as
'more and more women'.

Having worked with Bob to generate a picture of the woman gun-owner
as someone who faces problems of protection, Carol then goes on to
introduce the same sort of contrast case which was seen earlier in Ted's
conversation. It is 'criminals' and 'gang-bangers' who disregard licensing
laws and who 'are gonna be <u>carrying</u>' (lines 121–2). The effect of this
contrast is to support the idea that women only carry guns to protect
themselves whereas others carry weapons for criminal purposes. Women
are people who only carry guns through need, rather than through violent
or criminal intent.

The formulation which Bob and Carol have worked towards at this stage
is both similar and dissimilar to that developed by Bob and Ted. Women
can be viewed as normal citizens in that they are contrasted with criminals
and gang-bangers. However, Bob and Carol have also set this version of
women within a wider context of women needing to protect themselves.
This combination provides for a particularly easy move from gun-owner as
normal citizen to gun-owner as user of deadly force. However Carol, like
Ted, displays a particular orientation to this change. The gun-owner as
user of deadly force appears only by means of an extended extreme case
narrative.

Carol's deadly force narrative begins with a prefacing statement
(Jefferson, 1978). Her tale begins after a pause with the statement 'I'll
tell you the truth' (line 122) and is followed by Bob's appreciative 'wow'
which can be read as an expression of willingness to hear the rest of the
story (Goodwin, 1984). Carol's story sets out the same extreme cir-
cumstance as did Ted's: 'whoever gets into my bedroom'. Like Ted, her
expression of how she would respond to such circumstances makes it plain
that such a person might be met with deadly force (one reasonable
implication being that the intruder would be surprised by the appearance
of Carol's shotgun). However, as in Ted's case, this announcement
is softened in that no mention is made of actual shooting: '(whoever) . . . is
gonna be met with a big surprise'. Moreover, just as Ted was at pains to
picture himself as unwilling to use his gun, Carol then continues her story
with the claim that she would not be bothered if the robber merely wanted
'stuff'. The repetition of 'stuff' (lines 128–30) helps make clear that the
robber wanting stuff is one sort of case which differs from other sorts of
cases. This then leads naturally into the first conclusion of the narrative:
'you know and I know what's gonna happen'. This contrast between a

robber taking stuff and 'what's gonna happen' helps to make clear for Carol and Bob that the 'big surprise' only occurs in circumstances where the intruder wants something more than stuff. And the value of this, for Carol's account of herself, is twofold. First, it exemplifies just how extreme the case must be before she reverts to deadly force and, secondly, it functions as a form of blaming (Buttny, 1993) in which the cause of the 'big surprise' can be seen to derive from the intruder's unwillingness to settle for stuff.

From lines 132–3, the story takes on a more immediate character. The story switches from talk of two possible future scenarios 'what's gonna happen and (.) that is not gonna happen' to description of actual events 'it's happened to my friends'. In this account, presented of course as factual, the undesirable nature of the outcome is heightened by Carol's use of the 'crucified her' metaphor. This depiction of the unreasonableness of the treatment of her friend then allows Carol to close her story with a re-statement of the idea that 'that is not going to happen to me' although now the event which is not going to happen may be taken to be not so much rape itself as rape together with unfair treatment by the judicial system. Having set out these two alternatives: a 'big surprise' versus rape and unfair treatment at the hands of the law, Carol is then able to conclude that her willingness to use deadly force is 'as simple as that'.

Taken together, Ted's and Carol's conversations reveal the extraordinary complexity of the means by which the two interviewees characterize themselves as gun-owners. The simple gloss on their statements would consist of seeing them as people who categorize themselves as gun-owners, with the caveat that gun-owners are usually ordinary, non-criminal people. Of course, to this gloss it would have to be added that they also see themselves as people who would be willing to use deadly force; people who would 'try to make it them instead of me' or who would offer 'a big surprise' to intruders. Viewed in terms of simple group categorizations, these two self-categorizations seem apparently inconsistent. However, viewed from the perspective of the conversation analyst, they can be seen to be natural corollaries. In addition, the interaction between Bob and Carol demonstrates the way in which identities are often the outcome of a joint constructive effort. It is because Carol picks up on Bob's image of women as potential victims that she is able to accomplish the blending of the two apparently inconsistent aspects of being a gun-owner.

A Constructivist Account of Identity 'Salience' and 'Reality'

The outcome of the preceding sections is that there is empirical evidence in support of the view that people construct their social identities. This constructivist emphasis can be usefully contrasted with other views on the self. The notion of self and identity with which European social psychology is most familiar derives from the experimental work of Tajfel (1982a), and later Tajfel and Turner (1985). Tajfel defined 'social identity' as 'the individual's knowledge that he belongs to certain social groups together with some emotional and value significance to him of the group membership' (Tajfel, 1982b: 24). Contemporary versions of this experimental approach, most notably self categorization theory (Turner, 1987), stress that the identity-forming social categories we employ in making out a sense of self are 'external' entities. Identity is constructed in so far as we select a particular self categorization as apt for a given set of circumstances, but the 'building blocks' which underlie this constructive effort, the social categories themselves, are objective phenomena.

Self categorization theory therefore appears to offer two benefits to the analyst. On the one hand, it explains the empirical evidence of social constructions of identity available since Tajfel's early studies; social identity or self categorization appears to be mutable and is apparently affected by one's social interactions. On the other hand, it also offers a view of adoption of a social identity or self categorization as a process which is, at root, grounded in objective fact. Take, for example, an individual who is male, a Labour Party member and a supporter of Glasgow Rangers football team. Now suppose that individual finds himself, by a bizarre twist of fate, attending first a women's feminist discussion group, then a meeting of the local Conservative constituency party, and then an evening's night out for members of the (rival) Glasgow Celtic Football Club. According to self categorization theory, that individual's sense of self is likely to alter as he moves from one context to the next. And, indeed, it seems uncontroversial to suppose that his sense of self might well focus first on his maleness, then his political persuasion and then his football club loyalties as he moves from setting to setting. In this sense, his sense of self is changeable in that different social categories may come to seem more or less important. And yet what it is to exemplify these categories – to be male, or a Labour Party member or a Rangers supporter – is seemingly independent of the individual's act of self categorization and thus, in this sense, objective.

Now in order to provide a theoretical exposition of this blending of social construction and objectivity, the self categorization theorist must be able to demonstrate how the link is made between an individual's constructive efforts in selecting a contextually 'appropriate' self categorization and the objective world of social categories. If social categories are objective phenomena, standing outside any given social interaction, then self categorization theory must demonstrate what it is, beyond such social interaction, which determines choice of a specific self (or other) categorization in a specific context. Famously, this categorization determinant has been taken by self categorization theorists to be *salience*. In a specific context, many objective social categories may be (more or less) cognitively available, but determination of which category 'fits' that context is not achieved merely through social interaction. Rather, features of the context settle which of these social categories is likely to be perceived, by the interaction participants, as most obviously applicable.

The perceptual salience notion is, then, crucial to the success of self categorization theory. If social categories are not, in this sense, determinate, then they lose their objective character. If it were to turn out that any social category requires further interpretative work when it appears in social interaction before its perceptual 'fit' or aptness was acceptable to participants in the interaction, then there would be no sense in which it could be claimed that social categories are objective phenomena which are external to such interactions. But the objectivity of self categorizations is supposed to derive precisely from the objectivity of social categories. It follows that the objectivity of self categorizations, according to the theory, depends on the success of the notion that flexibility in use of social categories to categorize self and others is determined by contextual salience.

The conversation analyst's claim is that the salience notion cannot carry the burden of determining category 'fit'. Categorizations of self and others may involve much more than a passive perception of the scene. Instead, self and other categorizations can often be seen to be the focus of areas of interaction in which debate and re-negotiation flourish, although such debates and negotiations may never explicitly refer to categorizations and their salience *per se*. This claim need not be taken to imply that the empirical evidence adduced in support of self categorization theory is somehow in doubt. Nothing said earlier involves denial of the commonplace fact that some categorizations can become, or be made to become (e.g., through experimental manipulation), salient. The claim is, rather, that in everyday circumstances, the processes through which people make out, challenge or defend their sense of self for themselves (or for others) is often a complex matter of negotiation and active formulation in which identity can be seen to be discursively constructed.

It is worthwhile examining this notion of 'discursive construction of identity' more closely. One of the tensions that exists between proponents of experimental social psychology and conversation (or discourse) analytic social psychology is a difference in perspective on what constitutes social reality. Nowhere is this debate more sharply focused than on the issue of social identity. Self categorization theorists consider the self to be, in part, a product of interpretative processes. From the self categorization perspective, one understands oneself as a social being partly because one ascribes to oneself certain group memberships which, in a given context, are salient. However, the properties of group membership ascription, such as impact on self-esteem, adoption of stereotyped ways of thinking, and the influence of group membership on one's judgements and decisions, are themselves real phenomena which stand outside the ambit of the individual's social constructive powers. The discourse or conversation analyst takes a different view. The only notion of identity which the social psychologist has to work with is the idea of identity as a construct. The construction materials are those discursive accounts, such as descriptions, explanations, exonerations, corrections, and reformulations, which the analyst identifies as relevant to the subject's sense of, or display of, identity.

However, there is a danger, at least for the discourse or conversation analyst, were he or she to state the tension in just these terms. The danger lies in the apparently sensible conclusion that experimentalists such as self categorization theorists deal with real identity, while discourse or conversation analysts do not. This apparent problem can be resolved by a more precise understanding of what the discourse or conversation analyst means when it is said that identity is constructed in discourse.

It is central to the discourse analytic perspective that when people construct identity by providing accounts, this is a rational process. Accounts pertaining to identity are provided to address specific issues which arise in local contexts. This implies that people have a specifiable sense of identity which it is their business to develop or maintain or enhance or protect through their account-giving practice. Moreover, in looking at discourse between or among people, the discourse or conversation analyst will argue that the picture or demonstration of identity produced by one person may well become the focus of attention in subsequent discourse contributions of other people. Thus, for all of those involved in an everyday social interaction, the identity which is constructed is taken, by participants, to be a real phenomenon.

The distinction between the experimentalist and the discourse or conversation analyst in terms of the reality of identity can now be seen to boil down to a distinction between 'real' and 'taken, by participants, to be real'. The justification for the latter phrase is located in the common-sense distinction between varieties of talk where people take themselves not to be talking about something real, such as jokes, fantasies, lies, fictional accounts, metaphors, and those other varieties of talk where people take themselves to be picturing how things are. It is in this latter sense that people can be said to be presenting a picture of what their identity really is when they provide accounts of the sort examined earlier.

There may be a temptation to think that this 'taken, by participants, to be real' sense of 'real' is not, as it were, really real. But if one falls into this temptation, then one must provide a meaning for 'real' identity which goes beyond that offered which demonstrates that this further sense of 'real' identity is useful to the social psychologist. The discourse or conversation analyst's notion of real identity is that idea which, in a given context, a person has of him or herself as it is manifested in interaction with others. And, the discourse or conversation analyst's claim runs, it is just this phenomenon of a sense of one's own and others' real identities which the social psychologist should be pursuing. It follows that there is no additional benefit which accrues to the social psychological enterprise by introducing a further notion of 'real' identity which somehow transcends that on offer from the discourse or conversation analyst.

It is important to consider a final caveat in relation to this criticism of transcendental realism of identity. The discourse or conversation analysis conception of identity presupposes that account-giving is a rational affair – rational in the sense that accounts are offered to address potential problems within localized discursive contexts. This is meant to be common-or-garden rationality understood as actions performed for a purpose or reason. For the discourse or conversation analyst, however, these partici- pants' purposes or reasons do not, themselves, represent transcendently real phenomena which 'stand outside' accounts and provide a non- discursive explanatory framework. They 'stand outside' in the sense that they may not be explicitly mentioned within a given account. But their existence, as real phenomena upon which an analyst can draw in interpreting accounts, consists in the fact that they are discursive elements which could, themselves, be the subject matter of other, different accounts.

Concluding Comments

Analyses of the sort provided here show that identity is a complex phenomenon. First, people demonstrate an interest in constructing a sense of who they are in a number of different conversational contexts. These constructive efforts are seamlessly woven into other concerns as a conver- sation unfolds. Thus Carol tells Bob that gun ownership makes it possible to shoot intruders. At the same time, she informs Bob that gun-owners are the type of people who hate resorting to violence. Secondly, constructing an identity in talk may involve subtle negotiations about category memberships. For example, Ted questions the apparently obvious category distinction represented by 'members of the NRA' and 'opponents of the NRA'. He suggests that what matters is people's opinions on gun owner- ship. And these opinions are too varied to allow for the simple categ- orization of 'member' versus 'opponent'. Thirdly, constructing an identity is a collaborative enterprise. The interplays between Bob and Ted and Bob and Carol show that each one picks up on identity formulations offered by the other. For example, Bob suggests to Ted that some problematic cases of gun ownership are caused by 'fringe' elements. This is a formulation which Ted accepts and develops. However, when Bob points out that most gun deaths are caused by gun-owners, Ted rejects this characterization. Such deaths are caused by people in 'flash anger' and being a gun-owner is irrelevant.

These three features of talk about identity show that conversation analysis is a valuable tool in analysing how we make sense of ourselves and others. However, locating the explanation of identity at the conversational level raises tensions with other perspectives on identity and the self. Notably, what is abandoned by the conversation-analysis perspective is the idea that self categorization is a key explanatory mechanism. Identity construction does not require a conversational context of explicit self- categorization and does not even require that fixed or unchallenged categories be in use. Instead, what conversation analysis offers is a means of exploring the flexibility and variability, associated with self characterizations, which typify everyday interaction. It is the analysis of these conversational flexibilities and variabilities which leads to a deeper understanding of the role that identity talk plays for us as social beings.

'But You Don't Class Yourself': The Interactional Management of Category Membership and Non-membership

Sue Widdicombe

In this chapter, I shall be concerned with the ways in which speakers accomplish membership and non-membership of a potentially relevant category. The category membership at stake is that of a youth subculture such as punk or gothic. The data come from informal interviews with people who were approached on the streets of London or at rock festivals in the south of England on the grounds that their appearance suggested to us that they could be members of a particular subculture. In the first part of the analysis, I will outline some strategies used by speakers to warrant their non-membership of a subcultural category, and I will argue that these are designed to resist some inferential consequences of characterizing oneself as a member. In the second part, I will focus on two extracts from one interview in which one speaker affirms and the other rejects subcultural identity. I will thereby extend my observations on ways of warranting non-membership but I will also show that the negotiation of subcultural identity displays a sensitivity to the same problems of category affiliation: implied conformity and a loss of individuality. In the concluding comments, I will consider briefly how similar assumptions inform more traditional social scientific views which therefore fail to appreciate that categories and category membership are sites of negotiation and dispute.

My analytic interest in the descriptive strategies used for doing member-ship and non-membership differs from much previous conversation and discourse analytic work which has been more concerned with how categor-ies function in talk to accomplish particular social actions. These actions include ascribing motives (Watson, 1983), mitigating actions (Wetherell and Potter, 1989; Wowk, 1984), denials and refutations (Edwards and Potter, 1992), justifications (e.g., Potter and Reicher, 1987), and factual accounting (see Potter, 1996). These achievements rest on several general features of categories which, we shall see, also figure in doing and rejecting membership. For a start, notions of category membership and social identity are crucially linked: a reference to a person's social identity is also a reference to their membership of a specific category. In addition, categories are inference-rich such that they don't just provide us with convenient labels, they are also conventionally associated with particular activities and other characteristics. Membership categories also are loci for the legitimate (i.e., conventional and warranted) imputation of motives, expectations and rights associated with that category and its members (Watson and Weinberg, 1982). Therefore, category terms may be used to invoke activities or other attributes which may be expected or considered appropriate for people to whom the category term is applied (by them-selves or others). Conversely, a description of someone's activities may be used to invoke their category membership.

The fact that categories are conventionally associated with activities, attributes, motives and so on makes them a powerful cultural resource in warranting, explaining and justifying behaviour. That is, whatever is known about the category can be invoked as being relevant to the person to whom the label is applied and provides a set of inferential resources by which to interpret and account for past or present conduct, or to inform predictions about likely future behaviour (Sacks, 1979, 1992).

Nevertheless, the same features of categories which provide for their functional utility may also present inferential problems for those to whom the category is directly or indirectly applied. For example, it is likely that on occasions the ascription of category membership may be used to make available unfavourable inferences about a person (e.g., see Drew, 1987 on the way that teases can make relevant a deviant identity). More generally, Widdicombe and Wooffitt (1995) argued that there is a sense in which the ascription of a social identity is a form of social control. That is, once a person's category affiliation has been assumed, it is always potentially the case that the sense or purpose of his or her actions, beliefs, opinions and so on, may be understood solely by virtue of what is known commonly or expected about that category, and without consulting him or her. This may in turn provoke a sense of social injustice. Moreover, if it is assumed that the basis of a person's actions lies in his or her collective identification, this may constitute a threat to individual integrity and the authenticity of his or her actions (Widdicombe, 1995).

Rejecting Subcultural Identity

It is not surprising therefore that in our analysis of respondents' accounts (Widdicombe and Wooffitt, 1995), we identified a variety of ways through which respondents accomplished resistance to the appropriateness of the subcultural identity and to common assumptions about subcultures and the people who join them. Here, I will summarize several of these strategies, in particular those employed at the start of the interviews in which the interviewer asked two questions designed to elicit a subcultural self-identification. First, there was a vague question inviting respondents to say something about themselves, their style and appearance. If this failed to elicit the required response, it was followed by a more direct question about whether they would call themselves members of a particular subculture.

Resisting the Category-implicative Reference to Style

Widdicombe and Wooffitt (1995) discuss at some length how it was that participants could interpret the opening question of the interview, 'tell me something about yourselves . . .', as an invitation to specify their member-ship of a particular subcultural category. Nevertheless, we also observed that on many occasions, participants did not comply with this request. In the following extract, for example, the speakers criticize the question rather than produce what they can infer to be the appropriate or expected response.

(1a)   3:no specific group:F:T3SA [FP] [note: extracts 1a and 2a below are con-tinued later in extracts 1b, 1c and 2b respectively]

```
1       I:       can you tell me something about your style and the way
2                you look,
3                (.7)
4       I:       how would you descri:be yourselves
5                (.7)
6       R1:      °huhh°
7                (.7)
8       R1:      I dunno >I hate those sorts of quest ⌈ions< uhm
9       R2:                                          ⌊yeah horrible
10               isn't it
11               (.7)
```

Here, R1 formulates a negative attitude to the prior question, saying 'I hate those sorts of questions'. Her utterance constitutes a complaint about having to provide a characterization of herself, but it also functions as a way of avoiding the provision of any kind of self-identification in the place where it would have been appropriate. A similar effect is achieved in extract (2a) by MR's comment on the ambiguity of the question, 'I could answer that in a lot of ways'.

(2a)   2P and friend:M/F:T8SA [Cam] *[There were three participants in this interview; the appearance of two of them, MR and FR, suggested they could be punks, while NP's did not]*

```
1       I:       >↑O↓kay< ˙hh how would you descri:be yourselves an your style
                 an that
2                (0.8)
3       MR:      I could answer that in a lot of ways      ((laughing voice))
```

```
4     NP:    go on then
5     MR:    it's disgusting. heh heh, heh
6     FR:    urgh ·hh
7            (0.2)
8     FR:    it's colourful
9            (0.2)
10    I:     mm hm
11           (2)
12    FR:    I DUNNO:, I don't like describing it really it's just what you feel
13           (0.4)
14    I:     °mmhm°
```

However, explicit rejection of questions can jeopardize the smooth flow of interaction and in other extracts, speakers achieved the same effect through a more subtle device, specifically, by producing a question seeking clarification. This allowed the respondents to avoid giving a subcultural identification in such a way that their resistance did not become an explicit focus of the exchange. For example:

(3)   1R:M:T5SB [RRF] (from Widdicombe and Wooffitt, 1995: 94)

```
             ((Tape starts))
1     I:     how would you descri:be (.) yourself
2            and your appearance and so on
3            (.)
4     R:     describe my appearance,
5     I:     yeah
6            (1)
7     R:     su- su- slightly longer than average hair
             ((goes on to describe appearance))
```

Widdicombe and Wooffitt argued that through producing these questions and comments the respondents are able to recharacterize the business of that part of the interview. So that, instead of being question-answer sequences in which the respondents formulate a description of their identities, the subsequent utterances now focus on other concerns: descriptions of (superficial) appearances.

Moreover, requests for clarification are the kinds of response which would be produced by any normal, unexceptional person who could not infer what it was about them in particular that had motivated the interviewer to approach them and ask a question concerning style, appearance, and so on. Through their displays of not seeing the relevance for them of the reference to style or identity, speakers invoke an alternative identity, namely their identity as an ordinary person. Invoking the relevance of this identity implies in turn that they do not see themselves primarily or solely as punks, gothics or whatever; this therefore constitutes a further means of rejecting categorical identity. Sometimes this was achieved more directly. In the extract below, for example, the respondent displays an orientation to the salience of self-identification but describes himself by using a category which is applicable to anyone: 'I (jus feel like) a human being really'. He thereby achieves his ordinariness and simultaneously undermines the relevance of a specific subcultural category.

(4) 1 non-Punk:F:T3SA [KR] (from Widdicombe and Wooffitt, 1995: 104–5)

```
                    ((Tape starts))
 1      I:          how would you de((tape glitch))
 2                  your style and that
 3                  (.3)
 4      R:          Me::.
 5      I:          yeah
 6                  (.8)
 7      R:          well I haven't got (None of) that
 8                  I (jus feel like) a human being really you know
 9                  jus: am (.) what I am
10                  (.5)
```

Characterizing Motives

A second way in which speakers reject category affiliation is to describe the motivation for the way they look and reject the likely assumption that it has anything to do with group membership. Consider, for example, the turns subsequent to the speakers' criticism of the opening question in extract (1a) above.

(1b) 3:no specific group:F:T3SA [FP]

```
12      R2:         >I wouldn't really say< it's a- it's no definite style
13                  like I mean I just. I ⌈just
14      R3:                               ⌊cos
15      R2:         wear what I feel comfortable in and, just, what I like.
16                  (y)know=
17      R3:         =cos um everybody like has their own like varia:tion of it
18                  you know that way and it's just. it's just.
19                  personal preference if you wanna li- like be
20                  any particular way or look any particular way
21                  it's just up to you y'know
22      I:          mm hm
23      R3:         not it's not (.) it's >no:thing to do-< a lot of people think
24                  it's it's to do with other people sort of pressuring you
25                  into being the same as them but it's not, cos it's up-
26                  it's just up- whatever you want to be, °y'know°
27      I:          °mmhm°
28                  (.)
```

Here R3 makes explicit and rejects the kinds of motives that she claims others assume underlie category affiliation. Specifically, she contrasts 'what a lot of people think' (that 'it's to do with other people sort of pressuring you into being the same as them') with what is 'really' the case: 'but it's not, cos it's up- it's just up- whatever <u>you</u> want to be'. She thus claims that personal choice is the basis for appearance rather than a desire to affiliate. This is further reinforced (lines 17–19) by claiming that there is anyway no uniform image available to which people might conform even if they were so motivated. That is, she says that 'everyone has their own variation of it'. This is presented as a further warrant for the claim that 'it's just personal preference'. Similarly, R2 says that she wears 'what I feel comfortable in and, just, what I like' and thereby makes relevant practical and personal reasons for her choice of clothing.

Similar observations about the ways in which participants orient to underlying motives were made in our analysis of autobiographical accounts of how they began changing their appearance (Widdicombe and Wooffitt, 1995). For example:

(5)   3G:2M/1F:T17SA [KHS] (from Widdicombe and Wooffitt, 1995: 142–4).

1	MR1:	it's like I was <u>al</u>ways int'rested-
2		I <u>kno</u>w it sounds a
3		cliché looking like this- but
4		I was always interested in the:: (.) things like
5		<u>hor</u>ror (.) horror stories and horror.
6		and I was always writing
7		horror stories at sch<u>ool</u> <u>ev</u>er since
8		I can re<u>mem</u>ber (.)
9	I:	ahha
10	MR1:	and it's like (.) it was just a(.) an
11		es<u>cap</u>e from everything else and I was
12		<u>in</u>terested in things
13		like the super<u>nat</u>'ral (.) and I I jus
		((few lines omitted re: the supernatural))
14		and that's <u>why</u>: it started to <u>show</u>
15		with clothes, and hair, and make up
16		n everything as ↓well

In this extract, the speaker refers to category-bound attributes of the gothic subculture, and employs extreme case formulations (Pomerantz, 1986) to portray his interests as long-standing and consistent. He thereby establishes his deep-rooted commitment to those interests and conventions. So, the respondent reports that he was always interested in horror stories: a concern which is characteristically associated with the gothic subculture. By characterizing his interests as always existing, he suggests that they preceded subcultural affiliation. This is reinforced by specifying a period in his life in which they were manifest ('at sch<u>ool</u> <u>ev</u>er since I can re<u>mem</u>ber'). By constructing the enduring nature of his interests, the speaker implies that such features are not bound to membership of a subcultural category but are expressions of an intrinsic self-identity. That is, interests and aspects of appearance conventionally associated with a subcultural category are construed as vehicles through which to exhibit the 'true' self (see also Widdicombe, 1993). This is especially clear when the speaker says that his interest 'started to <u>show</u> with clothes, and hair, and make up n everything'. He thus rejects category-bound motives for the adoption of particular attributes and resists the problematic inferential consequences of affirming a subcultural identity.

Denying Possession of Criterial Features

Two further ways of resisting category membership can be seen in the following extract (a continuation of (1a) and (1b)) in the response to the interviewer's subsequent question which asks directly whether they would say that they were 'punks or anything like that'.

(1c) 3:no specific group:F:T3SA [FP]

```
29       I:      WOULD you, would you say that you were punks
30               or anything like that
31       R3:     n ⌈o
32       R1:      ⌊no
33       R2:      ⌊no
34       R3:     no
35               (.)
36       R2:     ˙hh cos we haven't got an attitude like, I mean,
37               when you think punk you think, you think punk is ˙hh
38               is not just the way you dress like you have to have
39               a certain way of thinking you know to be a punk and
40               we haven't got- well I certainly haven't got it anyway
41               you know I'm just ˙hh
```

In this extract the three respondents categorically reject membership of a subcultural category (lines 31–4). Denial of membership is an apparently straightforward strategy for resisting subcultural identity. Nevertheless, its inadequacy is indicated by the way that the interviewer does not produce the next question and, after a brief pause, R2 provides a warrant for their denial. Her warrant takes the form of claiming non-possession of an attribute which she then defines as criterial for being punk. That is, she first says that 'we haven't got an attitude' and she then goes on to portray two characteristics of punk: the way you dress and having a certain way of thinking. She thus orients to the way that their appearance was a likely resource in the interviewer producing the question about their identity as punks. However, she plays down the significance of appearance ('it's not just the way you dress') by describing a second basis for membership, having a certain way of thinking, which is defined as criterial by stating that 'you *have to have*' it. Finally, she reiterates her claim not to possess this way of thinking (this time changing from speaking for all of them to speaking for her own case only).

In summary, in the extracts above, there are several ways in which speakers portray themselves as not belonging to a specific category or group, in the especially accountable context of looking as if they could be, or are, members. The warrants for their denials are sensitive to the way that others may draw upon conventional knowledge about the subcultural category both to ascribe identity and to make further assumptions about its incumbents, for example concerning their motives for affiliation.

Participants' Orientation to the Problems of Category Affiliation

I have suggested that speakers' resistance to category affiliation is a way of addressing the inferential consequences that might follow accepting the categorical identity; in particular that affiliation is driven by a desire to conform and to be similar to others. The following extracts provide further evidence for participants' orientation to these issues, and a further set of interpretative resources about category membership; specifically that it is incompatible with or entails a commensurate loss of individuality. In these extracts, the inferential difficulties are made especially salient as one speaker affirms and negotiates his identity as a punk, but he does so in the context of criticism from the second speaker, who rejects the categorical identity.

(2b; continued from extract 2a)   2P and friend:M/F:T8SA [Cam]

```
16    I:     would you call yourselves punks
17    NP:    no
18           (.)
19    FR:    I wouldn't
20           (0.2)
21    I:     would you
22    MR:    mmhm ⌈ye:ah
23    FR:          ⌊(   )
24    FR:    you ⌈would you would
25    MR:        ⌊mm yeah ye:ah ye:::ah aie
26    FR:    I wouldn't, I wouldn't
27           (0.2)
28    FR:    I DOn't like people- I can't see people ack-=
29    NP:    =no
30    MR:    °mm mm°
31    FR:    c-calling themselves punks an that cos eh I dunno it's
             categorizing themselves
32           (.)
33    I:     mmhm
```

```
34    FR:    which I thought is what it's about
35           (0.2)
36    FR:    what it's against
37    MR:    aie it is against that y'know
38    FR:    yeah
39    MR:    it's be- being in- individual and that y'know wha' I mean
40    I:     ahha
41    MR:    it's being yourself. it just so ha:ppens that so many people.
42    FR:    they call it punk ⌈(      )
43    MR:                      ⌊just seem to look like each other
44           d'you know what I mean (I mean) they're in a cult (.) but
45           they still want to be individuals (y')know
46    FR:    aie
47    MR:    got a mind of your own instead of taking
48           what the government give you (.) (y')know
49    I:     mmhm
```

I want to consider first the exchange which occurs on lines 19 to 26, following the interviewer's question, 'would you call yourselves punks'. There are several interesting features of this exchange which constitute the background to the accounts subsequently produced (in lines 28–49). One is the asymmetry in the nature of their utterances which suggests that rejecting the subcultural category label is the preferred response. Specifically, FR's response, 'I wouldn't', is fairly immediate and direct. By contrast, MR's affirmation of category affiliation has the character of a dispreferred and reluctant response. He does not produce an answer to the initial question; instead there is a noticeable pause in the place where a response would be expected from him, that is, following FR's turn, and the interviewer repeats the interrogative part of the question. Moreover, his response, unlike hers, doesn't echo the key terms of the question; instead, it consists of 'mmhm ye:ah'.

A second feature of this exchange is the way that MR's acceptance of the category label is jointly accomplished. Note, for example, that FR begins speaking immediately after he has said 'mmhm' and although her utterance in the overlapping spate of talk is unclear, her immediately subsequent assertion, 'you would you would', is clear. The interruption, the repetition of 'you would', and the emphasis on the pronoun 'you' gives her utterance the character of a challenge or mild criticism of his display of reluctance to affirm the categorical identity. Moreover, her response embodies an implicit claim to possessing certain knowledge that he would, at least sometimes, call himself a punk, and there is evidence internal to the interaction which shows that her claim is treated as a factual claim. Specifically, his subsequent turn in no way challenges her utterance. Instead, he begins speaking before she has said more than 'you', and his utterance, 'mm yeah ye:ah ye:::ah aie', is more clearly affirmative.

The third feature of this exchange concerns the way that his acceptance of the correctness of FR's claim, 'you would you would', is followed by a re-assertion of her prior response, 'I wouldn't I wouldn't'. The symmetry in the two claims, together with the emphasis on the pronoun, indicates that she is orienting to, and emphasizing, the difference between them in relation to calling themselves punks.

These features of the initial exchange raise some interesting issues. First, though not surprisingly given my observations in the earlier part of this chapter, is the way that accepting or confirming the categorical identity is the dispreferred response, or the more defensive position. Secondly, generally in conversations people work to avoid interpersonal conflict and to ensure the smooth flow of interaction. Here, by contrast, the talk is designed to emphasize a difference between the two participants. The exchange thus has the potential to provoke 'troubles' in the interaction. In the subsequent turns, the participants each provide an account in which they address the problem of calling oneself a punk; their accounts display a sensitivity to the asymmetry in their initial positions and simultaneously attend to the potential troubles in the interaction.

Avoiding a Commitment to the Category

FR's argument is that people wouldn't call themselves punks because they are against categorizing themselves. The problem with this claim is that it simultaneously mobilizes and rejects the relevance of the category punk. In other words, her claim only makes sense if it is assumed that the people to whom she refers could potentially be classified as punks. It is also worth noting that the interviewer's question and the background of common-sense interpretative resources concerning their appearance, already brought into play, makes available the appropriateness of the category. None-theless, several features of her utterances on lines 28 to 36 suggest that they are designed to minimize the salience of the category membership of the people to whom she refers.

Consider, for example, her utterance on lines 28 and 31: 'I DOn't like people- I can't see people ack-c-calling themselves punks and that'. This utterance contains two significant repairs. First, she amends 'I DOn't like people' to 'I can't see people . . . calling themselves punks an that'. We can infer that had she simply continued the first part, her statement would have been something like 'I don't like people calling themselves punks'. This has significantly different implications to her amended formulation. To say that 'I don't like people calling themselves punks' implies that there are people who do so and that she disapproves of their actions. By contrast, 'I can't see people calling themselves punks' suggests that it simply doesn't happen, or that at least, it is unlikely. There is, moreover, further functional sig-nificance in this amendment in that it is less overtly critical or disapproving of MR's action of affirming that he would call himself a punk.

The second significant repair she makes in her utterance on lines 28 and 31 is the amendment of what we can infer to be the term 'acknowledging' in 'I can't see people ack-' to 'c-calling themselves punks'. To acknowledge some state of affairs, in this case claiming a particular identity, is to recognize or publicly affirm its truth. So that the implication of her initial formulation is that members don't admit or are reluctant to affirm their 'true' identity. This formulation is problematic in that it orients to punk as an intrinsic identity and implies that punks are being dishonest or perverse by not admitting their (true) category membership. By contrast, 'calling oneself a punk' is less problematic since it invokes the (unlikely) action of people using the label to describe themselves. Her modified version, 'I can't see people calling themselves punks', is thus designed to minimize her commitment to the category and hence reinforces her argument by indicating that the category term is irrelevant as a characterization of some people's identity. It is also worth noting that she refers to people calling themselves 'punk an that' and this implies that there is a range of labels, rather than a single potentially relevant categorical identity. Moreover, her references to 'people', 'themselves' and 'it' don't include herself. She thus avoids making available her affiliation with like minded others.

Other features of her formulation further warrant her rejection of the relevance of the subcultural category. For example, she describes categorization as something that 'it' is about or against, and although we can infer that 'it' is a reference to punk or punk lifestyle or ideology, she does not explicitly refer to punk. Wooffitt (1992) refers to this as a 'not naming device'. He suggests that naming some state of affairs or objects implies having some knowledge about and interest in the phenomena, but more importantly here, 'naming suggests a commitment to the in-principle existence of the object so named' (Widdicombe and Wooffitt, 1995: 151). Naming 'it' as punk would thus be damaging to her claim that it is unlikely that people would define themselves in terms of punk category membership. In addition, she formulates her observations as a personal estimation, that is something that 'I can't see people' doing and as what 'I thought is what it's about'. However, had she claimed that 'people don't call themselves punks' or to *know* what it's about, the recipient could then infer direct knowledge of the usual behaviour of punks and hence a commitment to the existence of that category. The preface to her account is thus sensitively designed to avoid reference to an actual group of people and their behaviour.

Negotiating Individuality and Category Affiliation

On lines 37 to 48, MR produces a modified version of what it's about which addresses more explicitly the problems of categorization and thereby deals implicitly with FR's criticism of his prior acceptance of category affiliation. At the same time, he deals with the potential interpersonal conflict that could arise by virtue of their differences. That is, on line 37, MR does agree with FR's argument, and he then specifies a basis for being against categorization. He says: 'aie it is against that y'know, it's being individual and that . . . it's being yourself'. This accomplishes what is ostensibly a collaboratively produced account of the problem of categorization; that it seems incompatible with being individual. However, by specifying a reason for being against categorization, he is then able to undermine this as the problem and hence provide an implicit warrant for his acceptance of the label. In other words, by invoking individuality as the reason for being against categorization, he indicates that being yourself is more important than resistance to categorization *per se*.

Moreover, in his subsequent utterances he contrasts the bases of category affiliation and individuality and he does so in a way that implies that the two are not incompatible. He says that 'it just so happens that so many people just seem to look like each other . . . I mean (I mean) they're in a cult but they still want to be individuals'. He thereby acknowledges both members' category affiliation and their desire to be individuals. Moreover, he suggests that the basis on which members can be described as being in a cult is their appearance, 'they seem to look like each other'. By contrast, he states that being individual means 'having a mind of your own', and he specifies what this means by contrasting it with 'taking what the government give you'. In other words, having a mind of your own and hence being an individual is characterized in terms of political views or activity. The implication is that since category membership and individuality are expressed in different ways, it is possible to be both a member and an individual.

Finally, through his description of the basis on which category membership is assumed, he rejects the problematic inference that its expression has anything to do with conformity. First, he avoids any reference to agency by describing similarity in appearance as something that 'just so happens'. Secondly, his reference to 'so many people' evokes the prevalence of this state of affairs while avoiding any explicit reference to the identity of the people to whom he is referring (even though in the context of his account we can infer their identity as punks). He thus minimizes the relevance of identity to similarity in appearance. Thirdly, his formulation draws on what has been referred to elsewhere as the 'appearance-reality device' (Edwards, 1991). Edwards notes that appearance is often used as a noticeable feature of some state of affairs in the preface to its denial. That is, people sometimes warrant accounts by invoking a distinction between superficial appearance (what things look or seem like) and an underlying reality which represents the true situation or a preferred version. This distinction recognizes the obviousness of appearances and so acknowledges the basis for one's own or another's possible understanding. At the same time, it subverts that version in favour of a purportedly more insightful and adequate analysis (see Potter, 1987, 1988). So, here, MR implies that although a lot of people seem to look like each other, this is only superficial or the way things may appear rather than a reality. In these ways, he orients to and rejects the idea that category membership actually rests on similarity in appearance or deliberate conformity to an image.

Doing Membership

The analysis of extract (2b) shows that in accepting and rejecting sub-cultural identity, participants orient to a background of largely negative assumptions about category membership. It is noticeable, however, that in the course of negotiating these problems, MR avoids making relevant his previously if reluctantly affirmed identity; that is, his account is impersonal. By contrast, in the following extract, MR does engage in the delicate business of doing his own membership of the subcultural category.

(6) 2P and friend:M/F:T8SA [Cam]

```
 1    I:     ↑d'you compare, yourself with other punks °ever°
 2    MR:    err
 3           (0.2)
 4    MR:    ˙hh there's like, tramp punks, ˙hh hard core punks
 5           and (0.2) ˙hh ju:st. street punks
 6    I:     what are tramp punks
 7    MR:    smelly ones ones wi' all the ripped clothes (.) (↑though)
 8           we all stick together but you know there's different-
 9           there's different cults in a cult >d'you know what I mean<
10    I:     °mm hm°
11    MR:    like the gothic are the- (.) the shit to us y'know
12           the punks ne- . don't like gothics (.) dunno why
13           y'know y'always err 'look at the state of them' gothics huh huh
14           me:ss heh heh heh hah ˙hhh
15    I:     so what sort of punk do you (.) associate yourself (wi')
16    MR:    just a- a s- street punk y'know (.) like I like
17           ⌈bondage (straps?) studs and leather
18    FR:    ⌊but you don't class yourself
19    MR:    I know but I don't really class myself-
20           I know I'm different from other punks
21    FR:    mm
22    MR:    d'you know what I mean I like bright colours in my hair you know
23    FR:    yeah but so do I but I'm  ⌈not
24    MR:                             ⌊aye
25    FR:    a punk at all
26    MR:    shut ya face=
27    FR:    >I don't think I'm a ⌈punk<
28    MR:                         ⌊shut your face
29    FR:    oh, sorry
30           (.)
31    FR:    ˙hh °huh huh° ˙hh
32    NP:    ⌈hah hah hah⌉
33    FR:    ⌊heh heh heh⌋ hah hah hah
34    MR:    ⌊forgot what I was going to say
35           (.)
36    FR:    hah hah
```

```
37   FR:    ⌈heh heh heh hah
38   MR:    ⌊just going to crawl back under my ⌈stone
39   FR:                                       ⌊Ne↑il
40   MR:    no I forgot now, you made me forget
```

In the first part of this extract (lines 1–15), MR makes relevant his identity as a punk in two ways: first, through invoking the idea of solidarity among members, and secondly by formulating shared, negative attitudes towards gothics. The interactional context is one in which he is invited by the interviewer to draw comparisons between himself and other punks. Instead of doing so, he mobilizes distinctions between different kinds of punks ('there's like, tramp punks, ˙hh hard core punks and (0.2) ˙hh ju:st street punks'). This in turn enables him to avoid the kinds of inferences which might be made available if he were to draw such comparisons (e.g., that self-identity is assessed according to the adoption of shared attributes or one's standing in relation to like-minded others).

Nevertheless, while this descriptive strategy provides a solution to one set of problems, it can also be taken to infer that the distinctions are in some way significant. In lines 7 to 13, he orients to and rejects this inference in two ways. First, he says '(↑though) we all stick together'. He thereby emphasizes solidarity among different types of punks and portrays punk as the significant category affiliation. Secondly, he specifies the boundaries of solidarity, such that cohesive relations are restricted to members of the punk subculture. He does so by producing an example of one cult, gothics, and a negative assessment of that cult. He says 'there's different cults in a cult . . . like the gothic are the- (.) the shit to us'. In this way he suggests that 'sticking together' is not indiscriminate nor, say, simply a feature of being attached to 'a cult'. In addition, his negative assessment of gothics is formulated as a collective view: 'the gothic are the shit *to us*', and '*the punks* ne- don't like gothics'. He thus reinforces the idea that there is cohesion among punks in so far as they share similar views. Moreover, through his use of the pronouns 'we' and 'us' in 'we all stick together' and 'the gothic are . . . the shit to us', he makes relevant his affiliation and identity as a punk.

In the following sequence of turns, the interviewer asks him to specify what kind of punk he is. She thus overlooks the inferential work accomplished in the prior sequences of playing down distinctions among types of punk. Instead, the invitation to produce a self-defining label has the character of an upshot: 'so what sort of punk do you (.) associate yourself (wi')'. In the utterances which follow a different set of resources is used to negotiate his identity as a street punk which simultaneously reinforce the status of that affiliation as less significant than membership of the category punk. First, he describes himself as 'just a- a s- street punk' (line 16). The term 'just' seems to be used here in the depreciative sense (Lee, 1987), conveying the impression that there is 'nothing special' about this categorical identity. Secondly, he describes three attributes which warrant his affiliation with this category: 'like I like bondage (straps?) studs and leather'. This description focuses on specific, mundane objects rather than his preference for the *style*, and these are characterized as preferences or things he likes rather than as features of his appearance. He thus implies that the label street punk is appropriate simply because he happens to like certain objects associated with that category.

In the first part of extract (6), therefore, MR mobilizes his identity as a punk and as a street punk in different ways: in the first case through invoking solidarity and shared views, in the second by specifying preferences which coincide with category-bound attributes. What is interesting here is that whereas his first action is not challenged, the second is. That is, at the point where MR begins specifying what he likes, there is an overlapping spate of talk in which FR says 'but you don't class yourself'. This suggests that the former is a less problematic way of doing identity. However, invoking relations between punks and a negative attitude towards another group (on the grounds that they look a mess) does not have the problematic connotations of stating one's possession of category-bound attributes since conformity is less likely to be inferred. In his subsequent turns, MR deals with the problems that arise by virtue of classing himself on the basis of category-bound preferences. First, he undermines his prior action by doing agreement with FR. He does so by recycling her claim, with the suitable pronoun change, and the addition of the particle 'I know' which functions as an acknowledgement or acceptance of the correctness of her claim. Moreover, his statement, 'I know but I don't *really* class myself', draws on the appearance-reality device; it suggests that his affiliation with the category street punk is only apparent or superficial rather than a claim to an intrinsic identity. (And the warrant for this claim has already been provided for in his prior action of playing down the significance of distinctions between punks, and formulating the mundane basis for his affiliation.)

A second way in which he warrants not classing himself is by saying 'I know I'm different from other punks'. This claim, unlike his statement about similarity, is formulated as a factual claim, or a statement of certain, personal knowledge. He justifies this claim by describing the way that he differs from other punks: 'I like bright colours in my hair.' 'Not classing oneself' is therefore equated with possessing attributes which make one different. This in turn orients to one problem with classing oneself which is that it implies similarity with other members and hence conformity to the image. (But it is also noticeable that he does not deny category membership altogether since his statement that 'I know I'm different from other punks' makes relevant one category membership, namely punk.)

Nevertheless, FR does not accept his negotiation of the problem of classing oneself and instead produces a further challenge with reference to herself: 'yeah but so do I [like bright colours in my hair] but I'm not a punk at all'. His response, 'shut ya face' suggests that he takes her challenge to be a successful one. Her claim to like bright colours and not to be a punk functions to undermine his argument by not accepting his justification for not classing himself. In other words, she suggests that showing that one is different from other punks can't be used as a warrant for not classing oneself. The implication is that it is irrelevant to not classing oneself. Instead, on the basis of her prior claims, we can infer that she equates 'not classing oneself' with rejecting category affiliation altogether.

A final point is that 'shut ya face' can be taken as an aggressive or abusive way to close a discussion. As in the previous extract, however, there follows the interactional management of the potential troubles such that interpersonal conflict is avoided. This is done in several ways. First, FR modifies her claim 'I'm not a punk at all' so that it is less emphatic. She says 'I don't think I'm a punk', thus making the claim to non-membership a personal viewpoint rather than a factual claim. MR, however, merely repeats 'shut ya face', this time more loudly. Secondly, FR apologizes, and after a brief pause, begins laughing. She thereby treats his comment as one not intended to be overtly aggressive. MR does not challenge this interpretation; instead he adopts the position of the 'injured party' by stating that she has made him 'forget what I was going to say' (implicitly a rejoinder to her challenge). Hence he saves face by implying that there was an appropriate counter-argument but he has simply forgotten it.

Concluding Comments

In this chapter, I analysed participants' responses to questions which invited them to characterize themselves and to speak as members of a particular youth subculture. A primary concern was to show that membership and non-membership of a potentially relevant category is an accomplishment, rather than something that can simply be assumed. A second concern was to show how identity work is sensitive to the inference-rich nature of categories: in particular, that respondents take account of the way that their appearance may be used to infer their category affiliation, and that this in turn may be used by others to ascribe motives to them which are largely negative, such as a desire to conform to the subcultural image, or to copy their peers. Such inferences are problematic in so far as they are shallow reasons for affiliating with a group and thus the related identity may be regarded as inauthentic (Widdicombe and Wooffitt, 1990, 1995). In addition, giving in to peer pressure, a desire to be similar to others, indeed group membership itself seems to entail a concommitant loss of individuality.

Therefore, in the analysis, I identified a range of descriptive strategies which were employed to deal with these kinds of problem. Some of these strategies were aimed at denying the appropriateness of the categorical identity, for example, through producing a straightforward denial (extracts (1c) and (2b)); by claiming that categorizing oneself is an anathema to those people for whom the label punk appears to be applicable (extract (2b)); and by mobilizing an alternative and implicitly more appropriate self identification as an ordinary person (extracts (3) and (4)). Other strategies challenged the category-boundedness of attributes like appearance. For example, in extract (1c), non-membership was accomplished by playing down the significance of appearance for being a member and by denying possession of other attributes which were formulated as criterial. Other respondents resisted the category relevance of their appearance and interests by characterizing their underlying motives such that they had nothing to do with group affiliation; instead, they were characterized as the expression of feelings or personal preferences (e.g., extracts (1b) and (5)). They thus made relevant their status as manifestations of a different identity, namely, an authentic self-identity.

The second part of the analysis provided further evidence for participants' orientation to the problems of category membership which were made especially salient for one speaker because of his prior acceptance of the categorical identity. For example, in extract (2b), MR oriented to and rejected the idea that category membership is incompatible with individuality. He did so by ascribing different grounds for claiming social identity and individuality; by playing down the importance of category membership in contrast to being individual; and by making use of the appearance-reality device to reject the common assumption that category affiliation has something to do with similarity among members.

In the final section of the analysis, I then considered how MR accomplished his identity as a punk, in the context of the kinds of inferential difficulties that such action may provoke. First, he described and played down the significance of his preferences for stylistic artefacts category-bound to street punks. But in the face of criticism from his companion, he emphasized his (implicitly more important) difference from others as grounds for not really classing himself. A second and apparently less problematic way in which he accomplished his category membership was by drawing on a further set of interpretative resources concerning categories; that they entail relations of solidarity and cohesiveness.

The negotiation of membership, like the rejection of the categorical identity, is therefore designed to address issues of implied conformity and loss of individuality. Widdicombe and Wooffitt (1995) point out that it is perhaps not surprising that such concerns permeate these accounts since they are manifest in lay reasoning about subcultures and the people who join them. By way of illustration, they cite an extract from a British newspaper article on youth subcultures which neatly encapsulates the kind of outsiders' understanding of, and accounts for, young people's affiliation to subcultures. This article states that '[A] teenager's desire to identify with a tribe – and to follow religiously its dress code – is entirely normal' (*Today*, London: 7 July 1990). Similar sentiments are echoed in the social scientific literature on youth culture. In their book on adolescent development, for example, Coleman and Hendry (1990) argue that peer groups encourage conformity and entail a transitory loss of individuality because they are oriented towards fostering identity, which in turn helps young people overcome the insecurity and fulfil the need to belong which are said to characterize adolescence.

Such reasoning is not, however, restricted to youth or to those who are so ostensibly members of a particular group; it is enshrined in the more general social psychological literature on group membership and identity. Self categorization theory (SCT) (e.g., Turner et al., 1987), for example, rests on the incompatibility between individuality and social identity. It claims to be primarily concerned with the processes underlying a cognitive transformation or change from an individual's subjective sense of a unique self to the perception of themselves as a member of a group via the process of depersonalization. This in turn is informed by the belief that there are two broad kinds of identity, social and personal, which have very different attributes associated with them. It is claimed that they are structurally different levels of the self-concept and that there is an inverse relationship between them in self-perception, so that when one type of identity is salient, other aspects of identity are suppressed. Depersonalization in turn requires the adoption of stereotypical features of the category so that one becomes identical to other members. It thus makes a virtue of the desire to be similar to others, and assumes that this is the basis for collective action. These theories, however, fail to recognize the problematic nature of the assumptions which are built into and formalized within them; they thus also fail to see that membership may be a controversial, problematic and disputed issue for those to whom a social identity is ascribed.

The analysis also highlights further problematic assumptions which are built into the literature. I have mentioned throughout that categories are inference-rich and that they have conventionally associated with them certain attributes. However, the orientation of category talk to this 'backdrop of normative knowledge' is often taken to imply that this knowledge is inherent in the way the world is (Edwards, 1991: 525). This belief informs the kind of essentialist models which are outlined in the epilogue to this book. Thus, at the sociological level, it is assumed that we can specify the content of this shared cultural knowledge. At a social psychological level, it is assumed that it is only by virtue of its status as a reflection of reality that we can make sense of how particular categories are constructed on occasions; that we can attribute characteristics to ourselves and others on the basis of category membership; and that we can determine whether someone is a member or not. For example, SCT's notion of depersonalization assumes a consensual set of stereotypical attributes which are adopted. Similarly, Edwards (1997: 233) discusses cognitive approaches to category membership which assume that category membership can be determined on the basis of a comparison between the features of a potential member and the 'prototypical' member or a list of typical category attributes.

By contrast, the analysis shows that in resisting subcultural identity, speakers acknowledge and undermine such normative cultural assumptions, by rejecting the category-boundedness of particular attributes and transforming their meanings so that they are expressions of personal identity.

These observations lend support to Edwards's (1997) argument that while shared, normative knowledge is clearly a resource in talk, speakers must evoke that knowledge, and make it relevant to the business at hand. In doing so, they act 'constructively upon that background, altering, challenging and recruiting it for the accomplishment of social actions' (Edwards, 1991: 525).

To conclude, in this chapter I have argued that particular social identities cannot simply be assumed; instead, we need to be sensitive to the ways that group membership and non-membership are negotiated, rejected or achieved. Moreover, denying membership of a potentially appropriate category, or warranting affiliation with the subcultural category, is a delicate business because of powerful but largely negative assumptions about categories and category membership. Finally, we cannot simply assume shared cultural knowledge about category attributes; rather, in the business of doing identity, the status of such normative knowledge should be treated as a participants' resource which may be invoked, transformed or rejected.

5 Identity Ascriptions in their Time and Place: 'Fagin' and 'The Terminally Dim'

Charles Antaki

In this chapter I want to have a look at identity ascription – calling someone this-or-that outright – when it is done jocularly. That is, when it is done by calling someone a name in such a way as to shy away from an accusation that one really meant it. It might seem at first blush that this sort of identity talk, since it is meant to be non-literal, and therefore – apparently – invokes things not there in the recorded talk, must play on 'culture', and perhaps on people's 'private meanings'. But I shall try to argue that even though it looks like a case for digging and decoding, it is not, and we need neither psychological speculation nor cultural interpretation to understand it. Taking my line from Sacks (1992), I shall try to argue that jocular identity ascription can (and ought) properly be grasped in its contemporary 'occasionedness': in its springing up in the transient local environment that fosters it and that is, in turn, changed by it.

I shall give two examples of what I mean. One is the ascription of a 'teasing' identity, and I shall say that it does an elegant bit of work to finesse a tangle of obligations that the conversation snags together; and I shall argue that even though the tease seems to invoke the cultural nugget of a fictional character-name ('Fagin'), the untangling work it does is hearable and intelligible without resort to any sort of 'cultural' or 'psychological' analysis, where the former means something like the interpretation of a code and the latter means the evaluation of inner states. The other example I want to work through is, from the same encounter, the trumping joke of the phrase '*the* terminally dim', and I shall try to show how one can understand the work it does, in its appearance in a conversational crescendo of upgraded assessments, again without recourse to cultural exegesis or psychological speculation.

The Encounter

This is the beginning of one of a number of mundane episodes that a colleague of mine videotaped in her home as a favour to me. I gave no specific instructions about when or what to tape, nor did I say what I was looking for other than (as was indeed the case) that I wanted some stretches of everyday interaction 'to look over'. This stretch is neatly topped and tailed by the participants, and most of the speech is easily audible, but otherwise there was no special reason for picking it out.

We might start with noting certain things about this encounter which – unless things are very peculiar – would in common sense be treated as 'facts' by the interactants themselves: that Lyn is Zoe's mother (the names are pseudonyms), that their ages are about 35 and 17 respectively, that Lyn and Zoe are white, British, female (whether all or any of these 'factual' identities are significant in any way is a matter we have to look out for, along with the management of other facts in the identities of whoever else is going to be brought on and off stage).

Preamble: Identities in Opening

The interaction begins like this (the line numbering in each extract is faithful to the chronology of the encounter):

(1)   (Up till now the videotape has shown Lyn in a domestic interior at a table reading and writing for some ten minutes)

1		((door? faintly, off camera))
2		(6 secs)
3	Zoe:	[off camera] Mum?
4	Lyn:	↑hel↓lo↑:
5		(3 secs)
6		I'm ↑he:↓re (..)
7	Zoe:	°o°kay- (..)
8	Lyn:	((coughs/clears throat))
9		((off camera: three ?crockery bangs for 2 secs))
10		(3 secs)
11		[door opens, Zoe appears]=
12	Zoe:	=↑hel↓lo↑::
13	Lyn:	↑hi:: (.)
14	Zoe:	↑where's the ci⌈gar↓ettes:
15		⌊[Zoe shuts door behind her]
16		(1 sec)
17	Lyn:	°in the° ↑kitchen:

From the very beginning we can see how Sacks's treatment of 'identity' (invoked throughout this book) is going to be helpful in giving a handle not on what people are, but on what they do, and how they do it. Identity work sparks the very start of the encounter. The summons and acknowledgement pair in lines 3 to 4 ('Mum?'/'hello') work a scene-change to bring Zoe and Lyn together on to the same stage and to a public awareness of each other. There would be more to be said even of this sliver of interaction, but let us press on to the jocular identity ascription that is coming up.

A Jocular Identity Ascription ('Fagin') in Appreciation of a Complaint

The first identity ascription at which I want to pause for a fairly long discussion occurs at line 33 below. It looks like a trivial ascription, but like everything else in an encounter, it does some work. Here's how the interaction carries on from the extract above:

(2)

18	Lyn:	˚in the˚ ↑kitchen:
19		(6 secs) *[in which Zoe comes and stands facing Lyn across the table]*
20	Zoe:	˚the˚ ↑camera's ↓on
21	Lyn:	=y↑e:s: (..)
22	Zoe:	are ↓you ↑t(hh)alk↓ing t(h)o it ↑while y(h)ou wO::RK?
23	Lyn:	↓n(h)o:: (..) ⌈↑heh heh-
24	Zoe:	⌊hh what (h)ye ↑DO:INg ↓then=
25	Lyn:	=hahh hahh hahh
26		(1 sec)
27		*[Zoe starts to move off]*
28	Zoe:	↓what's the ↑poin:t: *[[moves out off camera towards kitchen]]*
29		(1.5 sec)
30	Zoe:	*[off camera and out of sight of Lyn]* oh ↑go::d (.) look what ↑l'm wear↓ing=
31	Lyn:	=((explosive laugh)) >eheh ⌈hehh hehh hehh<
32	Zoe:	⌊hehh hehh
33 →	Lyn:	↓you ↑look ↓like (.) ↑Fa:↓gin =
34	Zoe:	=↑hahh ha ⌈ha
35	Lyn:	⌊ha hahh ⌈↑↑huh ((very high pitched at end))
36	Zoe:	⌊↑↑hhh ↓maybe I ↑am
37	Lyn:	(1 sec) *[in which Lyn starts to mimic pulling gloves on / off]*
38		we ↑just ↓need the ↑little ↓glov:es with the ↑fingers ↓out
39	Zoe:	˚↑very funny˚
40		(1 sec)
41		˚(d'you want one)˚

The moment of the identity ascription comes at line 33 ('you look like Fagin'), and it seems to fit nicely against the outline, at least, of Drew's analysis of teasing (Drew, 1987): it's some observation about Zoe, and it's met with a laugh and then a 'po-faced' rejection ('very funny'). But to get its full force we (like the participants) need to work up to it.

Back in line 20 Zoe has said that the camera is on; this information would obviously be known to Lyn, who is sitting facing it and, with her papers in front of her, must have been for some while. In other words, Zoe is not offering Lyn mere news. Rather, what she says is hearable as a 'noticing' (Pomerantz, 1984) like this one:

(3) (from Pomerantz, 1984)

1		Receiver:	Hello::
2		Caller:	HI:::
3		Receiver:	Oh:hi:: 'ow are you Agne::s
4	→	Caller:	Fine. Yer <u>line's</u> been busy
5		Receiver:	Yeuh my fu(hh) – 'hhh my father's wife called me [. . .]

What the caller 'notices' in line 3 is something patently obvious to the receiver; after all, if the receiver's line has been busy, it's because the receiver herself has been using it. So the utterance must work not as information but as something else, and Pomerantz's collection leads her to identify its work as the setting up of something as *accountable* – it makes expectable an account for why things are as the noticer observes (as we see in the extract, the receiver offers an account in terms of being called by her father's wife). This seems to be what is going on here. Zoe has observed something manifestly obvious to Lyn, to which the expected response from Lyn will be an account. Perhaps it might be an account such as 'yes, I put it on an hour ago' or 'yes, I'm just filming myself as I work'.

Instead we get a bare ('yes'), and this is treated by Zoe immediately (are ↓you ↑t(hh)alk↓ing t(h)o it ↑while y(h)ou wO::RK?) as inadequate; indeed, we can hear what she says, and in the next two turns (hh what (h)ye ↑DO:INg ↓then) and (↓what's the ↑poin:t:), as being repeat invitations for Lyn to improve her utterances into a satisfactory account. This never comes. Zoe moves away from the table, throwing a scarf around her neck. We might take it, then, that there is some unresolved business about the camera being on. We keep that in mind.

Zoe moves off and, in line 30, Zoe reports something about what she's wearing – which is, as Sacks remarks (Sacks, 1992, Vol. II: 97ff.), an example of the sort of thing that is owned by, and can preferentially be talked about by, the person who has brought it to the interaction. But we are in an environment where a camera has been signalled to be 'on' and recording; does that tell us anything about the report?

Let us see what we might get first from the formal structure of what Zoe says. It has the hearable force of a complaint or a self-deprecation, or both; perhaps a complaint via a self-deprecation. To hear it as (the start of) a complaint, compare it with this example:

(4) (from Heritage, 1984: 328)

```
1                  (.)
2      N:     uh Oh:: (.) ⌈my f f:face hurts ⌈=
3      H:            ⌊Bu:t              ⌊ =° W't-° (.) what'd'e do to you
4      N:     ↑GOD'e dis (.) prac'ly killed my dumb fa:ce
```

In this extract, the form of N's utterance is taken by H to be the start of a complaint, which H invites N to complete (=° W't-° (.) what'd'e do to you). Or is what Zoe said a self-deprecation? Compare it with somebody offering 'that she's "no bottle of milk"' (from Pomerantz, 1984: 85):

(5) [HG:II:2] (transcription simplified)

```
1      A:     [. . .] .hhh Oh well it's me too Portia, hh yihknow I'm no bottle a'
2             milk
3      P:     Oh:: well yer easy tuh get along with {. . .]
```

There, the form of A's utterance prompts P to treat it as something that prompts a consolatory disagreement. Now recall lines 30–3:

(6) detail from extract (2)

```
30      Zoe:   [off camera and out of sight of Lyn] oh ↑go::d (.) look what ↑I'm wear↓ing=
31      Lyn:   =((explosive laugh)) >eheh ⌈hehh hehh hehh<
32      Zoe:                           ⌊hehh hehh
33  →   Lyn:   ↓you ↑look ↓like (.) ↑Fa:↓gin =
```

Zoe's utterance 'oh ↑go::d (.) look what ↑I'm wear↓ing' shares at least two properties with both the complaint and the self-deprecation: she uses the 'oh' particle and draws attention to some unhappy aspect of her own circumstances. So her utterance is perhaps ambivalent, to be taken one way or another by Lyn in her disposal of it. And, of course, this is in the context, set up by Zoe, of the camera being (accountably) on; that is to say, in an environment where recording is taking place and someone is responsible for it. In other words, an environment where the putative complaint might be something to do with Lyn being responsible for unwarrantedly catching Zoe on tape, perhaps not looking at her best.

Were Lyn to treat it as some kind of complaint, she might follow it up with an invitation to Zoe to continue (as 'what'd'e do to you' does in extract (3)). Were Lyn to treat it as negative self-assessment, she might offer a palliative disagreement, perhaps a description contrary to the one expressed or implied in the deprecation (as in 'yer easy tuh get along with', in extract (4)). In this case it could be something like 'no, you look fine' or an equivalent. But what in fact does Lyn do? Initially, at least, neither of these – she explodes into laughter. Now laughter will do various things in various places (as Jefferson, 1984, shows), but here it is hearable as (at least) a temporary withholding of an appreciation of what Zoe says as either a complaint or a self-deprecation. Assessment of Zoe's problem is deferred. Zoe's own next contribution (at line 34) is a laugh which can be heard both to ratify Lyn's laugh but not to delete Lyn's obligation to crystallize it into an explicit diagnosis. The ball is back in Lyn's court. What is expectable now is something from Lyn that will show that she accepts that Zoe has either made a complaint or a self-deprecation, or both.

This is the point at which Lyn's 'you look like Fa:gin' comes. In a moment, I shall offer a suggestion about what Lyn's utterance is doing here in the environment of Zoe's camera-relevant complaint and self-deprecation. But first let me do one of the things I want to emphasize in this chapter: say why I think that 'you look like Fa:gin' is, whatever else it is, the ascription of an identity, and why neither of the participants in the interaction, nor we observers, need special cultural decoding or mental speculation to make that clear.

Do We Need Extra-textual Knowledge of Who Fagin Is?

There are two rival sorts of evidence that the sound I have transcribed as *Fa:gin* is 'the name "Fagin"' and not something else – for example (as an English colleague playfully, and a Dutch colleague sincerely, once heard it) a laconic version of the morphemically possible English verb 'fayging'. One sort of argument that it is indeed the name Fagin is via an extra-textual, culturally informed reading; the sort of analysis that identifies things in the text by appeal to analysts' common cultural understandings. The other, which I shall prefer, is just on the basis of what would make sense to any user of the English that Lyn and Zoe are using, 'culture' apart.

It is important to rehearse the difference between these two, I think, because in its more commonsensical form the former argument is what gives licence to social scientists (even social identity psychologists, as Chapter 1 argues) to claim that their subjects are usefully describable by names which signal culturally 'obvious' characteristics (male or female, white or black, and so on); and it also informs a lot of work done under some understandings of 'discourse analysis'. Not the textually principled and conversation analytic variety familiar in the work of, for example, Widdicombe (e.g., Widdicombe, 1993) and Widdicombe and Wooffitt (1995) (see also their individual chapters in this book), and perhaps still more canonically the discursive psychology of Edwards and Potter (see, for example, Edwards, 1997 and his chapter here; Edwards and Potter, 1992; Potter, 1996). I mean, rather, the sort of discourse analysis which, crudely speaking, is more interested in the 'content' of the talk rather than its sequential organization, and reserves the right to invoke extra-textual fact or interpretation in its claims about what is going on (and I mean to refer to such styles as critical discourse analysis, thematic analysis, narratology, and so on; see, for example, the collection in Burman and Parker, 1993).

The 'content' argument here would be that I, as a reader of the text and viewer of the videotape, being British, know that the (British) participants know that Fagin is an (English) fictional character about whom there is a freight of stereotypical characteristics which has passed into the common stock (in Britain, and possibly beyond). This includes his thievery, his band of child pickpockets and (especially as personified in a well-known film version, which has become iconic, at least in British popular culture) his image as being hook-nosed, stooped, and dressed in layers of rags. By virtue of all this, I understand that when Lyn utters the sound 'fa:gin' she is mentioning a personage, and I know what its features are for her, for me and for Zoe, and I understand what she is up to. This seems plausible and intuitively satisfying. But it could be wrong. More to the point, it won't tell us what as analysts we want to know, which is whether all of the above (debatable) features of Fagin's identity are active, or, if only a part, which part; and, most importantly of all, what that part does.

Analysis of the unfolding sequence, Sacks's argument goes, gets us all of this. If we look simply at what happens, we see that we can recuperate all that is then important about Fagin – all that matters to the people involved – simply from what they do. Thus, Lyn's offering of 'Fagin' is unmarked, implying an easy reference, therefore a reference to a known name, or to someone her audience could treat as being a known name. Zoe gives a signal (her echoing overlapped laughter) that she appreciates what Lyn has said, and that she is aware (or willing to be taken to be aware) that Lyn is referring to a named person, and the aptness of that naming in relation to the matter in hand.

All I have said so far is that the sound 'fa:gin' is taken by the participants to work as some sort of unproblematic entry into a sentence slot which is normally filled with a name; the point is, though, that I haven't needed extra-textual knowledge to say so. There will be readers who are not, in fact, familiar with the Fagin character, but nevertheless I predict (or hope) that what I've said so far, and the reading of the interaction that follows, works just as well for them. The point, of course, is not just about whether it is necessary for an analyst to identify some specific fictional character or other, but the general epistemological one of how we know that an identity (and which one) has been invoked by the people in front of us.

What Does the 'Fagin' Ascription Do Here?

What, then, does this name do? Here the content based discourse analyst does seem to have a point of entry. After all, the name is the name of a well-known fictional character – surely we have to use our knowledge of his characteristics to make sense of what Lyn and Zoe do with it? Well, let us see. We noted above that Zoe's utterance was hearable as a complaint or self-deprecation to do with the camera being on, and that Lyn's utterance was hearable as a candidate specification of something about that complaint or self-deprecation. What does the jocular, possibly 'teasing' use of the Fagin identity accomplish in that specification?

To start with, we note that it is done in what is recognizably an idiom: the stem 'you look like' affords completion by all sorts of idiomatic phrases ('something the cat dragged in', 'a dog's dinner', 'you've just seen a ghost', and so on). Drew and Holt (1988) have shown that idiomatic expressions of this sort do tend to signal what they call 'inauspicious environments' – for example, where the speaker might believe that the audience may think differently about some gripe or grievance that he or she is rehearsing. In that context, the formulation can be taken as an opportunity for the conversation to move on to less contentious things. Look at the idiom 'it'll iron itself out' here:

(7)   (from Drew and Holt, 1988)

```
1      P:      different things'll pick up when it begins to be spring of the year and
2              everything
3      M:      yah
4  →   P:      ˙hh but I think it'll iron itself out
5      M:      I sure hope ⌈so
6      P:                 ⌊I'll see you Tuesday
```

What P does is to offer something a platitudinous gloss on the specific trouble he had reported earlier – a gloss much easier for M to assent to. Note the importance of the recognizability of the platitude: 'it'll iron itself out' is, to speakers of British English at least, instantly recognizable as ready-made. Now consider what this might tell us about what Lyn does with 'you look like Fa:gin'. Recall again what Lyn and Zoe say:

(8) detail from extract (2)

```
30     Zoe:    [off camera and out of sight of Lyn] oh ↑go::d (.) look what ↑I'm wear↓ing=
31     Lyn:    =((explosive laugh)) >eheh ⌈hehh hehh hehh<
32     Zoe:                               ⌊hehh hehh
33 →   Lyn:    ↓you ↑look ↓like (.) ↑Fa:↓gin =
```

Lyn uses it in a response to Zoe's complaint or self-deprecation about what she's wearing. So we might hear Lyn's use of an idiom like this as a rather strong affiliation with Zoe, providing her with the sort of expression Zoe herself might have used. And, of course, by its platitudinous, ready-made feel, it avoids specificity, and that leaves it undecided as to whether Zoe is indeed complaining or self-deprecating. And it turns out, this is the key to what Lyn is doing here. If we dig a little more, we find that there are two further features of 'Fagin' which allow Lyn to express support for Zoe without asking her for further explication.

First, the environment in which 'Fagin' is used is one that privileges an identity-label, one of whose features ought to be relevant to something in Zoe's original utterance. Since she said 'oh go::d look what I'm wearing', we are doing no extra-textual interpretation if we take what is relevant to be something to do with 'clothes and clothing' (and just in case there is any interactional doubt about it, Lyn mimes 'gloves'). Moreover, Fagin comes in a idiom ('you look like . . .') which formulates a complaint by swinging it out towards something marked for extremity ('. . . a dog's dinner', 'something the cat dragged in', and so on), so the thing to do with 'clothes and clothing' is going to be peculiarly vivid. In other words, the environment picks out what it is we are to understand the relevant category-bound feature, as Sacks calls it, of 'Fagin' (here) to be. But it does no more than that: it does not, we notice, provide an environment which would support 'Fagin' as being a different sort of uptake on a complaint, namely to treat it as an accusation and provide an account in some sort of exoneration. The environment that Lyn exploits makes 'Fagin' work as the nasty personification of 'troublesome clothes and clothing', and so communicates Lyn's appreciation of 'troublesome clothes and clothing' as Zoe's problem. But it does not support Fagin being used to explicate the currently unsaid *cause* of Zoe's having such trouble with her clothes.

The elegance of this is that it does the business of giving a sympathetic hearing to Zoe's utterance – be it complaint or self-deprecation – without in any way passing judgement on its cause. Compare, for example, what Lyn might have said in reply to Zoe: 'what's wrong with them?' or 'what do you mean, are you cold?', and so on. By putting the ascription to Fagin just in this way, Lyn unostentatiously delivers some sort of affiliative response without the requirement that Zoe's complaint be unpacked into something which might put such affiliation to the test (e.g., it might be that Zoe is complaining that Lyn keeps her in rags, or that she is mean about heating the house, or that, in the context of the camera being 'on', Zoe has been recorded looking unkempt).

There is more. The second property of the ascription of the clothing to Fagin is to offer Zoe an end to the matter, in two ways. One is to exploit the hearer's axiom that Sacks (1974) notes, that to link up an activity to the category it belongs to is to do what is sufficient to account for it (along the lines of accounting for 'mischief' by saying 'well, they're just kids'). 'Fagin' offers a categorical reference that mops up the clothing worry. The other way that Lyn's utterance might be heard as a possible end to the story is its idiomatic expression. Drew and Holt (1988) demonstrate that idioms come at the hearable end of a complaint sequence, not at the beginning. Either way, the ball is back in Zoe's court should she want now to reveal the motivation for her complaint. She does not do so, and instead offers a *sotto voce* acknowledgement of the jocularity of Lyn's ascription, and, in the absence of any other development, offers a cigarette and moves on to a different topic:

(9)   (Repeat of part of extract (2))

39   Zoe: °↑very funny°
40   (1 sec)
41   °(d'you want one)°

It is not hard to hear Zoe's under-emphatic turns as exactly what Drew calls a 'po-faced' response to the tease (Drew, 1987). Her complaint or self-deprecation – whichever it is heard as – has been dealt with 'teasingly' and what the teasing has achieved, under its jocular coating, is an identity ascription which leaves Lyn non-committal about the cause of Zoe's problem.

To sum up the action so far then, the playfulness of 'Fa:gin' is part of the way it allows Lyn to manage the delicate business of not doing something expected – here, appreciating the cause of Zoe's troubles. By ascribing a jocular identity to Zoe, Lyn delivers something that identity ascriptions provide for: picking out a salient activity that goes along with it, and offering an account that mops it up. Lyn has mobilized the categorical implications of Fagin exactly to deal with the symptoms of Zoe's trouble – and as a means of not diagnosing them.

It would not have helped to have been a Dickens scholar to have said this, nor would it have helped to have asked a sample of people in the street what Fagin meant. Suppose one *was* an expert on Dickens and could point to Fagin's associations with Victorian London, criminality, stooped-ness, to stereotypes of the poor or of Jews, and a dozen other retrievable or arguable features. None of these would help us because none is made relevant by Lyn and Zoe. Nor would there be an infinity of other features; that Fagin was played by Ron Moody in the stage and film version; that Fagin is a man and not a woman; human and not animal, and so on, endlessly, and in all directions. What does matter about a category is its indexical use, as Sacks observed (an account Edwards (1997) has recently developed in an argument against the psychological account of categorization in general). What matters about a category is what is made of it then and there. Indeed, one could go further along the line with Edwards and point out that what we have said about Fagin – that we understand the word in its local use – is a feature of understanding all and any words; the problems of participants' understanding of 'Fagin' are no different from those facing us in their understanding of 'you', 'look' and 'like'.

A Jocular Identity Ascription ('the Terminally Dim') in an Appreciation

I used the Fagin extract above to labour the point about not needing cultural exegesis to understand the work it does, and now I want to say something more about the way an identity ascription is occasioned by the dynamics of the interaction – as policing, keeping tabs on, or in some other way indexing the footings on which participants are taking part (Antaki et al., 1996). This time the ascription – of the category 'the disabled' and of alternatives, one of which is 'the terminally dim' – happens in the context of a troubles story. As with what we did with the Fagin reference, we have to lead up to it as it comes, as did the participants. We know so far that Lyn and Zoe have set up a mother–daughter frame, and, within that, that Zoe has choked off the examination of her complaint about her clothes. This is how it continues:

(10)

42	Lyn:	°(↓well) (.) (I've already had a cigarette) of ↓yours°
43	Zoe:	°that's al↓>right< cos I know you're going to ↑buy: me ↓some°
44		(3 secs)
45	Lyn:	↑this is ↓really ↑DI::↓re
46	Zoe:	(°I kno::w°)
47	Lyn:	this ↑per↓son gave ↑me ↓this (.) ↑es↓say: (1 sec) be↓cause she ↑got such a
48		↓crap ↑mark >from ↓me< for the ↑first ↓one she (↑ge-) (..) she ↑ga:ve ↓me
49		↑this (.) to ↓look (1 sec) at bef↑o::↓re (1 sec) she gave it ↑in:
50		(1 sec)
51		↑an' ↓I- (.) ↑I'd (.) >sort of ↓skimmed ↑it an'< I said ↓yeah °it's° (1 sec)
52		↑don't ↓worry a°bout it it's not too (↓bad)° *[[tails away]]*
53		(2 secs)
54 →	Zoe:	°and it's ↓boll↑ocks°=

After the cigarette has been verbally accepted, Lyn introduces a 'troubles' story tied to something she was doing (the 'this' in 'This is DI::re' in line 45), and goes on to specify it as 'this person gave me this (.) essay' (line 47). This story-introduction quietly offers to Zoe a casting of what she and Lyn are, in principle, both capable of understanding (but to which Lyn has first access). Unless Zoe acts to the contrary, Lyn's talk about 'this' will place Lyn and Zoe in an agreement about what sort of interactants they have now become, for present purposes at least (Sacks, 1992, Vol. I: 313–19). Up to now, it was their categorization as mother and daughter that was live, if only by the default of having been the original summons and response ('Mum?' and '↑hel↓lo↑: (3 secs) I'm ↑he:↓re'). Now, Lyn has oriented them both to the 'this' set up in line 45. A change is afoot.

In the visible context of the interaction as it ran at the time, the deictic reference of 'this' is what is on the table in front of Lyn. Minimally that could be 'papers'; the addition of the assessment 'DI::re' turns that into, maximally, 'the sort of papers that could be dire in my judgement'. Lyn treats whatever those objects are as being no news to Zoe. Zoe's positive, if *sotto voce*, endorsement ('I know') confirms that. Lyn does a bit more specification ('this person gave me this (.) essay'), and any uncertainty is now cleared up. Lyn is ascribing to herself, and treating Zoe as appreciating, the sort of identity which deals in judgements of essays. This display of a category-bound activity does its business quietly; that is to say, neither Lyn or Zoe adverts to it openly – there is no need to. Compare the example from Sacks in which a caller (B) to a counselling service looks backwards to a reference to being a hairdresser he had made earlier in the call:

(11) (from Sacks, 1992, Vol. I: 46; line numbers added)

1	A:	Have you been having some sexual problems?
2	B	All my life
3	A:	Uh huh. Yeah.

4	B:	Naturally. You probably suspect, as far as the hairstylist and uh
5		either one way or another, they're straight or homosexual,
6		something like that.

For B to tie 'hairstylist' to sexual preference, is to treat 'hairstyling' as a category-bound activity which would or could be taken as a clue to a category ('straight or homosexual, something like that'). Lyn is not doing that corrective hinting of her identity; she is merely *displaying* it. Her talk unobtrusively shows her as a person with some kind of authority (perhaps an 'academic' or a 'teacher', or a 'trainer' and so on, temporarily or permanently) to assess an essay and, since it is not set up as news, Zoe's identity as someone already aware of such authority.

Using Identity Ascription for Contrast and Escalation

Now that we have a sense of the surrounding scene, let us look at what part the jocular identity ascription plays within it. The matter in hand is, we know, the telling of a troubles story; so far we know that it is some trouble with an essay, but we don't know what sort of trouble. This is how Lyn and Zoe take the talk on from extract (8) above:

(12)

55	Lyn:	=↑well ↓no: ↑it's ↓no:t (.) no ↑it's ↓not (.) it's just ↑it- >a- a-< hhh::: (.)
56		for a ↑star:t I told ↓her f- (..) ↑↑do not ↓↓u::se (.) ↑the ↓ter:m
57		(1 sec)
58		the dis:↑a:b↓led (..) and (.) ↑the ↑handi↓capped cos it ↓gets up my ↑no:se (..)
59	Zoe:	⌈(mmm yeh)
60	Lyn:	⌊>I ↓just (.) ↑can't stand ↓it and she's ↑done it< ↑a::ll the °↑way ↓throu:gh-°
61		(1 sec)
62	Zoe:	well ↑that's ↓just ↑stu:↓pid °isn't it° (.) °>(if somebody)<° (.) if
63		↑some↓one's been ↑specifically ↓to:ld not to ↑do: ↓some↑thing (.) >↓I ↑mean<
64		↓no↑one
65		(1 sec)
66		hhh ↑no ↓one would'↑ve ↓er:m:
67		(1 secs)
68		I ↑mean you ↓couldn't ↑use that ↓term ↑any↓wa:y (.) >°(I mean at)°<
69		university ↑now?°
70		(2 secs)
71	Lyn:	↑(wh-ah: ↑n-) >the ↓point is ⌈↓that<
72	Zoe:	⌊you ↑should↓n't be able ↑to::
73	Lyn:	↑they've had ↑ten ↓wee:ks (..) of me ↑say↓ing=
74	Zoe:	((cough))
75	Lyn:	↑(day) (.) ↓one
76	Zoe:	(yeh) [nods]
77	Lyn:	↓don't ↑s- (.) don't ↓say ⌈↑>any of this< s-
78	Zoe:	⌊↑it's ↓gene↑ra↓lize ⌈(syll)
79	Lyn:	⌊°↑it's< ↑not: (..) a ↓good

80		↑ide:↓a:::>* ((*'strangled' funny voice*))
81	Zoe:	↑like (.) being ↓called (.) <the ↑nor:m↓al> ↑huh or >↓huh huh< ye ↑said it's
82		↓not- >(.) (ye-) ↑gott↓a (even) ↑word
83		(1 sec)
84		isn't ↓it
85	Lyn:	(n↑o::↓::)=
86	Zoe:	=↓like ↑say↓ing
87		(1 sec)
88		hhhh (.) ↑peop↓le with ↑legs every↓time you ↑t(h)alk (a(h)↓bout) ˙hhh
89		↓huhh ↑huhh (.) ↑huhh (..) ↓it's ri↑DICu↓lous
90		(1 sec)
91 →	Lyn:	↓we:ll: (..) ↓hhhhh:: (.) ↑she's-
92		(1 sec)
93 →		↓terminally (..) dim:::=a-
94 →	Zoe:	↓may↑be we should ↓ca:ll ↑her- (..) the ↓terminally ↑dim::
95		(1 sec)

We can gloss the trouble as revolving around Lyn's student's persistent use of the term 'the disabled'. Of course, there is a great deal we could say about the ins and outs of the story as Lyn tells it and Zoe appreciates it, but I shall skip over all that so as to get quickly to the point at which Lyn, as the teller of the tale, offers the description of the student as 'terminally dim'. Lyn's description 'she's- (1 sec) ↓terminally dim::::' (lines 91–3) is an extreme-case formulation (Pomerantz, 1986) appropriate as the punchline to an anecdote. Now how do we understand – how do *they* understand – the curious identity ascription that Zoe makes in her next turn: '↓may↑be we should ca:ll ↑her- (..) the ↓terminally ↑dim::' (line 94).

Whatever else it is, Lyn's description at lines 91–3 is of an anonymous third party and it is a simple, person-relevant adjective, with no great implication of group membership. The person Lyn is referring to, *she*- the student, *qua* just any student, is terminally dim. That is the environment in which Zoe's utterance comes. Notice two things. One is that the extreme case formulation in Lyn's description is right at the limit: if someone is not just dim but *terminally* dim there's not much more room to express just how dim you think he or she is. The second thing to note is that Zoe nevertheless sets what is to follow ('↓may↑be we should ↓ca:ll ↑her . . .') as being an escalation of what Lyn has offered. So we are to hear what she says ('the ↓terminally ↑dim::') as being a still more punishing way in which someone can be called dim.

Those are two things about the form of Zoe's utterance, and the general point to make is that these formal properties tell us interesting things about what must be the case about the sense that these participants make (and they are ordinarily competent members of society) of personal and group identities. For the contrastive structure of Zoe's contribution (the student is 'terminally dim' versus the student is (one of) 'the terminally-dim') to make the sense it does, then being 'terminally dim' is to be understood as incompatible with, or trumped by, the collection 'the terminally dim'. The former is just a description of one person's characteristics, whereas the latter is evocative of a whole category. To use the description '*the* terminally dim' transforms the idiosyncratic personal label into one with a burden of known, routinized features shared with other people.

Note, though, that none of this is meant to be a story about the 'mutual knowledge' that the participants must have, at least not in the sort of sense that cognitive psychologists mean. It is just the way that the language works; there would be no reason for English to discriminate between the form 'terminally dim' and '*the* terminally dim' unless the contrast meant something, and I know what that something is, just as you do and Lyn and Zoe do, by virtue of being a competent speaker. There is no claim that Lyn and Zoe have special knowledge or are working to some pre-rehearsed code; they are speaking English.

If the class-based term is not to misfire as an escalation, then it must 'do more' than the personal adjective. How do we know what 'more' is being done? Our intuition just from reading the extract is to think of the 'more' as being 'more negative', but we feel vague about it. In fact, there is good evidence if we look a little further. If you look back at the body of the story, you'll see that Lyn's talk has been about the student's failings in calling people 'the disabled' and 'the handicapped'. Now the most economic comeback to a piece of calling, Sacks observes in remarks on 'naming' (Sacks, 1992, Vol. I: 544), is to turn the term back on the caller ('You're stupid', 'I'm not – you are'): economic because it casts the original caller's activity in naming as now being the accountable thing. But we need not worry about the details here. The important thing is that we hear in what Zoe is doing, in calling the student 'the terminally dim', the use of that comeback form as a vehicle. She mobilizes the insult and turns it back on the caller – and that is (at least part of) how we and the participants know that the sense of the ascription is pejorative. The way it contrasts with and escalates the personal description is by being a sharper, better designed, insult. We see then, that the escalation of Lyn's description is towards the 'generality' and 'indiscriminateness' already set up by Lyn's complaint.

Is there any further evidence, apart from the contrastive, escalatory structure of Zoe's utterance, and its insult-comeback content? Indeed there is, as the participants immediately go on to confirm exactly what we have noticed so far:

(13)

96	Lyn:	↓YEH ↑HA (.) HA- >hahh hahh hahh hahh hahh< ↑hu::h (..) ˙hhh >hehh
97		⌈hehh hehh hehh<
98	Zoe:	⌊↑we're ↓gonna ↑ca:ll ↓you the t(h)erminally ↑di:m:
99	Lyn:	↑uh:=
100	Zoe:	=and ↑re↓fu:se to ↑cite ↓you as the >indi↑vidu↓al< or a ↑per↓son (.) un↑til
101		you ↓stop ↑labell↓ing ↑peop↓le (.) the dis↑ab(hh)↓led or (.) the ↑men↓tally
102		˙hh ↑handi↓capped ˙hh ((sniff))
103		(1 sec)

104	Lyn:	((audibly exhales smoke)) ↓we:ll that's an ↑interest↓ing ↑i↓dea ↓Zo↑e:
105		(2 secs)
106		↓er::: (.)I don't think ↑it's (.) ↓poss::i↑BLE [funny voice]

There is the possibility that the delay and exaggerated explosion of laughter with which Lyn greets Zoe's utterance is an index that Lyn has appreciated the heights to which the escalation has reached. But that is a bit indirect, so let us note instead that Zoe further underlines the group nature of the ascription by repeating it explicitly in the voice of an ascriber at the appropriate membership categorization device level (Sacks, 1992, Vol. I: 40 and thereafter), namely another group (*'we're* going to call you . . .'). The group is indeterminate, but is (at least) 'those with some lien over you'; the important thing is that it is indeed a group (and not Zoe speaking for herself, as in what would be, in this context, the awkward-sounding *'I'm* going to call you').

It is noticeable also that Zoe uses the expression 'we're going to call you the terminally dim'. Explicitly saying that you are 'calling' someone some-thing is a sharper way of doing it than merely calling them that without reflection, which is perhaps the default way in which descriptions are used for interactional work (as investigated by Edwards and Potter, 1992, chapters 4 and 5, for example). And explicitly saying you are calling someone something affords, as we can see again in Sacks's discussion of 'naming' (1992, Vol. I), usually only a category description, rather than a personal adjective; compare the oddness of the utterance 'we're going to call you dim'. And finally, in what is a simple bonus for us as analysts, Zoe makes wholly explicit what this means: she says (in line 100) 'and refuse to cite you as the individual or a person', showing up just exactly that the contrast is between being 'an individual' and a group member, making just the distinction that was the motivating trouble of Lyn's story.

What was the point of all that? Well, I wanted to make the case that what we have in front of us is identity ascription occasioned by the specifics of their interaction. It is part of a dynamically emerging trajectory of the conversation, namely the escalation of assessments in the environment of a story punchline. Lyn and Zoe are active agents in the production of the shape the conversation takes, of course, but once it has started they are also bound by its demands, until and unless one of them calls a halt to it and sets the trail going elsewhere.

Concluding Comments

Identity ascription is neither an all-powerful incantation nor one with unique effect. It does many things, and whatever it does, it does as part of an ensemble of devices brought together in the right place and the right time. Of course it provides a special service (such as the implication of a feature from a category, or vice versa), but what that service delivers is coloured by the particular company it keeps on every outing. Here in this encounter I wanted to show how jocular identity ascription was used, with various companion devices, and according to the time-line of the encounter, to do two things: to deliver a sympathetic (but evasive) formulation of a problem, and to upgrade an assessment of a story's punchline while appreciating its motivating complaint. Neither of those fit neatly into the standard sort of list that social science allows 'identity work' to do. They are not, to burlesque a list of standard cultural and psychological motivations, anything like: outgroup derogation, self-esteem maintenance, perceptual-category sharpening, and so on or, at least, they are not taken by the participants themselves to be any of those things. They do what they do in their place and time.

By tracking through the opening few minutes of one entirely unremark-able domestic encounter I tried to show that identity ascription (to oneself, the person one is addressing, and people outside the interaction) is occasioned by what is happening, and that it reacts to those things and changes them: it is, as Schegloff puts it, both context-sensitive and context-renewing (Schegloff, 1992b) and it does its work effectively and without fuss. To ascribe an identity to someone in the routine complexity of social life is to appraise the local state of affairs as allowing or requiring such an ascription; then you make the ascription, accomplish what you accomplish, and move on.

Note

I am grateful to Jonathan Potter and Derek Edwards for comments on an earlier draft of this chapter.

PART II

DISCOURSE IDENTITIES AND SOCIAL IDENTITIES

6 Identity, Context and Interaction

Don H. Zimmerman

The concept of 'identity', particularly in relation to discourse, can be variously specified, for example, as an independent variable accounting for participants' use of particular linguistic or discourse devices; as a means of referring to and making inferences about self and other; as a constructed display of group membership, as a rhetorical device, and so on. In this chapter, I propose to treat identity as an element of context for talk-in-interaction. Indeed, any of the previously listed applications of the concept would depend in some way on identity as a contextual element of a given discourse. I note here that I use the term 'discourse' in this chapter as shorthand for referring to talk-in-interaction, the domain of concerted social activity pursued through the use of linguistic, sequential and gestural resources. In this usage, it is primarily a behavioural rather than symbolic domain, less a 'text' to be interpreted than a texture of orderly, repetitive and reproducible activities to be described and analysed. Shortly, I will elaborate on the notion of identity-as-context and distinguish between different types of identity. First, however, I briefly consider the link between interaction and the social order.

Erving Goffman (1983) proposed that there is a domain of face-to-face interaction – what he termed the interaction order – that is only loosely coupled with what is generally taken to be the 'macro' social order. This proposal suggests that the organization of social interaction can be looked at as a phenomenon in its own right, and although conversation analysis antedates Goffman's valedictory formulation, it nevertheless abundantly confirms that suggestion. However, I want here to go a step further and propose that although social interaction has a detailed organization that is largely independent of social structure, the 'loose coupling' that Goffman refers to, it nevertheless is tightly articulated with the environing social world. I propose further that participants' orientations to this or that identity – their own and others' – is a crucial link between interaction on concrete occasions and encompassing social orders (see Wilson, 1991). Indeed, in so far as a social order presupposes recurrent patterns of action, its fundamental substrate is the organization of interaction – a view of which Goffman was wary (1983: 8–9). However, to view the interaction order as furnishing the building blocks for a social world beyond the instant situation is not to say that the 'larger' social order is 'nothing but' interaction; rather, that the interaction order provides the mechanisms that enable not only interaction between social actors, but also larger formations that arise from such activities (see Schegloff, 1991, 1996: 54).

The main focus of this chapter is how oriented-to identities provide both the *proximal* context (the turn-by-turn orientation to developing sequences of action at the interactional level) and the *distal* context for social activities (the oriented-to 'extra-situational' agendas and concerns accomplished *through* such endogenously developing sequences of interaction). Discourse identities bring into play relevant components of conversational machinery, while situated identities deliver pertinent agendas, skills and relevant knowledge, allowing participants to accomplish various projects in an orderly and reproducible way. Activities in a given setting achieve their distinctive shape through an *articulation* of discourse and situated identities for each participant and an *alignment* of these identities across participants, linking the proximal and distal contexts of action. Thus, in the most general sense, the notion of identity-as-context refers to the way in which the articulation/alignment of discourse and situated identities furnishes for the participants a continuously evolving framework within which their actions, vocal or otherwise, assume a particular meaning, import and interactional consequentiality (see Goodwin, 1996: 374–6).

The linking of proximate and distal contexts of action through the alignment of discourse and situated identities is a fundamental interactional issue. This can be seen most clearly when troubles of articulation or alignment occur. Consider the following to an emergency number in the mid-western United States:

(1) (MCE 20–10/196)

```
1      CT:    Mid-City police an fire
2             ((background noise and music on the line))
3      C:     (YA::H ) Thiz iz thuh (      ) ((voice is very
4             slurred))
5             (1.5) ((loud background noise))
6      CT:    Hello:?
7             (0.4)
8      C:     YEA::H?
9  →   CT:    Wadidja want'?
```

```
10              (0.5 )
11      C:      Yea::h we- we wan' forn'ca:y (h) heh
12              (0.6) ((background voices, noise))
13  →   CT:     'Bout wha::t?
14              (5.3)
15              ((noise, voice: 'hey gimme dat. . .'))
16      C:      Hay=I've=uh ri:ddle for ya::
17              (0.3)
18      CT:     HU:::H?
19      C:      I have uh ri:ddle for ya
20              (0.3)
21  →   CT:     I don't have ti:me f'r riddles=do-ya wanna
22              squa:d'rno:t=
23      C:      =NO: jes' uh simple que::stion,
24              (0.4) ((loud music)) Wha' fucks an leaks
25              like uh ti:ger,
26              (0.2)
27      CT:     HU:H?
28      C:      What fucks an leaks like uh ti:ger,
29              Huh? ((background noise))
30      CT:     Good bye
31      C:      Why::?
32              ((disconnect))
```

Below, I will discuss in more detail the organization of calls to emergency numbers, and particularly how this organization aligns caller and the answerer. For present purposes, the call may be glossed as follows (see Zimmerman, 1990). To begin, the caller seeks explicitly to take the discourse identity (see below) of a story teller or a riddler (line 16, 'hay=I've=uh ri:ddle for ya'). When the call-taker refuses to be a recipient for the riddle and asks (lines 21–2) if he needs police services (thereby explicitly proposing the capacity in which he should be calling), he appears momentarily to shift identities, countering that he wants 'an answer to a simple question', which, of course, turns out to be the riddle (lines 23–5).

Each party proposes a different footing for the call, that is, a different alignment of situated identities within which the sense and relevance of the exchange is to be understood and responded to. While the call-taker speaks 'seriously', that is, in her identity as call-taker, the caller aligns himself not as a 'serious' complainant, but as its alternative, a non-serious identity, 'prank' caller.

Thus, to the extent that this sequence is in fact a 'prank' being played on the complaint-taker, this is an instance of an attempt to alter the routine framing of citizen calls to the police (Whalen and Zimmerman, 1990; Zimmerman, 1984, 1992a, 1992b). It is important to observe in this regard the almost heroic character of the call-taker's attempt to manage the call on a routine footing. For example, in lines 9 and 13 she seeks to elicit some indication that the call is a request for service. When the caller then offers to tell her a riddle, the dispatcher rebukes him with 'I don't have ti:me for riddles', but mounts yet another attempt to allow the caller to disclose a possible emergency with her query ('do=ya=wanna squa:d'rno:t?') in line 21. When it becomes clear to her that the caller proposes a different footing for the encounter (line 28), she initiates a closing of the call (line 30).

Note that the problems of this call stem from the misalignment of situated identities across the participants. Moreover, this call shows that alignment is an interactional issue, that is, it is something that cannot be secured unilaterally. Neither party was successful in inducing the other to align with their proposed identity sets and this impasse ultimately leads to the termination of the call. This suggests that when alignment is achieved, it must entail interactional ratification by the parties involved, and also that the interaction will be troubled to the extent that alignment is problematic (see the discussion of the Dallas Fire Department call, below).

The riddle call is useful in that it permits us to see how crucial the alignment of discourse and situated identities is for the conduct of an emergency call. I want to turn now to a brief examination of the nature of discourse and situated identities, and of a third type, transportable identities.

Discourse, Situational and Transportable Identities

Discourse, situational and transportable identities have different home territories. Discourse identities are integral to the moment-by-moment organization of the interaction. Participants assume discourse identities as they engage in the various sequentially organized activities: current speaker, listener, story teller, story recipient, questioner, answerer, repair initiator, and so on (see below). In initiating an action, one party assumes a particular identity and projects a reciprocal identity for co-participant(s). As suggested in the discussion of the riddle call just above, such projections are subject to ratification (the recipient assuming the projected identity) or revision (in the case where, for example, a recipient of a question locates some aspect of that action as a trouble source, becoming a repair initiator instead of the answerer).

Situated identities come into play within the precincts of particular types of situation. Indeed, such situations are effectively brought into being and sustained by participants engaging in activities and respecting agendas that display an orientation to, and an alignment of, particular identity sets, for example, in the case of emergency telephone calls, citizen-complainant and call-taker. In turn, the pursuit of such agendas rests on the underlying alignment of discourse identities.

Finally, transportable identities travel with individuals across situations and are potentially relevant in and for any situation and in and for any spate of interaction. They are latent identities that 'tag along' with individuals as they move through their daily routines in the following sense:

they are identities that are usually visible, that is, assignable or claimable on the basis of physical or culturally based insignia which furnish the intersubjective basis for categorization. Here, it is important to distinguish between the registering of *visible* indicators of identity and *oriented-to* identity which pertains to the capacity in which an individual should *act* in a particular situation. Thus, a participant may be *aware* of the fact that a co-interactant is classifiable as a young person or a male without orienting to those identities as being relevant to the instant interaction.

The distinction between *apprehension* of the transportable identity of the other, and the *orientation to* incumbency in that category as the basis of action, is critical for empirical investigation. Parties to an interaction may recognize at some level that they and their co-interactants can be classified in particular ways. Moreover, such classificatory information could be used to refer to or characterize individuals as a means of *accounting for* the course of some interactional episode. This does not entail that such identity assignments provided the *operative* context for the interaction, although such tacit identity work may affect how participants subsequently describe or evaluate the interaction. Thus, for example, a given interaction may, behaviourally, be gender neutral while participants' perceptions or professional accounts of it may invoke gender-relevant meanings and inferences (see Garcia, 1998). That such perceptions occur, or that gender-based accounts are offered, are, of course, significant phenomena in their own right, and can have important consequences (see Ridgeway, 1997).

In the analyses of emergency calls reported below, however, there is little evidence that participants treat transportable identities such as gender as relevant to their interaction. To be sure, reference to such matters as the age, sex and race of third parties do occur in emergency calls, but this is for the purpose of locating and apprehending those persons. For reasons of space, I will confine my attention in this chapter to oriented-to discourse and situated identities. This is not, I emphasize, to suggest that the latter identities are unimportant, for it is clear that they are a way of encoding some of the major structural features of a society in a fashion that is capable of bearing directly on concrete social activities. I turn next to a closer examination of discourse and situated identities.

Discourse Identities

First, notice that the parties to an interaction do different things over the course of talk. They ask questions, tell stories, issue and defend against complaints, do repairs on problems of hearing and understanding, offer and respond to assessments of persons and events – this list is far from exhaustive. Moreover, who is doing what varies over the interaction, and the procession of discourse identities is interactionally contingent rather than determined, that is, one party's initiation of a discourse activity does not preclude a shift to another activity by another party. The mundane activity of talking with one another is coincident with assuming and leaving discourse identities.

Discourse identities furnish the focus for the type of discourse activity projected and recognized by participants, what they are *doing* inter-actionally in a particular spate of talk. For example, for all types of spoken discourse, the pervasive identities are that of *speaker/hearer*. It matters for participants who has the floor to speak, and who is assigned the tasks associated with listening. For specific types of discourse such as telephone calls, the relevant identitites are *caller/answerer*. It matters who placed the call and who received it. For specific segments or sequences within a discourse, *story teller/recipient, inviter/invitee, or questioner/answerer*, and so on become important. In so far as an activity is enabled and advanced through discourse, participants recognizably act in the capacity of one or another discourse identity. For example, in locating topics for discussion, a participant may ask a question directed at some aspect of another's situated identity, thereby inviting a recipient to pursue a particular line of talk, and an invitation a recipient can accept or decline (see Maynard and Zimmerman, 1984).

I argue that discourse identities emerge as a feature of the sequential organization of talk-in-interaction, orienting participants to the type of activity underway and their respective roles within it. Indeed, the alignment of discourse identities figures in the maintenance of sequential ordering and the 'architecture of intersubjectivity' it sustains (Heritage, 1984: 254–60). The initiation of a given sequence projects (but does not assure) a restricted range of next actions and selects particular parties, either individuals or larger units (see Lerner, 1992, 1993) as the animator of those actions.

Consider the following call to a mid-western emergency dispatch centre:

(2a)   (MCE 30–20.18)

```
1        CT:     Mid-City emergency
2    →   C:      ˙hhh Yeah um I'd like tu:h report something weird
3                that happened abou:t (0.1) um five minutes ago?
```

Notice that the caller/citizen-complainant (C) initiates what at first looks to be the first component of the standard report format: *I'd like to report* + *categorization of problem*, for example, an accident/robbery/loud party, etc. Routinely, call-takers respond to this format by initiating a series of questions, which I have called the 'interrogative series' as in the following:

(3)   (MCE 23–14.22)

```
1        CT:     ˙hh Mid-City emergency.
2        C:      ˙h Yes um (.) I would like to:: (.) u:h 'port uh,
3                ˙hhh uh break in.
4    →   CT:     To your home?
```

```
5       C:      Yes. (.) Well: (.) we're babysitting.
6       CT:     Okay what's the address there?=
7       C:      =It's forty one forty four (.) ⌈eighteenth avenue.=
8       CT:                                    ⌊uh huh,
9   →   CT:     Is this a one family dwelling or a duplex.
10              (0.5)
11      C:      It's u::h h=
12  →   CT:     =Is it a house or a dupl⌈ex.
13      C:                               ⌊It's like ˙hhh yeah a
14              duplex. We're- ⌈ih- upstairs.
15      CT:                    ⌊Up 'r down.
16  →   CT:     And what's thuh last name there?
```

However, in the case of the previous extract (2a), the 'report' is transformed into a characterization of an as yet unspecified event, 'something
weird'. This can be considered an instance of what Goodwin (1996: 384)
calls a 'prospective indexical', namely, an expression which orients recipient
to the 'yet to be discovered' sense of the event (in this case, its status as a
'policeable' matter). Examining an extended version of this transcript (2b)
we see that the characterization of the problem is followed by try-marked
temporal and locational information. The call-taker's 'yeah?' (line 4)
displays a readiness to receive an explication of the 'weird' event (see
Goodwin, 1984: 226). The caller then continues, completing the locational
information and launching into a narrative account of how they came to
encounter the 'weird' happening:

(2b)   (MCE: 30–20.18)

```
1       C:      ˙hhh Yeah um I'd like tu:h report something weird
2               that happened abou:t (0.1) um five minutes ago?
3               In front of our apartment building?
4   →   CT:     Yeah?
5       C:      On eight fourteen eleventh avenue southeast,
6   →   CT:     Mmhm,
7       C:      ˙hh We were just (.) um (.) sittin' in the room and
8               we heard this cra:nking you know like someone was
9               pulling something behind their ca:r an' we
10              looked out the window ˙hhh an' there was this (0.1)
11              light blue: (.) smashed up u:m (0.1) station wagon
12              and ˙hh a:nd (.) thuh guy made a U-turn=we live
13              on a dead end ˙hh and (.) thuh whole front end of
14              thuh- thuh car was smashed up ˙hhh and (.) he jumped
15              out of the car and I remember he- he tried to push
16              the hood down on something and then he jus' (.)
17              started running an' he took off,
18  →   CT:     Mmhm.
19      C:      A::nd we think that maybe 'e could've (.) you know
20              stolen the car and abandoned it or something.
```

```
21  →  CT:    What kinda car is it?
22     C:     'h It's a blue station wagon 'hh hh We just (.) have
23            seen it from the window.
24     CT:    We'll get somebody over there. . .
```

The caller, by moving from report format (which projects the call-taker as report-recipient and usually leads, as indicated above, to the initiation of a series of questions) to a narrative format, projects the call-taker as, in effect, story recipient. CT exhibits her orientation to a multiple turn unit in progress by issuing continuers. When the narrative is apparently brought to a close in lines 19–20, the call-taker initiates questioning at that point. A report or request format thus initiates one type of discourse structure (interrogation) early on in the call (recall extract (3)) whereas a narrative or story format initiates another (extracts (2a) and (2b)) namely an extended turn by the caller supported by continuers from the call-taker. Interrogation, if it occurs, comes after the completion of the narrative.

Conversational sequences and their discourse identities thus provide the resources for the pursuit of an array of activity types, for example, question-answer sequences as a species of adjacency-pair organization provide the means to pursue activities as courtroom examinations (Atkinson and Drew, 1979; Drew, 1992), police interrogations (Watson, 1990), television news interviews (Heritage and Greatbatch, 1991), and many types of service calls, including emergency telephone calls (Drew and Heritage, 1992: 43–5; Zimmerman, 1992a, 1992b).

Situated Identities

By virtue of their ubiquity as an element of the general organization of talk-in-interaction, discourse identities do not by themselves account for the variation in the nature of these activities, for example, the difference between courtroom interrogation and a television news interview (both of which involve questioning and answering). Discourse identities can shift turn by turn. In the immediately preceding example, the situated identities of citizen-complainant and call-taker remain constant, while the discourse identities shift, or rather, become layered, as the caller assumes the task of narrator and the call-taker the narrative recipient. The shifting of identities repositions the parties to address particular tasks as they arise, in this case, the characterization of an event that the caller could not, or would not code in the report format. When the narrative is concluded, the call-taker becomes interrogator, the caller the interogatee, as further information of a particular sort is elicited. This play of discourse identities is tied to the situated identities of the parties, which in turn link these local activities to standing social arrangements and institutions through the socially distributed knowledge participants have about them. For Wilson (1991), the term 'social structure' is a covering concept for orientation to such extra-situational formations:

. . . social structure consists of matters that are described and oriented to by members of society on relevant occasions as essential resources for conducting their affairs and, at the same time, reproduced as external and constraining social facts through that same social interaction. (Wilson, 1991: 27)

In these terms, oriented-to situated identities circumscribe and make available those extra-situational resources participants need to accomplish a particular activity by articulating with the discourse identities embedded in the sequential organization that enables the accomplishment of these activities. They are the portal through which the setting of the talk and its institutional surround (Wilson's 'social structure') enters and helps to shape the interaction, which in turn actualizes the occasion and its institutional provenance.

A perspicuous example of how situated identities function in talk-in-interaction can be found in Heritage and Sefi's (1992) study of Health Visitors in Britain. Health Visitors are nurses who, by law, must call on mothers who have recently given birth. Heritage and Sefi observe (1992: 365–6) that these interactions were mutually regarded as a service encounter (see Jefferson and Lee, 1992): the mothers oriented to Health Visitors as 'baby experts' and hence knowledgeable judges of mothers' competence as caregivers, and the nurses usually comported themselves as such. This is shown, in extract (4), by a mother's (M) uptake of an observation by a Health Visitor:

(4)   (from Heritage and Sefi, 1992 [4A 1:1])

```
1       HV:    He's enjoying that ⌈isn't he.
2       F:                         ⌊°Yes he certainly is=°
3       M:     =He's not hungry 'cuz (h)he's ju(h)st (h)had
4              'iz bo:ttle ˙hhh
```

Heritage and Sefi point out that HV's observation is regarded by M as offered in her professional capacity, *qua* Health Visitor, and hence, as an implicit negative assessment of her (the mother's) care of the infant. M's response exhibits both her orientation to the situated identity of the Health Visitor, which comprises, among other things, expertise in matters of infant care, and her orientation to her own identity as a mother who, in that capacity, may feel accountable with regard to any noticing offered by HV concerning the state of her infant. As Heritage and Sefi observe, F and M have a different take on the upshot of the assessment: F apparently does not view the query as professionally motivated (i.e., at just this juncture, produced by reference to the Health Visitor identity) whereas M does, shaping the defensive stance of her answer.

In what follows, I will use materials from several studies of emergency telephone calls that my collaborators and I (separately or together) have done, drawing them together in a fashion that focuses more closely on the problem of identity-as-context.

Identity and Interaction in Emergency Calls

Drew and Heritage (1992: 43–4) in their introduction to a collection of studies of talk in institutional settings observe that in contrast to ordinary conversation, which, apart from opening and closings, is not constrained by some overarching organization or 'standard pattern', institutional interactions follow a 'task-related standard shape', whether this be prescribed or the product of 'locally managed routines'. The 'locally managed routines' characteristic of service calls can be characterized as follows:

Pre-beginning / summons
      Opening / identification / acknowledgement
           REQUEST [caller's first turn]
                 INTERROGATIVE SERIES [contingencies of response]
           RESPONSE [promise or provision of service]
Closing

FIGURE 6.1   *The organization of service calls (modified from Zimmerman, 1992b: 419)*

For present purposes, I will consider identity-as-context with respect to the pre-beginning, opening identification/acknowledgement, the caller's first turn, and interrogative series 'phases' of the call.

Pre-beginnings and Openings

Conversation on the telephone is, of course, conversation, and is organized in much the same way as face-to-face encounters. However, parties to telephone talk cannot see one another, and special steps have to be taken to achieve the mutual recognition accomplished in other circumstances by a glance (Schiffrin, 1977; see also Schegloff, 1979: 71).

The accomplishment of identification and, thereby, an alignment of identities, provides for reciprocal understanding of just what sectors of one's self and one's social knowledge are now relevant to the upcoming interaction. To fully appreciate this fact it is necessary to consider what occurs just before the opening in such calls.

A call to an emergency service like 9-1-1 in the USA begins prior to the opening identification sequence. There is, in short, a 'pre-beginning'. Generally, it consists of the activity of dialling a telephone number, which summons another to interact (Schegloff, 1968). For most casual telephone calls, the answerer does not and cannot know who, in particular, is calling and for what reasons, although prearranged calls can overcome these constraints. The caller has selected a recipient, although, similar to the answerer's circumstances, the caller cannot be certain who will answer (the number dialled may be incorrect, or answered by some party other than the one sought).

In the case of dialling the number of a service port like the police, the situation is modified in several respects. First, the caller is selecting an organization (and a service) rather than a particular individual, although individuals known as agents of the organization may be sought. Secondly, the answerer can presume that callers who have correctly selected the number are members of a class of callers who have appropriate business to transact. The organization of identity alignment in emergency calls can be summarized as follows:

1 In answering the telephone summons, the answerer from the outset treats incoming calls to that number as selected by callers in terms of the purposes which that number exists to serve. Incoming calls to emergency numbers are thus treated as *virtual emergencies* (Whalen and Zimmerman, 1990; Zimmerman, 1992b); the *placing* of the call itself assuming the status of a *request* for service.
2 By providing a self-identification appropriate to that number, the answerer announces to the caller the character of the service port reached.
3 The caller, upon hearing the answerer's self-identification, ordinarily acknowledges having reached the intended service port, completing the opening identification sequence.

In terms of identity, then, what transpires in the pre-beginning is a *pre-alignment* (caller/called and citizen-complainant/call-taker) subject to ratification in the opening/identification sequence. In a routine opening sequence where the caller has dialled 9-1-1, the call-taker answers with a categorical self-identification and an offer of assistance.

The sequences themselves, including those that figure in the emergency telephone calls, are indifferent to the particular situated identities of the parties who animate them. Yet, as Wilson (1991: 37–8) argues, they can be articulated with particular discourse identities such that, for example, call-takers ask the questions, and callers return the floor when they complete their answer, allowing for a series of question-and-answer pairs (see below). Speaking of the distribution of events found across emergency calls, Wilson goes on to observe that:

> In effect, routine use of the mechanisms of interaction passes an antecedent distribution [citizen requests for service] through to a final distribution [call takers ask questions]. In this sense, then, one can account for the distribution of subsequent events as a product of sequential mechanisms, but only if the distribution of antecedent events is already given. . . . [T]he initial distribution of requests, such that these are made by citizen complainants rather than complaint takers, arises from the institutional context that the participants establish as relevant. Thus, ultimately, distributional phenomena in interaction may reflect elements of institutional context. (Wilson, 1991: 37–8)

This distributional regularity is achieved by virtue of the way in which participants *enter* the sequential space within which the interactionally organized pursuit of the institution's work is sustained, namely, through a set of sequences initiated by the pre-beginning. The 'institutional context' Wilson refers to is first provided by the designation of a 7-digit or 3-digit telephone number as an emergency number, and secondly, embodied in the call-taker who is positioned in her identity by the alignment in the opening sequence to perform the interactional work necessary for the institution's purposes.

The point I wish to stress here is that the opening of the call, and in particular, the first component or components of the first turn of the answerer and caller are regularly devoted to establishing a mutually oriented-to set of identities implicative for the shape of what is to follow – the *footing* (Goffman, 1981: 128), as it were, of the encounter. Moreover, the sequence of events – dialling 9-1-1 (or other emergency number), answering the summons with a categorical self-identification, acknowledging having reached the intended number – projects a particular line of activity and, to use Wilson's phrase, a 'continuity of relevancies' (1991: 25). This not to say that this initial establishment of the relevance of the institutional context automatically 'covers' all else that follows. As Wilson (1991: 25–6) notes, to establish a presumption is one thing, to fulfil it, and fulfil it recognizably, is another. The notion of continuity suggests that (i) relevance does not have to be *established anew* at each turn, but it does have to be *extended*, and (ii) failure to extend or reconfirm by producing some behaviour understandable in a different context is a method of renegotiating what is going on in the situation – recall here the discussion of the riddle call (extract (1)) above. The issue of the 'continuity of relevance' underscores the irreducibly interactional character of the alignment.

I want to turn now to the more routine features of call-processing to explore how identity-as-context functions to undergird the practical activity of seeking and receiving emergency services.

Caller's First Turn

The caller's first turn ordinarily consists of an acknowledgement token (which completes the ratification of pre-alignment identities) followed by one or more possible utterances. Such utterances function as some version of the 'reason for the call'. The format by which callers engage emergency dispatch services reflects their analysis of both 'who' they are addressing (recipient design), the nature of the problem, and their own relationship to it, that is, their 'stance' (Whalen and Zimmerman, 1990). That is, the format of the caller's first turn projects a further identity alignment of caller and the answerer. These formats include *reports*, *narratives* and *requests*:

(5)   (MCE 21–16a/21) Report format

1	CT:	Mid-City emergency.
2	C:	hh u:h Yeah I wanna report a:: (.) real bad accident h hh

(6)   (MCE 20–15/207) Narrative format

1	CT:	Mid-City police an' fire
2	C:	Hi um (.) I'm uh (.) I work at thuh University
3		Hospital and I was riding my bike home
4		tanight from (.) work-
5	CT:	Mm
6	C:	'bout (.) ten minutes ago, ·hh as I was riding
7		past Mercy Hospital (.) which is uh few blocks
8		from there ·hh ( ) um ( ) I think uh couple vans
9		full uh kids pulled up (.) an started um (.)
10		they went down thuh trail an(h)d are beating up
11		people down there I'm not sure (.) but it
12		sounded like (something) ·hh

(7)   (MCE 21–4a/4) Request format

1	C:	I need the paramedics please?

The report format ('I want to report . . .') is typically an account of a 'codeable' problem delivered to an 'authority' by a citizen. A codeable problem is one that can be named or characterized in a word or two. Its codeability is reflected in the fact that little, if any, elaboration is requested; rather, the call-taker will proceed to determine location and ancillary features of the reported problem, for example, whether personal injuries were sustained. Narratives are chronologically organized descriptions or accounts, often extended, leading up to a discursive characterization of a possible trouble, as was seen in extract (2a) and (2b) discussed above, in which what began as a report was transformed into a narrative. Finally, the request format is a request for service delivered to a service provider. It can be the sole component of the caller's first turn after the acknowledgement token, or be followed with a statement of a codeable problem.

Callers also employ a proprietary format which can deploy one or both of the following components: a categorical self-identification ('This is . . .') and a proprietorial we ('We have a . . .):

(8)   (MCE 7–3.56) Categorical self-identification

1	CT:	Mid-City emergency.
2		(.)
3	C:	tch ·hh u::h This is u:::h ( ) Knights of Columbus
4		Hall at uh: twenty twenty ni:ne West Broadway
5		North?=
6	CT:	=Mmhm, ((keyboard sounds))
7	C:	U:::h we had some u::h women's purses u::h stolen,

(9) (MCE 21–13.10) Proprietorial Format

```
1      CT:    Mid-City emergency.
2      C:     ˙hh tch Hi: we got u::h (.) this is security at thuh
3             bus depot, Greyhound bus depot?=
4      CT:    =Yes ma'am=
5  →   C:     =An' we got a guy down here that's uh::
6             (0.6) ((background noise))
7      C:     over intoxicated. hhh ˙hh He just- he's passed out.
```

In employing a report format, the caller assumes a particular stance, as a gloss, a 'citizen' reporting an incident to an 'authority' for whom the information is a warrant for taking action of some sort. Indeed, engaging in such an activity displays the caller's orientation to the call-taker as a representative of the organization.

Narrative accounts deal with problems that are less readily codeable, which is to say that they are less clear-cut and seem to require some explanation of how the caller came to know of them and why they might think them worthy of report to authorities. This format allows callers to present their noticing of ambiguous events in a way that portrays them as ordinary, disinterested, reasonable witnesses (see Bergmann, 1987).

Requests, while they intimate that some type of policeable trouble or medical emergency is involved, do not specify the exact nature of the problem, projecting a particular response without providing its warrant. A report establishes the substantive reason for a call, although it does not clarify the caller's identity beyond that of 'citizen' (e.g., whether the citizen-caller is a victim or a witness).

Proprietorial formats establish a communication from 'my organization' to 'your organization', that is, as a report of a 'responsible party'. Proprietorial formats also report particular types of repetitive incident (often dealing with problems occurring within the realm of the caller's occupational responsibilities).

Whatever the format, the call-taker will usually have further work to do in processing the call. The work involved in identity alignment, and the role that identities play in shaping the character of reported troubles and the trajectory of the call can be found in situations like the following which present ambiguous features to call-takers. Consider the following:

(10) (MCE 21–27/39)

```
1      CT:    Mid-City emergency
2      C:     Yes sir uh go' uh couple gu:ys over here ma:n
3             they thin' they bunch uh wi:se ((background
4             noise))=
5      CT:    =Are they in yur house? or is this uh busness?
6      C:     They're over here ah Quick Stop (.) They (fuckin)
7             come over here an pulled up at thuh Quick Stop
```

8		slammin' their doors intuh my truck.
9	CT:	Quick Stop?=
10	C:	=Yeah.
11 →	CT:	Okay Uh- were you uh customer at that store?
12	C:	Yeah.
13	CT:	What thee address there or thee uhm:. . .

The call-taker's question 'in yur house? or is this uh business' (line 5) is not simply locational in its import. She is asking for the setting of the problem, and hence, on the basis of the inferential tie between setting and identity, 'in what capacity' the caller is reporting. His answer adds further ambiguity for, although he selects 'business' as opposed to 'home' (line 6), he does not clarify his relationship to the business establishment. This much is evident when the call-taker asks if he is a customer (versus an employee) at the store in question (line 11). There are several issues implicated here. The police-relevant nature of the trouble is shaped by its location, and by who reports it. A disturbance of some sort on a public street is a different event from a disturbance occurring on private property, and the person reporting the problem may stand in a different relationship to it depending on the nature of his or her tie to the territory in question. 'Citizens', for example, may report disturbances occurring in public places, while 'proprietors' may report disturbances occurring in stores or other places of business (and may be heard as more reliable sources of information since they are accountable for managing such events as part of their occupational responsibilities). The categories of place, identity and problem are thus linked in consequential ways for the handling of emergency calls.

As I hope to show in the following section, the identities thus far displayed and aligned in the opening of the call (and as subsequently developed within it) will continue to play an important role in the intelligibility and practicability of the work of emergency dispatching.

The Interrogative Series

As noted earlier, the core organization of the emergency call, like many service calls in general, is a single adjacency repair (request/response) with an insertion sequence – what I have called the 'interrogative series' (see Figure 6.1). An insertion sequence, a series of one or more question-answer pairs, serves to clarify or determine matters necessary to provide a response to the initial 'pair part', in this case, the request for service. Sequentially, reports (including narratives) and requests are oriented to by citizen-complainant and call-taker as initiating the first adjacency pair, that is, each of these forms achieves functional status as a request for service (see Wilson, 1991). The embedding of a series of adjacency pairs within an adjacency pair requires participants to sustain the relevance of each embedded pair to the ultimate provision of a response to the initial pair part, in this case, the 'request for service' (however formatted).

The interrogative series is the sequential space in which the call-taker addresses the *contingencies of response*, that is, he or she (i) determines that there is a legitimate need for police, fire or paramedic services, and (ii) assembles the information necessary to dispatch the response effectively. Such information includes the location to which the responding unit or units are to be sent (which can involve fairly extensive questioning) as well as relevant features of the problem itself, for example, the nature of medical problems (for which 'pre-arrival instruction' in first aid may be indicated), whether or not a reported auto accident involves injuries, and details pertinent to any reported crime (whether it is in progress or just completed, suspect descriptions, direction and mode of flight, the presence of weapons, etc.). These questions stem from, and exhibit the special occupational competence and responsibility of the call-taker; indeed, their form and manner of execution constitute the call-taker's activity as call-taker. The caller's recognition of this, implied in the alignment of identities and the receptiveness such alignment establishes, provides for the routine character of most emergency calls.

It is instructive to consider instances where alignment is problematic or not maintained. In one instance, a woman called Central County 9-1-1 and made a terse report of some activity at the corner of her street and then hung up. The enraged CT called the woman back and chastized her for breaking off the contact after an initial, if inadequate, report of possible trouble:

(11)   (Central County (VIDEO TAPE) ((CT1 has redialled a caller who has hung up prematurely; transcript displays only CT's side of the conversation))

1	CT1:	HELLO! CAN YOU HEAR ME?
2		((CT2 looks towards CT1))
3	CT2:	I can.
4	CT1:	This is 9 1 1 emergency (1.0) W-I you don't report
5		something an' just hang up

Note here that CT1's identity as call-taker – a position that carries with it the responsibility to determine the need for police or other forms of assistance as well as a location to which they can be sent – provides a warrant for insisting on cooperation from callers.

We can begin to see how identity works in this fashion by first considering the constraints call-takers' situated identity places on their mode of responding to callers. The first such constraint is the requirement that a problem of an appropriate sort exists. Expressed need for service is insufficient, as is clear in the following call from an Ambassador Hotel operator to the Los Angeles Police Department on the occasion of the shooting of Robert Kennedy in the hotel kitchen:

(12) (RFK)

1	CT:	Police Department.
2		(.)
3	C:	Yes This is the Ambassador Hotel Em
4	CT:	Ambassador Hotel?
5		((echo: *Hotel*))
6	C:	Do you hear me?
7		(.)
8	CT:	Yeah I hear you.
9	C:	Uh they have an emergency=They want thuh
10		police to thuh kitchen right away.
11	CT:	What kind of an emergency?
12	C:	I don't know honey They hung up I don't know
13		⌈what's happening
14	CT:	⌊Well find out. (.) We don't send out without=
15	C:	=I beg your pardon?
16		(.)
17	CT:	We have to know what we're sending on,

The delay in responding to this incident may have embarrassed the police department, but it is evident that C, a hotel operator, was not in a position to provide the required information. Pressing her to obtain the information, the call-taker explicitly formulates the critical issue: 'We have to know what we're sending on'. The mere assertion that an event is an emergency is, other things being equal, not enough.

In the case of the assassination of Robert Kennedy, the caller was initially unable to provide a characterization of the problem satisfactory to the call-taker. The difficulties that plagued a call to the Dallas Fire Department (Whalen et al., 1988) was largely due to a *misalignment* of caller and call-taker (a 'nurse-dispatcher' in this case). As a consequence, the dispatch of an ambulance was delayed, and the afflicted party was dead upon its arrival. The encounter begins when the Dallas Fire Department operator (who screens and routes calls according to their need for fire or medical response) answers a call:

(13) (Dallas FD/B1)

1	O:	<u>Fire</u> department
2		(0.8)
3	C:	Yes, I'd like tuh have an ambulance at forty one thirty
4		nine Haverford please
5		(0.5)
6	O:	What's thuh <u>problem</u> sir?
7	C:	I: don't know, 'n if I knew I wouldn't be <u>ca:l</u>ling you all

The caller begins with a request for service which is followed by a routine query by O concerning the nature of the problem (line 6). The caller responds by averring that he does not know the nature of the problem, and indeed, should not be expected to know (line 7). After an attempt by O to clarify the caller's inability to address the problem query (not shown in extract (13)), he is transferred to the nurse-dispatcher who initiates a series of questions concerning the destination to which the paramedics are to be sent and the caller's telephone number. She then asks the caller about the problem. However, C responds with an utterance nearly identical to that of line 7 in extract (13). The nurse-dispatcher interrupts and attempts to align the caller as the answerer in the question-answer sequence she has initiated. This time, the caller responds with a characterization of the problem (someone having difficulty breathing) that could count as a 'priority symptom', one requiring an immediate response of the mobile life support ambulance dispatched by the Fire Department.

For reasons that I won't go into here (see Whalen et al., 1988: 351–2), the call from that point on rapidly dissolves into a dispute focusing on the caller's 'refusal' to let the nurse-dispatcher speak with the caller's step-mother who is experiencing the breathing difficulties. The identity align-ment of caller and nurse-dispatcher has become significantly (and as it turned out, disastrously) altered, the two parties re-aligning as *disputants*. In their capacity as disputants, what each says to the other is in the service of the pursuit of an argument rather than the orderly elicitation and provision of information satisfying the contingencies of response for dispatching a paramedic ambulance. The nurse-dispatcher treats the caller as uncooperative, refusing to answer questions and comply with requests, while the caller treats the nurse-dispatcher as incompetently impeding the satisfaction of his request.

As noted above, queries as to the nature of the problem for which help is sought are routine, and are routinely answered. Against that background, the caller's denial of knowledge about the problem and indeed, the legitimacy of the question itself requires explanation. Whalen et al. (1988: 346) suggest that the caller, for whatever reason, misunderstood the contingencies of the service offered by the Fire Department, treating it as relatively unconditional like, for example, the request for the delivery of a pizza for which only an address and an order are necessary. I am enter-taining a conjecture not reported in the 1988 paper, namely, that on the assumption of unconditional service, when the caller was confronted with a request for a statement of the 'problem', he understood it within the device *lay versus professional* (see Sacks, 1972a, 1972b), that is, in terms of the distribution of competency on such matters in the population. Classifying himself in this situation as a *layperson* to the Fire Department's *pro-fessional*, he rejected the question as beyond his scope but within that of Fire Department personnel. That is, within such an understanding, the specifically medical reasons for requesting an ambulance are not relevant, it being the responsibility of Fire Department paramedics to deal with such matters. Hence, the hearing of the problem queries as requests for *diagnosis* rather than for a descriptive statement of the observable features of the medical emergency. Of course, virtually any caller would call in the capacity of a layperson *vis-à-vis* any call-taker, but an insufficient understanding of the nature of the professional constraints on the latter (in the case of Dallas, call screening in terms of a medical protocol) can also lead to insufficient understanding of what matters fall within a layperson's capacity (being able to describe the publicly observable features of the problem). And, as we saw, when re-alignment momentarily occurred, the caller was able to produce such a description.

The Dallas call rather dramatically underlines the importance of appropriate identity alignment for the routine (and successful) processing of emergency calls – as well as for the necessity of call-taker and dispatchers to *recognize* and deal effectively with misalignments when they occur (see M. Whalen (1990) for other circumstances that can affect the nature of the alignment between caller and call-taker).

Concluding Comments

In the preceding discussion, I tried to show how discourse and situated identities provide both the proximal and distal contexts for a range of activities within the domain of emergency telephone calls. Discourse identities implicate a sequential machinery by which participants manage their interaction. On this view, conversational organization is the fundamental resource for engaging in social (i.e., intersubjectively coordinated) action, the platform on which activities of various sorts are built. The substantive shape of these activities, the agendas they embody and the goals that they pursue, emerge from the situated identities of participants. Co-orientation to particular, articulated discourse and situated identities joins a given sector of distributed social knowledge (both tacit and explicit) and interactional know-how to produce repetitive, reproducible, recognizable activities. This emphasis on participants' orientations to features of the interactional situation (such as discourse and situated identities) does not presuppose that they possess 'theories' of discourse or of society, but rather that they can manage their local affairs in systematic ways that have consequences, intended and unintended, some of which are beyond their reach or notice. To echo a theme from early on in this chapter, while the interaction order is loosely coupled to social structure, it is tightly articulated with it. Indeed, the coordination of activities within the interaction order provides the fundamental sociality which makes socially structured actions of diverse sorts possible.

The empirical case in point, which I used to illustrate these ideas, is the emergency telephone call. What recommends this sort of call as a focus of investigation is that it is at once close kin to 'ordinary', non-institutional telephone interactions while at the same time bearing the imprint of a particular institutional arrangement. That is, it displays the generalized shape of a service call (a sequence organization that can be found in many transactions with businesses of various sorts). Such calls allow us repeatedly to encounter the contingent achievement of this form of activity while displaying in relatively accessible ways the workings of discourse (i.e., interactional) and situated (i.e., institutional) identities, and in particular how these identities are articulated and aligned. I have tried to show in this chapter how such articulation and alignment operate to generate the routine features of emergency calls, and I have also attempted to point out how failure of articulation and alignment produces trouble for this type of activity. More important, it should be clear from the discussion that the articulation of discourse and situated identities is a *contingent* matter: the alignment of identities is an achievement, and the shape of the interaction that results is a local crafting out of the resources of talk-in-interaction and materials of human social agendas.

Note

I want to thank Thomas P. Wilson, Angela Garcia and Gene Lerner for their helpful comments on earlier drafts of this chapter.

7 Mobilizing Discourse and Social Identities in Knowledge Talk

Robin Wooffitt and Colin Clark

There has been, in recent years, a number of studies which adopt an approach to the study of language and social identity which draw from conversation analysis, particularly Harvey Sacks's (1992) early work on membership categorization devices. These studies have shown how categorizations of self and others can be accomplished with respect to interactional and inferential concerns generated by the trajectory of verbal exchanges. Antaki and Widdicombe in Chapter 1 have already characterized some important aspects of those studies which mark them off from more conventional social science accounts. The key point is that those studies regard social identity in terms of lay or vernacular social categories, the ascription of which is inextricably tied to the details of talk-in-interaction. This is a radical departure from those psychological (and commonsense) accounts which treat identity as a fixed set of properties or operations residing in the individual's cognitive make up, and which regard language as a largely docile medium through which dimensions of a person's identity (among other psychological characteristics) may receive occasional expression.

Studies of identity (a term which will be used interchangeably with 'social identity' throughout this chapter) and language informed by Sacks's work have three characteristics. First, the data are naturally occurring, not artefacts of contrived laboratory arrangements. Second, analysis focuses on the socially organized inferential processes through which people themselves orient to the relevance of categorizations of self and others. Thirdly, these studies are rigorously empirical, in that analysis is not motivated by theory, intuition or a priori assessments of the significance of events represented in the data. Perhaps because of these features, conversation analytic methods (and findings) have proved useful to those researchers who wish to provide an empirically based critique of accounts of social identity in cognitive social psychology, specifically, social identity theory (Tajfel, 1981, 1982a) and self categorization theory (Oakes et al., 1991; Turner, 1987). The critique of cognitive social psychology was a central concern, for example, in Widdicombe and Wooffitt's (1995) analysis of accounts produced by young people who were members of youth subcultures. In this book, Edwards in Chapter 2 and McKinlay and Dunnett in Chapter 3 offer compelling reworkings of some of the principal claims of self categorization theory.

These critiques are to be welcomed. However, there has been a tendency to use empirical observation illustratively, as a means to highlight the weakness of essentialist or poststructuralist approaches when set against the fine-grained analysis of naturally occurring data. While the analytic observations generated from these critiques have been insightful and important, this approach could take attention away from more focused analysis of members' identity work in its own right. Consequently, the objective of this chapter is to encourage analysis of the systematic properties of identity work *per se*. Specifically we want to outline two sets of resources through which social identity may be established in interaction. First, we examine some data fragments to show how a discourse identity – a status derived from the speaker's relationship to the ongoing unfolding of interaction – can be invoked in such a way as to mobilize the relevance of a vernacular, or 'common-sense' social categorization. Secondly, we make some observations about the resources for identity work made available in sequences of conversational actions.

To illustrate these issues we will consider data taken from a study of interaction between mediums and people for whom they provide information or messages purportedly from the spirit world. The fragments come from a tape of seven 'edited highlights' of performances by Doris Stokes, a famous British medium, recorded during three consecutive appearances at the Dominion Theatre in London. The live fragments consist of episodes in which Stokes relays messages from the spirit world to individuals in the audience, while other members of the audience listen. This tape was purchased by the second author at the headquarters of the Spiritualist Association of Great Britain based in London.

It may be objected that focusing exclusively on Stokes's performances ensures that our analytic observations may have little relevance to forms of language use in other contexts. However, we are not here trying to make an argument about specific interactional phenomena. Rather, the primary concern is to illustrate that the study of identity work in talk can benefit from attention to the relationship between discourse identities and social categories, and the inferential resources made available in sequences of exchanges.

Stokes was a very successful medium: her books about life after death, gleaned from her spirit contacts, sold in large numbers, and her public performances were always well attended. However, there is a sense in which Stokes's success depended upon her ability to establish the proof of her claims and the authenticity of her paranormal powers. This was almost certainly due to the fact that, as is the case with all mediums, the basis of Stokes's performances rested on the acceptance of a series of contentious assumptions and claims: that some aspect of the human personality survived death; and that she could communicate with the dead and relay information to the living, either through direct communication with the spirits of the dead, or via an intermediary spirit guide. Stokes herself was aware of the need to warrant her claims about life after death, often beginning her public demonstrations with the statement that that evening she was going to 'prove' the existence of the afterlife. Thus her identity as a medium (as opposed to, say, 'charlatan') was crucially linked to her ability to establish that her statements for and about members of the audience came from a paranormal source, and that the information she supplied was not available to ordinary people who did not possess her special powers.

During the late nineteenth and early twentieth centuries, the proof of the medium's paranormal powers were often demonstrated physically: musical instruments would fly across the room, ectoplasm would stream from whichever of the medium's orifices were visible and tables would rock and rise above the ground. However, such physical demonstrations of the medium's claims are rare in contemporary mediumship; consequently, the proof of the medium's power is almost always demonstrated verbally: through the kinds of information which the mediums produce. Any proof that is given, any evidence that is provided, is accomplished in the interaction itself; what is communicated between the medium and the sitter is thus the sole basis from which judgements can be made about the existence of the afterlife.

In the following sections we will examine some transcribed fragments of Stokes's performances to identify systematic properties of the way in which she establishes the paranormal source of her information, and thereby authorizes her social identity as a medium.

The analytic focus on the way that Stokes used language to establish her identity as a medium may be interpreted as an exercise in debunking. However, there is a difference between studying the way in which the authority of a claim to have special powers may be established in interaction, and assessing the validity of those claims. In this chapter we are only concerned with the socially organized resources through which Stokes establishes the authority of her (implicit) claim to have a certain kind of identity. Furthermore, whether Stokes was in touch with the spirit world, or was simply complicit in a thoroughgoing deception, the information she provided still had to be accepted, rejected and negotiated through talk-in-interaction. Relatedly, it is important to remember that we are concerned only with the properties of socially organized patterns in language use. These are taken to have robust properties which are independent of, and not propelled by, individual intent. Therefore, our observations about Stokes's use of language should not be taken to imply that we consider that she was intentionally designing her talk to achieve specific interactional ends.

Discourse Identity and Social Identity

Discourse identities are characterizations of participants' status in relation to the ongoing production of talk, and which arise from the trajectory and organization of the talk. For example, in any two-party interaction, the discourse identities of 'speaker' and 'recipient' will be relevant; and in a telephone conversation, the identities of 'caller' and 'called' may become salient for some features of the conversation. Of course, such identities are not fixed; clearly, in any normal conversation the status of 'speaker' and 'recipient' will vary. But the relevance of discourse identities is not simply a matter of alternate distribution: rather, their relevance for any spate of interaction has to be occasioned in the talk. Therefore, to ascribe the relevance of a discourse identity to a spate of interaction, the analyst needs to demonstrate that the behaviour of the participants themselves displays their orientation to the relevance of that identity, at that moment. This can be illustrated if we consider a study by Goodwin (1987).

The data for Goodwin's analysis comes from a video and audio recording of a group of friends having dinner. Goodwin's analysis concerns a sequence in which one of the group is reporting on a television programme he has recently watched. While making this report, the speaker seems to forget momentarily the name of the show's host. Instead of treating this apparent loss of memory as an indication of a cognitive or psychological aberration, Goodwin investigates the 'forgetting' as a distinct spate of interaction – as a display of 'not remembering' – and focuses on its sequential placement to see what kinds of interactional purposes it serves. His analysis is grounded in the speaker's orientation to the relevance at that time of two sets of discourse identities.

Goodwin argues that, at the time of telling his story about the television programme, the speaker faces a delicate problem: his audience consists of people who fall into two categories: his spouse, who already knows the story he is about to relate (either because she has heard it before, or because she was watching the programme with her husband, and therefore saw for herself the events upon which her husband is about to report), and the others present at the dinner who do not know the story. Goodwin's analysis shows how the speaker's actions, both verbal and non-verbal, display his orientation to the relevance of two discourse identities at the time he is telling his story: knowing recipient (his spouse) and unknowing recipients (the others). Goodwin argues that at the time that the speaker seems to forget the name of the television personality, he turns to his spouse, soliciting help with the problem. He thereby orients to her identity as a knowing recipient: someone who knows the details of the story on which he is embarked. But by doing this the speaker is able to warrant her involvement in the interaction, an involvement that would not have occurred had the speaker simply oriented his behaviour to the unknowing recipients in his audience. So, Goodwin argues that the momentary lapse of memory displayed strategic interactional properties, in that it allowed the speaker to negotiate the delicate situation of pursuing a projected course of action – telling a story – without excluding the one person present who was already familiar with that story.

However, as Goodwin points out, the way in which the relevance of a particular discourse identity is invoked may also in turn occasion the relevance of wider social identity. Recall that Goodwin's focus was the way in which a speaker's apparent forgetting of a detail of a story was produced with respect to his spouse, the only other person present who knew of the details of the story he is telling. To involve his wife, who may have been otherwise momentarily excluded from interaction by the telling of the story, the speaker invoked the relevance of the discourse identity 'knowing recipient'. But consider: the speaker was reporting a story which concerned a late-night television show; for another person to be identified, then, as a 'knowing recipient' of details of the story relevant to that show invokes certain assumptions about the relationship between the speaker and that person. Conventionally, couples who live together, or who are married, have a stock of common experiences and stories; so, by invoking a discourse identity of 'knowing recipient' the speaker also occasions the relevance of that person's social identity as his spouse.

With this in mind we can examine some features of Stokes's use of language in her public performances. The following extract begins with Stokes telling the audience generally that she has received some information from the spirit side. The audience member to whom that information is relevant responds by providing further information. What is analytically interesting is the way in which Stokes invokes the discursive identity of knowing recipient to establish that the information now publicly available, and which clearly came from a human source, was in fact known to her all along and originally came from the spirit side.

(1) *('DS' is Doris Stokes, 'S' is the sitter. Throughout this chapter we shall use the word 'sitter' to refer to the member of the audience for whom Stokes provides messages or information from the spirit world.)*

```
1     DS:   I heard a voice, an' it gave me a telephone number,
2           an' the name was Mott.
3           (0.8)
4     DS:   Does it mean anything to anybody?
5           (0.4)
6     DS:   Let me hear your voice love
7           (2.0)
8     S:    Yes, ah'm-, I'm Yvonne Mott.
9     DS:   ((smiley voice)) Oh! Ah te-, said 'er name was Yvonne,
10          in the dressing room. ((laughs))
```

In the medium's first prediction in this extract all we get is a surname (i.e., 'Mott'); there is no mention of Yvonne or the fact that the person being referred to is female until after this information is revealed by the sitter in the response, 'Yes, ah'm-, I'm Yvonne Mott'. (While it is true that Stokes did seem on occasions to have access to detailed knowledge about her audience, there is evidence that the source was not the spirit world. For a sceptical assessment of Stokes's claims, see Wilson (1987) and Hoggart and Hutchinson (1995).)

The discursive identity relevant here for Stokes is 'recipient' (of information): she has been told something. However, she then paraphrases part of a conversation, the topic of which was the sitter Stokes is now addressing. Given that this report occurs in the context of a demonstration of mediumistic powers, it seems reasonable to suggest that the other participant in that exchange would be taken to be a spirit entity. Furthermore, by reference to the location of the exchange (the dressing room) Stokes establishes that it occurred prior to the start of the performance, thereby making it inferable that she already knew the name and sex of the audience member prior to the public disclosure of this information. Thus Stokes establishes her discourse identity as 'knowing recipient' with respect to the information provided by the sitter. Note also that the claim that she already knew the person's name is prefaced with 'Oh! Ah te-' which is hearable as the beginning of 'Oh I'm terrible'. This projected display of mild self-admonishment conveys the sense of a momentary lapse in memory. This not only further reinforces the identity of 'knowing recipient', but also provides an account for the failure to produce these details in the first instance.

This crude strategy can be used more subtly: in extract (2) Stokes reports an earlier conversation between herself and the spirits to overcome a potentially tricky situation: what to do when a prediction or claim is wrong.

(2) *(It has already been established that the sitter was once in the Royal Air Force.)*

```
1       DS:    are you in insurance now
2              (.3)
3       S:     I have been
4       DS:    ((laughing)) I said 'What's he been doing since he
5              came out of the mob like?' (.8) an he said 'Oh,
6              insurance, y'know'.
```

Here Stokes produces a question which embodies a claim about the current employment of the sitter. The sitter replies that he used to be in insurance. Consequently, that he used to work in insurance is now publicly disclosed in the meeting; and, parenthetically, that the medium's claim was incorrect. At this point she recites a conversation she has already had (again presumably with her spirit source). This conversation is produced to be heard as having happened prior to the moment in which it is rehearsed in the sitting, thereby establishing that whatever passed between Stokes and the spirit happened before the sitter's disclosure about having been in insurance.

What is subtle about this extract is that the spirits' own words are reproduced with respect to the nature of the mistake in Stokes's initial prediction/question. That is, in the initial question she imposed a specific time frame for the sitter's occupation (that he was in insurance now). The sitter's response indicates that this prediction was wrong, although, interestingly, he doesn't topicalize the error. The subsequent reproduction of the spirit's words establish that she knew only that the sitter's employment in insurance was at some point after he left the Royal Air Force, referred to here as 'the mob'. This information is actually correct. Thus her knowledge of the sitter's employment is subtly negotiated in the light of his response to reveal that she already knew of the connection with insurance prior to the sitter confirming that he had been in that line of work. So, what Stokes now knows to be the case is produced as information she knew beforehand, and is reproduced in such a way as to account for her 'error' of focusing on insurance as being the sitter's employment at the time of the exchange. Moreover, 'the mob' was a common way of referring to the Royal Air Force at the time of the Second World War. Thus her use of this term adds credibility to her claim that she was in communication with someone of that era.

In these extracts Stokes has dealt with two tricky situations: in the first instance, she had to demonstrate knowledge of specific information which had just been publicly displayed by the sitter; in the second, she had to repair an error embodied in her description of the sitter's employment. In both cases, she invokes her discourse identity as knowing recipient, generated via a report of (prior) discussion with communicators from the spirit world. This discourse identity in turn mobilizes the relevance of her social identity as a genuine medium: that is, in touch with spirit sources, as well as human ones.

Identities in Sequence

Conversation analysis examines the systematic and recurrent properties of sequences of discursive actions, and the inferential and interactional resources made available by those sequences. In this section we want to examine the way in which Stokes exploits the properties of a sequence of overlapping talk. Here are two examples:

(3) *(S is female.)*

```
1        DS:     Oh, there's two of you they tell me.
2        S:      There's my sis⌈ter
3        DS:                     ⌊Sisters.
4        S:      Mmm.
```

(4)   *(Stokes is reporting information about two men, supposedly known by the sitter, who had died.)*

```
1      DS:    because (0.4) she's telling me, (0.3) an' one older
2             than the other,
3      S:     yes.
4      DS:    yes. (0.3) Because I'm getting one not very old and
5             one,
6      S:     ol⌈d
7      DS:      ⌊olde⌈r
8      S:           ⌊yes
```

Let us note some features of these two cases. First, the medium's utterance prior to the spate of overlapping talk stands as a claim or prediction about the sitter: 'Oh, there's two of you they tell me' and in extract (4) the medium is describing people in the spirit world known by the sitter: 'he's telling me, (0.3) an' one older than the other'. These claims are not very specific: they reveal very little about the sitter for whom the information is provided, or the entities in the spirit world who are meant to be related in some way to the sitter. For example, there are no names mentioned. Furthermore, although 'two of you' (extract (3)) subsequently transpires to be a reference to the sitter's sibling, it does not unambiguously imply sisters: 'two of you' could refer to a close friend or a spouse. Consequently, the medium's claim about the sitter in both cases reveals only 'soft' information, and contains ambiguous references.

Secondly, this information is produced so that the sitter (and the other members of the overhearing audience) is clear that the source is the spirit side, or some paranormal agency. This is achieved by the phrases 'they tell me', 'she's telling me' and 'because I'm getting' to preface or follow the claim or prediction.

Thirdly, immediately after Stokes's 'soft' claim or prediction, the sitter produces an utterance which either confirms that information, elaborates upon it, or supplies further detail. So, 'there's my sister' specifies the referent of the utterance 'oh there's two of you'. In extract (4) the sitter's utterance ('old') anticipates that the prior turn was establishing a relationship between the two men in terms of their (unspecified) ages. So, although there may be variation in the positioning of the sitter's turn with respect to Stokes's ongoing turn, in both cases the sitters elaborate upon or confirm the information provided in the prior (or ongoing) utterance.

Finally, while this elaboration or specification is being provided, Stokes begins to talk in overlap; and her overlapping talk begins while the sitter is in mid-production of the word which actually elaborates upon the prior soft prediction.

Stokes's overlapping utterance is closely related to the sitter's turn in production, although not a direct echo. In extract (3) the sitter says 'sister' and Stokes says 'sisters'. And in extract (4) the sitter says 'old' and

Stokes says 'older'. So we have minor reformulated versions of the sitters' utterances.

Initially, it might be assumed that Stokes is trying to echo exactly what the sitters say, but simply gets it wrong on the basis of their assessment of that part of the sitter's utterance which has been produced prior to the start of the overlap. But there is evidence that there may be something more strategic going on. In extract (3), for example, before she gets to the focal point of the utterance, the word, 'sister', the sitter has already said 'there's my' thereby elucidating and 'filling in' Stokes's prior claim that she is obtaining knowledge about two people. So from an inspection of 'there's my' Stokes can infer that the syllable 'sis' is part of the word 'sister' and not 'sisters', because that would imply more than two, and the sitter has said nothing to reject or query that part of the medium's prior claim.

To understand the interactional benefits from the production of such a strategic reformulation it is necessary to consider the broad kind of work done though this form of overlap organization. The overlapping talk in extracts (3) and (4) are instances of what Jefferson (1983) has called recognitional overlap. This occurs when the next speaker's start is designed to display their appreciation or understanding of some aspect of the turn in production. For example, extract (5) comes from the beginning of a call to a flight information service (Wooffitt et al., 1997). Immediately after a greeting sequence, the caller addresses someone present with her, asking for a piece of paper which contains information she needs before she can produce a request for specific flight details. Later in this turn she then starts to tell a story which accounts for why she had to go 'off line' earlier in the call. The agent's enthusiastic '(BR)i:ght' overlaps with this story while it is in progress, thereby displaying her recognition that what the caller is currently reporting is not relevant to the 'business at hand', for which task she already possesses sufficient information.

(5)   ('A' is the agent of the flight information service, 'C' is a caller.)

```
 1        A:      flight infor↑mation,
 2                (.)
 3        C:      ˙hh oh good morn↓ing flight >i(c)- c-
 4                can I have that piece of paper david
 5                please=you took from me, (.) ˙hhh
 6                >˚right˚< >sorry< >thank you<=˙hh
 7                flight infor↓mation, I'm checkin' on the
 8                fli:ght bee ay two nine ↓six >I think they
 9                gave it out but my son walked
10                off with [(the contact) [˙h h h show (k-) chicago
         A:                [(BR)i:ght) ho [ld on
```

Recognitional overlap, then, is a way of demonstrating 'mind on' with respect to proceeding talk. As such it is a vehicle for a range of affiliative actions. For example, the production of an overlapping utterance which partially echoes parts of the ongoing talk is a common method of displaying agreement. The following extract comes from Pomerantz's (1984) study of the ways in which speakers may agree or disagree with assessments produced in prior turns.

(6) (from Pomerantz, 1984: 67)

```
1      E:      ...'n she said she f- depressed her terribly
2      J:      Oh it's ⌈terribly depressing.
3      L:             ⌊Oh it's depressing.
4      E:      Ve⌈ry
5      L:         ⌊But it's a fantastic ⌈film.
6      J:                               ⌊It's a beautiful movie
```

In this case there are two agreements with prior assessments: L's agreement with J about the impact of a film and then J's agreement with L's assessment of its quality. In both cases the agreement with the prior assessment is produced in overlap with the prior turn.

The point is then that recognitional overlap, built around a full or partial repeat of a key word or phrase in the ongoing turn, is one way of performing broadly affiliative action, such as agreement. Consequently, if Stokes's overlapping turn simply echoes the sitter's prior turn, then it is likely that she will be heard as engaging in the activity of doing agreement. And simply agreeing with information being provided by the sitter would run counter to the (implicit) claim that people with mediumistic powers receive information from paranormal sources. However, a minor reformulation of key information in the ongoing turn at least establishes the possibility that Stokes's subsequent turn may be interpreted as doing the action of informing. And it does seem to be the case that that's how the sitters themselves treat the work of the overlapping utterance: in both cases the subsequent turn is built from a minimal acceptance or agreement token.

There is a related point. It is well known that people who visit mediums inadvertently reveal a lot of information about themselves. Sceptics argue that the mediums' apparent knowledge of intimate or private details of their sitters' lives is simply a consequence of the ways in which information provided by the sitter is consciously or tacitly recycled during the session. Indeed, analysis of extracts (1) to (4) reveals how Stokes is able to establish herself as already knowing or actually providing (a version of) information which is publicly available. However, the placement of Stokes's incursions in extracts (3) and (4) may furnish a further resource. In these cases, just as the sitter provides specific information, Stokes begins to speak in overlap to produce a reformulated version of that information. The speed with which these incursions begin relative to the prior turn has at least the chance of establishing an equivocality as to whether Stokes provided the information first. That is, while it may be relatively easy to recall the sense or gist of conversation, it is not so easy to recall tacit, socially organized sequential or structural features of talk. Consequently, the speed with which the overlapping turn is produced, relative to the start of the prior turn, provides an organizational basis for doubt as to who said what first.

Extracts (3) and (4) have some systematic properties which can be schematically represented as:

Turn	1	Medium:	Soft prediction or claim
Turn	2	Sitter:	Elaboration/specification
Turn	3	Medium:	Minor reformulation of prior information produced in overlap with key word or phrase from prior turn
Turn	4	Sitter:	Minimal acceptance or agreement

What seems to be crucial in this sequence is Turn 3, both in its design and its placement: it can be exploited to enhance the likelihood that Stokes's utterance may be heard as doing informing, thereby establishing her identity as a knowing recipient, which in turn invokes her membership of the category 'medium'. Furthermore, there is evidence that Stokes herself is tacitly sensitive to the inferential significance of this sequence, and the production of the third turn in particular.

(7) *(Stokes has mentioned a place regularly visited by the sitter.)*

```
1        DS:    So, (.) er, (.) you do have, (.) memories the⌈re,
2        S:                                                  ⌊Yes.
3        DS:    don't you?
4        S:     Sad ⌈ones. ((laugh⌈s))
5        DS:        ⌊And erm,   ⌊No, I was just going to say, you
6               jumped in the⌈re,
7        S:                   ⌊Oh.
8        DS:    ˙hhh Erm, (0.9) not altogether, as you would want them
9               to be. Do you understand?
```

Again we get the soft prediction 'So, (.) er, (.) you do have, (.) memories there,' which is confirmed and elaborated by the sitter's utterance 'Sad ones'.

It is interesting to note that the sitter does not immediately elaborate upon Stokes's soft prediction. Instead, she merely agrees with the prior turn and offers no further information. Consequently, Stokes produces a tag question. Tag questions routinely occur at the end of turns, and, according to some researchers, can be used to press for a specific form of turn from the next speaker. The production of 'Don't you?' at this point proposes that Stokes's utterance prior to the tag question was incomplete, thereby recycling the transfer relevance place and providing another opportunity for the sitter to speak, while at the same time enhancing the likelihood that the sitter's next turn will address the topic of her memories of the deceased. This is precisely what she does, elaborating upon the initial soft prediction.

During the sitter's turn Stokes begins to speak; however, the sitter begins to laugh. Stokes stops, waits until the sitter's laughter has ended, and then says 'No, I was just going to say,' which implies that what she is about to say she would have said earlier were it not for the intervention by the sitter. She then rebukes the sitter for interrupting, before producing the utterance which, presumably, she was attempting to start in overlap with the sitter's specification/elaboration. That is, that part of the sequence which provides opportunities for Stokes to establish interactionally her claimed medium-istic powers has been lost, due to the sitter's intervention. This intervention is then directly addressed by Stokes in the next turn in the form of a mild complaint.

There is a similar event in the next extract, which begins with the sitter's specification of the prior soft prediction. Note that Stokes attempts two, or, if the in-breath is counted as projecting a start, possibly three incursions into the sitter's ongoing turn. The first attempted start is produced at that point in the turn where the sitter begins to provide specific information about the final contact with a relative before his death.

```
(8)

 1    S:     That was the l⌈ast time ⌈I spoke t⌈o him=.
 2    DS:              ⌊˙hhhh    ⌊And,    ⌊this
 3           =this would be (h)a(h) you jumped in again=
 4    S:     =((laughing))       ⌈˙hhhh S⌈orry.
 5    DS:                 ⌊Er,    ⌊This would
 6           be, (0.3) the last time,
 7           (0.5)
 8    S:     Yes,
 9    DS:    That he had words with you.
10    S:     Yes it was.
```

These attempted incursions are unsuccessful, and the sitter continues until the next recognizable transfer relevance place, at which point Stokes produces the turn she was trying to establish in overlap. She says 'this would be' which seems to be the beginning of a paraphrase of the sitter's prior turn. She then produces a self-repair, terminating that trajectory of the utterance, and instead jokingly chastises the sitter for interrupting. Finally, Stokes provides a mildly reformulated version of the turn projected prior to the self-repair: 'This would be the last time'.

It is ironic that Stokes should chastise the sitters for their interruptive behaviour when it is her turns which are initiated while the sitter is speaking. But there may be a reason for these gentle rebukes. First, as we have seen, the likelihood that the overlapping utterances will be heard as displays of paranormally acquired knowledge rests on the degree to which they can be initiated as close as possible to the start of the word or phrase in the sitter's turn, and, crucially, completed. However, in extracts (7) and (8) Stokes initiates but fails to complete her turn because of laughter or further talk from the sitter.

Furthermore, when Stokes does subsequently complete the turns which were initiated in overlap, they are less likely to be heard as providing information from a paranormal source. So, in extract (7) the sitter's utterance 'That was the last time I spoke to him' is reformulated as 'This would be the last time that he had words with you'. And in extract (8) 'Sad ones [memories]' becomes 'not altogether, as you would want them [the memories] to be'. Consequently, it now appears more likely that Stokes's claims will be heard as having been derived directly from the sitter's prior response. Hence the principle in operation here seems to be: the longer the medium's message is produced after the sitter's information the more obvious it will appear that the medium's message has been generated out of what the sitter has said. Putting it bluntly, Stokes's reformulations are more transparently paraphrases of what the sitter has just said. And paraphrasing what the sitter says is not what mediums claim to do, and moreover, not what they are paid to do.

In the light of these observations we have an account for Stokes's mild rebukes. Her admonishments are designed to ensure that the sitter defers when Stokes initiates utterances, thereby increasing her chance of exploiting the inferential possibilities made available by the precise placement of overlap within that sequence of utterances. In short, Stokes is socializing the sitter into forms of verbal behaviour which enhance the likelihood that her claim to possess extraordinary powers, and her identity as a medium, will be accepted.

Concluding Comments

In this chapter we have not been concerned to use our analytic observations as a basis for a critique of cognitive theories of social identity which seem to hold currency in contemporary psychology. This is not because such critiques are not merited, but simply that others are providing precisely that kind of critical examination, and are probably better equipped to do so. Our concern has been much more prosaic: to focus exclusively on some of the mechanics of identity work. To this end we have investigated some fragments to demonstrate how a discursive identity can be mobilized in such a way as to invoke the speaker's membership of a broader social category. Moreover, we have shown how the mobilization of the discursive identity of knowing recipient is tied to the patterned properties of one sequence of exchanges. Indeed, the careful exploitation of some of the properties of this sequence seems to be a method by which to establish or maintain the validity of the claim to have specific kinds of paranormal power, which is arguably the main criterion of being a medium. That is, instead of asking what characteristics does a person have to have for others to infer that a category ascription may be legitimately applied, we have asked: what are the sequential properties of verbal interaction which facilitate the likelihood of the ascription of those psychological characteristics or personal qualities deemed sufficient to merit membership of a specific category?

While the data from which we have derived our observations may be far removed from everyday instances of talk-in-interaction, the ways in which discourse identities may be occasioned in the business of talk, and the sequential organization of discursive actions, are generic features of various forms of interaction. By focusing on the way in which identities may be made salient through these mundane properties of the organization of interaction, we hope to have sketched some key dimensions for future study of the ways in which social identities may be mobilized in the mechanics of actions.

8 Talk and Identity in Divorce Mediation

David Greatbatch and Robert Dingwall

As Harvey Sacks (1992) pointed out, and is often noted in this book, participants in talk-in-interaction can be accurately categorized in terms of numerous social identities, including those related to age, race, sex, religion, social class, occupation, family, geographical region, institutional setting, education and the interactional activities in which they are engaged. This raises important methodological and theoretical issues for research into the social organization of talk. In particular it poses the question of how professional analysts can establish which, if any, of the social identities that can be applied to participants are relevant to understanding their interactional conduct (Schegloff, 1991). Many approaches to the analysis of identity solve this problem by warranting the invocation of social categories on grounds extrinsic to the interaction, as Widdicombe in Chapter 12 describes. By contrast, conversation analysis (CA) restricts its focus to the endogenous orientations of the participants as displayed in the specifiable details of their interactional conduct: it describes how the participants *themselves* make social identities relevant within their interactions (Schegloff, 1991).

CA research distinguishes between, on the one hand, discourse identities, such as 'questioner–answerer' and 'inviter–invitee', which are intrinsic to talk-in-interaction and, on the other hand, larger social identities (Goodwin, 1987), such as sex, ethnicity and occupational role, which derive from wider societal and institutional formations and thus reach beyond the talk itself. Some CA studies restrict their focus to discourse identities, explicating sequentially organized domains of talk-in-interaction which are relatively autonomous of other aspects of social organization. However, others explore how participants make larger social identities relevant within their talk and how the invocation of such identities can constitute both a constraint on and a resource for the accomplishment of the activities in which the participants are engaged.

We take advantage of both streams of work to show not only that the discourse identities that the participants can make relevant change moment to moment, but also that these identities can make larger social identities visible in the talk. As an example of what we mean, Goodwin (1987) shows how a speaker at a family gathering makes relevant his spousal relationship with a co-participant by producing a display of uncertainty about household affairs which positions the latter in terms of the discourse identity 'knowing recipient' and the other participants as 'unknowing recipients' (Goodwin's analysis is more fully described by Wooffitt and Clark, in Chapter 7). Similarly, research on the news interview shows how discourse identities (and the activities in which they are embedded) invoke the institutional identities news interviewer and news interviewee by positioning the broadcast journalists as neutralistic report elicitors, the guests as report producers, and the audience as primary recipients of the talk (Clayman, 1988, 1992; Heritage, 1985; Heritage and Greatbatch 1991).

In this chapter, we show how both discourse identities and larger social identities are made relevant in an extract from a divorce mediation session. Our analysis illustrates that participants may invoke multiple identities, often simultaneously, and that these may change even within the production of a single turn at talk (C. Heath, 1992). After showing how discourse identities are a platform for larger social identities, we show how other 'macro' identities are invoked by the topical focus of the talk and by the use of an identity category. This leads to a discussion of how participants may constitute particular identities as occupying either a 'foundational' or a 'definitional' relationship with respect to other identities. We conclude by discussing some of the problems associated with the analysis of social identities which reach beyond the talk of the moment but which nonetheless may be invoked within it.

Data

The data extract is from a divorce mediation session. Advocates of divorce mediation describe it as a process in which a neutral third party helps separating couples to reach their own agreements. Increasingly, it is used as an alternative to court hearings in which settlements are imposed by judges or other 'neutral' adjudicators. We have audio recordings from 121 divorce mediation sessions conducted in ten different agencies in Britain. The transcribed extract below is from one of ten sessions recorded in an independent agency serving a large city in Northern England.

In this case, a divorcing couple agree that their two daughters, aged eight years and five years, should live with their mother, but disagree about contact (visitation) arrangements for the father. In particular, the mother objects to the father's request that their daughters be permitted to stay overnight with him. Two mediators are present. Both are qualified social workers. The extract begins with the mother accusing the father of not hearing one of the children, Kathy, crying at night because he was drunk. W addresses her talk to the mediators. We shall first show all of the extract and, as we go through the body of the chapter, pick out details for specific analyses, concentrating on lines 7 to 11. (In parenthesis, the reader will easily see the participants' talk displaying the sort of orientation to accountability that Edwards has elegantly brought out in his chapter on similar material.)

Full extract. *[L2:11-13:19.50. In this, and in the selections from it below, W is the wife, H the husband, and M1 and M2 are the mediators]*

```
1    W:        And er (.) I've had to go out to work. And my next door neighbour's
2              have said is Kathy: (.) this was when she was smaller not so much
3              no:w ˙hhh when she was smaller was crying all ni:ght. (.)
4              You know. And (.) because he were- he'd come in and he was so drunk
5              he never heard her.
6              (0.3)
7    H:        You see ⌈you bring this up- hang ⌈ o:n hang on love (.) you=
8    M2:               ⌊Jo:hn's              ⌊(    )
9    H:        =bring this up now:, it wasn't brought up at a::ll (.) when you know
10             when we went to cour⌈:t for access.
11   M2:                           ⌊Ri:ght
```

Discourse Identities

Before describing the discourse identities invoked by H and M2 at lines 7–11, it will be useful to consider the identities invoked by W in her prior talk at lines 4–5.

(Detail 1)

```
4    W:        You know. And (.) because he were- he'd come in and he was so drunk
5              he never heard her.
```

W's talk invokes several discourse identities. She constitutes herself as speaker, M1 and M2 as addressed recipients, and H as an overhearer. In addition, she invokes the identities accuser for herself and accused for H. Because her accusation is addressed to M1 and M2, and takes the form of a description of H's alleged actions, W also makes relevant the identities report producer (for herself) and report recipient (for M1 and M2). Moreover, because she does not refer to or solicit the opinions of M1 and M2, she constitutes them as non-aligned recipients.

It will perhaps be helpful if we set out the identities that are made relevant for each of the speakers. We shall list the company always as W, M1, M2 and H, in that order, and, to the right of each, indicate the discourse identities they are respectively ascribed. Thus, W's utterance at line 4 makes relevant the following discourse identities for herself, for M1 and M2, and for H:

The discourse identities made relevant by W in line 4

> W: Speaker, report producer and accuser
> M1: Addressee and non-aligned report recipient
> M2: Addressee and non-aligned report recipient
> H: Overhearer and accused

That is to say, W's utterance casts herself as speaker, report producer and accuser; the mediators are cast as the people addressed, and H as the overhearing accused. After a brief silence at line 6, H responds to W's accusations ('You see you bring this up-').

(Detail 2)

```
7    H:      You see ⌜you bring this up-
8    M2:             ⌊Jo:hn's
```

H makes relevant a number of discourse identities. First, by addressing his talk to W ('you . . .'), H positions M1 and M2 as overhearers, rather than report recipients. Like W, however, he positions M1 and M2 as non-aligned participants: his talk neither involves nor projects reference to the opinions of the mediators. Secondly, H's talk does not comprise or project a simple refutation of W's accusations. Nor does it adumbrate an alternative description and/or interpretation of the events discussed by W. Instead, the content and the tone of H's talk suggest that he is about to comment negatively on W having made the accusation, and thus that he is constituting himself as accuser and W as accused. Simultaneously, in so far as his accusation-in-progress is designed to rebut W's accusation, H makes relevant the identities accuser for W and accused/defendant for himself:

The discourse identities made relevant by H in line 7

> W: Addressee, accuser and accused
> M1: Overhearer and non-aligned party
> M2: Overhearer and non-aligned party
> H: Speaker, accused/defendant and accuser

H's contribution projects a different trajectory for the subsequent talk than is projected by W's prior contribution. During H's utterance, however, M2 makes a bid for speakership ('Jo:hn's') which may be designed to resist H's emerging utterance. Thus M2 begins to speak just as it becomes apparent that H is directly addressing W and, by virtue of his argumentative tone, that he is adopting an oppositional stance. In addition, M2 refers to H in the third person and thus positions him as a non-addressed recipient (although it is not clear whether M2 is addressing W or M1). Note also that, although M2 drops out after one word, her speech delivery conveys a commitment to producing her projected talk. Thus she employs practices that are associated with continuation of speaking in the context of overlapping talk: she (i) elongates the word by extending a sound within it and (ii) completes the word without an abrupt cut off.

The discourse identities made relevant by M2 in line 8

> W: Addressee (perhaps)
> M1:   Addressee (perhaps)
> M2:   Speaker
> H: Overhearer

What M2 says in line 8 can't be taken to be addressed to H, since it names him as a third party ('Jo:hn's'), so he must be casting either W or M2 (or both) as the addressee(s). Although M2 does not immediately say more, H, in continuing, displays an orientation to aspects of her bid for speakership. On the one hand, H, by interrupting himself and producing the imperative 'hang on', treats the issue of speakership as yet to be resolved, even though W has not continued beyond naming him. On the other hand, he emphasizes his commitment to completing his projected utterance, and thereby underlines the importance he attaches to what he has to say about W's accusation.

(Detail 3, continuation within lines 7 and 8)

```
7    H:      hang ⌈ o:n hang on love (.)
8    M2:           ⌊(    )-
```

By asking M2 to delay until he has finished speaking ('hang on'), H makes relevant the identities 'overlapping speaker-overlapping speaker'; he also invokes the identities 'orchestrator' and 'orchestrated' for himself and M2 respectively. Moreover, by signalling a commitment to continue with his aborted utterance, he positions W as incipient addressee.

As H produces the imperative 'hang on', M2 speaks again. On this occasion, she (M2) cuts off abruptly, perhaps in response to H's overlapping talk. Accordingly, her contribution does not strongly project continuation. Nonetheless, H repeats his imperative and then appends the address term 'love'. Thus he continues to speak under the auspices of the discourse identities made relevant by his preceding imperative.

The discourse identities made relevant by H in line 7's continuation

> W: Overhearer and incipient addressee
> M1:   Overhearer
> M2:   Addressee, overlapping speaker and orchestrated
> H: Speaker, overlapping speaker and orchestrator

After a brief silence ((.)), H restarts his aborted utterance (lines 7 and 9: 'you bring this up <u>n</u>ow . . .') and in doing so reinvokes the identities with which he began in Detail 1: H as speaker/accuser/defendant; W as addressee/accused/accuser; and M1 and M2 as non-aligned third parties.

(Detail 4, continuation of H's utterance in line 7 into line 9)

```
7     H:     You bring this up now:, it wasn't brought up at a::ll
```

Then, having begun to extend the clause 'it wasn't brought up at all', H interrupts himself (after 'when you know'), and upon restarting repositions W, M1 and M2 in relation to his talk.

(Detail 5)

```
9     H:     when you know when we went to cour⌈:t for access.
10    M2:                                        ⌊Ri:ght
```

Thus instead of continuing to address W (as he was doing with 'you bring this up <u>n</u>ow'), H addresses M1 and/or M2: this shift is marked by a distinct shift in tone. In so doing, H constitutes himself as a report producer and M1 and M2 as non-aligned report recipients. Thus he concludes his utterance by constituting himself and his co-participants in terms of the following discourse identities:

The discourse identities made relevant by H in Detail 5

> H: Speaker, report producer, accuser and defendant
> M1:   Addressee and non-aligned report recipient
> M2   Addressee and non-aligned report recipient
> W: Overhearer, accused and accuser

In responding to his utterance, M2 merely acknowledges what H has said (line 10: 'Right') and thus positions herself, as H as done, as a non-aligned report recipient.

In sum, H and M2 make relevant a number of discourse identities, for themselves and their co-participants, and more than one at a time (e.g., in line 9, as we have just seen, H casts himself as speaker, report producer, accuser and defendant). Some of these discourse identities are generic in that they are potentially relevant throughout any occasion of talk-in-interaction: for example, 'speaker', incipient addressee, addressed recipient and, in multi-party settings, overhearer. Others are tied to the specific actions and activities in which the participants are engaged: for example, report producer–report recipient and accuser–accused/defendant. The participants invoke, accept and/or contest these discourse identities on a moment-by-moment basis.

Below, we show how some of the discourse identities invoked by the participants make relevant larger social identities which are associated with the institution of divorce mediation.

Institutional Social Identities

So far in the encounter the participants have displayed a pervasive orientation to tasks and constraints that are indigenous to divorce mediation. Among other things, they have invoked discourse identities that are consistent with the identities 'divorce mediator'–'disputant'. In particular, they have collaboratively constituted incumbents of the mediator role as neutralistic facilitators with special rights to manage both the organization of turn-taking and the topical focus of the talk. They have done this, *inter alia*, through the selective and asymmetric invocation of discourse identities.

Thus M1 and M2 have adopted a neutralistic stance by refraining from aligning openly with either H or W. Moreover, H and W have contributed to the maintenance of this stance. On the one hand, they have not treated M1 and M2 as advocates of personal or institutional positions, even when M1 or M2 have produced utterances that are presuppositionally weighted for or against their own standpoints (Greatbatch and Dingwall, 1989). On the other hand, they have not directly asked M1 and M2 for their opinions. In both these respects, H and W have refrained from treating M1 and M2 as 'partisan'.

M1 and M2 have also constituted themselves as 'facilitators' rather than, for example, 'disinterested third parties'. Thus, in addition to advancing a neutralistic stance, they have confined themselves to a range of enabling actions such as requesting clarification, introducing and changing topics, and soliciting or suggesting possible compromises. H and W have ratified M1 and M2's authority to undertake these facilitative actions, even when they involve negative sanctions.

What about our example? H begins by invoking discourse identities which are consistent with the identity relationship 'divorce mediator–disputant' for he positions M1 and M2 as 'non-aligned overhearers'. This stance is consistent with their incumbency of the identity divorce mediator as collaboratively defined within this session to date (line 7, below; and see also the earlier analysis of Detail 2, above).

(Detail 2)

```
7      H:      You see ⌈you bring this up-
8      M2:             ⌊Jo:hn's
```

In contrast, H's subsequent imperatives ('hang on hang on love'), which are responsive to M2's bid for speakership ('Jo:hn's'), involve H moving out of the 'mediator–disputant' identity-relationship. M1 and M2 undertake the explicit management of H and W's conduct on several occasions: for example, by asking one to let the other finish. In contrast, with this one exception, H and W do not do this in relation to either M1 or M2. This asymmetry, which is found throughout our data, betrays an orientation to the special rights of divorce mediators to orchestrate the interaction. Consequently, by making relevant the discourse identities orchestrator for himself and orchestrated for M2, H constitutes his relationship with M2 in a way which is at odds with the mediator–disputant relationship they have thus far collaboratively sustained. With this said, this is marked as a temporary departure and H does nothing to undermine the neutralistic stance of M2.

(Detail 3, continuation within lines 7 and 8)

```
7    H:      hang ⌈ o:n hang on love (.)
8    M2:           ⌊(    )-
```

In restarting his aborted talk, H reinvokes the discourse identities with which he began: as he again addresses W, he positions himself and W as the principals in a dispute and M1 and M2 as non-aligned overhearers.

(Detail 4, continuation of H's utterance in line 7 into line 9)

```
7    H:      You bring this up now:, it wasn't brought up at a::ll
```

Recall that, although H begins by addressing W, subsequently he addresses M1 and M2 as he produces the clause 'when we went to cour:t for access' (Detail 4). However, H does not produce talk which is explicitly designed to draw M1 or M2 into the dispute. Instead, he continues to treat them as non-aligned third parties and, by extension, lends support to their occupancy of the identity 'divorce mediator'. Notice, moreover, that M1 and M2 collaborate in this process by not assessing or commenting on what H says. Thus, although M2 responds ('Riiight'), thereby confirming her status as an addressed recipient, her response merely acknowledges what H is saying and does not involve her aligning with or against H or W. In other words, M2 advances a neutralistic stance.

(Detail 5)

```
9    H:      when you know when we went to cour⌈:t for access.
10   M2:                                        ⌊Ri:ght
```

Throughout the extract M1 and M2 are positioned by H and themselves as 'non-aligned', a stance which is consistent with the formers' incumbency of the role 'divorce mediator'. Although H's imperatives invoke discourse identities which are not associated with divorce mediation, they project the continuation of talk which is consistent with the identity relationship divorce mediator–disputant.

Other Social Identities

The institutional identities of mediator–disputant are not the only 'macro' identities invoked within the talk by H and the other participants. Others are invoked through the topical focus of the talk and the use of the identity category 'love'.

Social Identities Invoked by Topic

In this and other divorce mediation encounters the disputant role is variably defined in terms of identities which are associated with a small number of social relationships: (i) the disputants' relationship as parents; (ii) the disputants' relationship as spouses/ex-spouses; (iii) the disputants' relationships with new partners; and (iv) the disputants' relationships with their children. In the light of this, the topic of H's talk can be seen to invoke identities that are contingently linked to the identity disputant-in-divorce-mediation (Greatbatch and Dingwall, 1997). First, W invoked H's identity as a parent in the preceding utterance by focusing on his behaviour when looking after the children. By explicitly referencing this topic through the pro-term 'this', H himself makes relevant his identity as a parent in lines 7 and 9. Secondly, H then asserts that W did not mention her accusation when the problems surrounding access were dealt with in court and thereby invokes identities which centre on his relationship with W. These include 'separating spouses/parents', 'spouses/parents in disagreement about access arrangements', and 'legal disputants'.

Social Identities Invoked through the Use of an Identity Category

H also invokes identities through the use of the identity category 'love' (as an address term) which invokes an informal relationship with M2 and possibly categorizes her in gender-related terms. This occurs when H repeats the imperative, possibly in response to M2's overlapping talk. However, the repeat differs from the initial imperative in that H appends the address term 'love' ('hang on love'). In mainstream British English (and leaving aside dialect usage not otherwise signalled in this talk), women may use this term when addressing members of either sex, but normally men only use it when addressing females, and in all cases there is a strong suggestion of informality.

Thus by referring to the female mediator M2 as 'love', H appears to make relevant 'male' (for H) and 'female' (for M2) and place them both in some less-than-formal relationship. This represents a marked departure from conventions associated with the formalities of institutionalized mediation, and perhaps professional–client interaction in general (see Edwards, this volume). Throughout our corpus of divorce mediation sessions, the participants rarely categorize incumbents of the mediator role in terms of other social identities, including those related to gender, social class, age, and ethnicity. To date in this encounter the same pattern has been collaboratively sustained by the participants. By collaboratively insulating the divorce mediator role from such identities, the participants contribute to the maintenance of a neutralistic stance for divorce mediators. For the latters' actions are not linked, at least officially, to forms of thinking and behaviour which may be associated with particular social groups.

The use of the identity category 'love' may serve to soften the force of H's imperatives. Nonetheless, given that its use involves a departure from the convention whereby mediators are categorized in social identity-neutral terms, it also upgrades his resistance to M2's bid for speakership and thereby further emphasizes the importance he attaches to his response to W.

The Foundational Status of the Identities Mediator–Disputant

The participants invoke a number of larger social identities. These identities, which reach beyond the participants' talk, are made relevant by discourse identities, by the topical focus of the talk, and by the use of an identity category in an address term. Throughout, however, the identities divorce mediator–disputant seem to occupy a foundational status. That is to say, they remain relevant to the production and interpretation of the participants' talk.

This is not to say that these identities *automatically* have a foundational status in this or other mediation sessions. The relationship between these identities and discourse and other larger social identities is managed by the participants themselves and may change moment by moment. Thus, in our example, the foundational status of the identities 'mediator–disputant' is locally achieved in at least two ways. First, with the exception of H's imperatives, H and M2 make relevant discourse and larger social identities which are consistent with the identities divorce mediator–disputant, as collaboratively defined thus far in the encounter. Secondly, although H produces talk which involves a movement away from the identity relationship divorce mediator–disputant, the positioning and design of his talk continues to privilege this relationship. It is produced as an interruption of, and interpolation in, an ongoing utterance which makes relevant his identity as a 'disputant-in-mediation'. Consequently, the talk he addresses to M2 not only involves 'H doing something conversational' and/or 'H, a male, speaking to M2, a female'. As noted above, it is also formulated as a temporary departure from talk that is consistent with a role-based identity.

Thus, although H is not acting under the auspices of the institutional identity disputant-in-mediation, this identity perhaps remains relevant to understanding his talk.

Concluding Comments

We have argued that one cannot assume that particular identities or sets of identities are pertinent to talk-in-interaction. The identities that participants make relevant for the production and interpretation of their talk may change within even a single turn at talk. It is therefore necessary to examine how participants invoke and accept or contest the relevance of identities on a moment-by-moment basis.

In the case of discourse identities this involves dealing with identities which are intrinsic to talk-in-interaction and the activities being accomplished within it. With larger social identities, however, it is necessary to explicate links between the details of talk-in-interaction and identities which reach beyond the talk itself. As we said above, this involves explicating how such identities may be invoked by discourse identities, the topical focus of talk, the use of identity categories, or other details of the talk. It also requires consideration of how participants may privilege particular identities, and of how they may invoke particular relationships between different identities such that some may be treated either as definitional of others or as occupying a foundational status in relation to others.

To address these issues, without engaging in stipulative analysis or unsubstantiated speculation (or both), poses a serious analytical challenge. Thus, for example, to establish linkages between discourse identities in a particular episode of talk-in-interaction and larger social identities associated with divorce mediation we have referred to wider patterns of conduct not only within this encounter, but also within others recorded in the same agency. We have also relied upon a range of knowledge about the participants and their relationships with each other, as well as about the conventions associated with divorce mediation sessions. Clearly this raises questions about how we may warrant the introduction of such information into the analysis of a particular strip of interaction.

Perhaps the most problematic aspect of our analysis concerns the use of the address term 'love'. On the one hand, this is not part of a systematic pattern of address involving gender-related categorization of the participants. On the other hand, neither M2 nor the other participants explicitly treat H's use of this identity category as invoking gender. Consequently, it is not possible to support our contention that the category makes gender relevant by reference either to wider patterns of conduct or to the participants' displayed understandings. The danger is that by proceeding without such support we may open the door to unsubstantiated speculation.

Although satisfactory answers to these problems have yet to be found, we should not be deterred from considering the invocation of identities which are not intrinsic to talk-in-interaction. By undertaking such analysis, we will develop clearer understandings of the problems and of how they may best be handled. However, it is essential that we anchor our observations in the overt details of the talk and, where possible, in the understandings that participants display of each other's conduct. We should always begin with painstaking analysis of the 'indigenous features of talk-in-interaction' (Schegloff, 1991: 67), before moving to equally painstaking analysis of the ways in which these features may (but need not) make relevant larger social identities.

PART III

MEMBERSHIP CATEGORIES AND THEIR PRACTICAL AND INSTITUTIONAL RELEVANCE

9 Describing 'Deviance' in School: Recognizably Educational Psychological Problems

Stephen Hester

The identity of the 'deviant' is an everyday feature of school life. Its availability for members and for sociologists alike is accomplished through a wide range of imputations and descriptions. With a few exceptions (Hester, 1990, 1992; MacBeth, 1990, 1991; Mehan, 1983; Mehan et al., 1986; Payne, 1982), little ethnomethodological (and sociological) analytic attention has been paid to the naturally occurring local detail of the talk-in-interaction through which 'problem children' are identified as deviating or departing from category-predicated rules and norms (see Matza, 1969) and/or as having other kinds of 'special educational needs' and perhaps, in the cases judged the most 'serious', as requiring exclusion from school.

This chapter uses membership categorization analysis (MCA) (Eglin and Hester, 1992; Hester and Eglin, 1997a, 1997b; Sacks, 1992) in an investigation of some organizational features of descriptions of 'deviance' in schools. The context in which these descriptions were witnessed and recorded for analysis consists of 'referral talk' between teachers and educational psychologists. In such talk, children considered by schools to have 'special educational needs' and to warrant the practical intervention of educational psychologists are discussed. Following an outline of the approach of MCA, the aims of this chapter are twofold: to examine some categorical organizational features of the description of such children as deviant, and to consider some ways in which teachers' categorizations are recognizably designed for their recipients, namely educational psychologists. In short, the focus is on the recognizably educational psychological character of deviance in referral talk.

Membership Categorization Analysis

As a variety of ethnomethodology, and as indicated elsewhere (Hester and Eglin, 1997a), the focus of membership categorization analysis is on the locally used, invoked and organized 'presumed commonsense knowledge of social structures' which members of society, conceptualized as lay and professional social analysts, are oriented to in accomplishing (the sociology of) 'naturally occurring ordinary activities', including professional socio-logical inquiry itself. This knowledge is conceived as being organized in terms of membership categories, membership categorization devices and category predicates.

Membership categories, as defined by Sacks and much invoked by the contributors to this book, are classifications or social types that may be used to describe persons, for example 'factory worker', 'postmodernist', 'police officer', 'sister', 'drunk driver', 'boy', 'friend', 'lover' and 'historian'. These various kinds of category may be interactionally linked together, on the occasions of their use, to form classes, collections or 'membership categorization devices' (MCDs).

The two rules identified by Sacks for applying membership categories are the economy rule and the consistency rule. The economy rule provides for the adequacy of using a single membership category to describe a member of some population. Of course, sometimes more than one category may be used, but standardly in describing persons a single category will suffice. The consistency rule holds that 'if some population of persons is being categorized, and if a category from some device's collection has been used to categorize a first member of the population, then that category or other categories of the same collection may be used to categorize further members of the population' (Sacks, 1974: 219). Thus, for example, if a person is categorized as 'first violin' then further persons may be referred to in terms of other membership categories comprising the collection 'members of the orchestra'. Sacks also identified a corollary or 'hearer's maxim' with respect to the consistency rule. This maxim holds that 'if two or more categories are used to categorize two or more members of some population, and those categories can be heard as categories from the same collection, then: hear them that way' (ibid.: 219–20). The now famous example in Sacks's work is the child's story, 'The baby cried. The mommy picked it up' (Sacks, 1992, Vol. I: 236–59). Here, with reference to the hearer's maxim, the two categories, 'baby' and 'mommy', may be and are routinely and commonsensically heard as both belonging to the collection 'family'.

Another key concept of membership categorization analysis is that of the category predicate. Sacks introduced the concept of 'category-bound activities' to refer to those activities that are expectably and properly done by persons who are the incumbents of particular categories. He notes that categories selected to categorize some member performing a category-bound activity and categories selected to categorize that activity are co-selected. Thus, although it is possibly correct to say of a baby crying that it is a male shedding tears, it is not possibly recognizable as a correct or appropriate description of the scene. The 'preference' for category co-selection is a strong and generative one and helps us to understand some of the organizational and selectional features of such utterances as the one with which Sacks began: 'The baby cried. The mommy picked it up.' Subsequent researchers have extended Sacks's work on category-bound activities to encompass other properties or predicates which may be presumed of particular categories (see Jayyusi, 1984; Payne, 1976; Sharrock, 1974; Watson, 1976, 1978, 1983). Other predicates include, for example, rights, entitlements, obligations, knowledge, attributes and competences.

Categorizing Deviance in School

With that background in mind about what it might mean to 'categorize' someone, it is worth looking at previous studies of deviance in schools, and especially of cases where children are referred to outside authorities. A distinction between two aspects of deviance becomes apparent. On the one hand, descriptions of deviance may be investigated in terms of what they allude 'to' (i.e., the kind of problem pointed to), while on the other hand there is the issue of what the designation consists 'of' (i.e., *how* it alludes to the problem). Previous researchers have largely restricted their studies to the first of these aspects, that is, to the kinds of 'problem' defined as deviant and for which the children are referred. In so doing, it would seem to be standard sociological practice to group members' vernacular categorizations into various analyst's classifications. One such classificatory scheme of 'reasons for referral' might include the following:

(1) Learning problems/problems of educational retardation
(2) Problems of maturity/development
(3) Attainment problems
(4) Social problems
(5) Behavioural problems
(6) Emotional and psychological problems
(7) Physical problems.

Such a concentration on 'underlying' problems treats members' talk as a resource rather than as a topic of inquiry in its own right. Thus, such abstractions do not illuminate *how* the participants in settings such as this describe deviance for each other. Analysts' classificatory schemes, abstracted from the 'lived detail' of members' descriptive practices, entail a neglect of the phenomenon of 'deviance' as it is known, understood and talked about by members themselves.

It was Garfinkel who emphasized that sociology's preference for generalized description entailed a neglect of the specifics of settings and activities: what he referred to as a 'missing whatness'. In terms of this conception, then, members' categorizations of 'deviance' require investigation as a topic in their own right. Furthermore, in doing so, and in contrast to sociological approaches such as realism and social constructionism (see Chapter 12), the aim is not to theorize deviance but to describe and analyse what deviance is for the members of society. For ethnomethodology, deviance is not an issue about which any theoretical stance needs to be or should be taken. Rather, ethnomethodology seeks to examine the ways in which concerns with 'deviance' inform members' locally ordered practical action and practical reasoning. The concern is fundamentally a descriptive one; it seeks to describe the mundane practices in and through which persons are oriented to issues of what is deviant and engage in its 'analysis' in the course of such activities as reporting, describing, questioning, interpreting, deciding and explaining what is or is not deviant. The aim is to draw attention to the various locally situated ways in which deviance is identified, described, explained, understood, made sense of, and treated as the grounds for various kinds of remedial intervention. In short, its focus is on how deviance is ordered in specific sites of talk and interaction.

In what follows, first, some methods used in describing deviance in referral talk will be examined. Attention will then be focused, secondly, on the issue of recipient design in relation to these descriptions.

Categorizing Deviance in Referral Talk: Category Contrasts

Category contrasts are 'occasioned' devices for describing deviance in that they are constructed for the local situation at hand, to make just this point. They comprise two parts, elements or items which are hearably contrastive in some way. Several varieties of the method of category contrast are observable in the data to hand. Consider, for example, the following extract (1).

(1)   (RMSJ/550)

```
1    HT:    He's he's such a ahm you know so many children if they are telling you lies
2           you ⌈it sta⌉nds out a ⌈mile⌉ the lying but with=
3    EP:         ⌊Mm ⌋          ⌊Mm⌋
4    HT:    =Robin.
5    EP:    He's good.
```

6	HT:	((*sotto voce*)) He's very good.
7	EP:	He's quite I can't re⌈member the the exact assessment⌉.
8	HT:	⌊He's very good and so innoce⌋nt
9		looking.
10	EP:	Yeah I seem to remember he's at least average intelligence
11		isn't he?
12	HT:	Oh yes about average ⌈(1.5) something like that. ⌉
13	EP:	⌊He's not he's not ( ) no.⌋
14	HT:	Yeah yeah but er.
15	EP:	Yeah.
16	HT:	He's a child you just can't tell whether he's lying or not.
17	EP:	Mm.
18	HT:	Most of the time I must admit I think he is lying but you try
19	EP:	Mm.
20	HT:	You would never get him to show it.
21	EP:	Mm.

In this extract, then, the category contrast consists of 'so many children' versus the particular pupil under discussion ('Robin') with respect to the observability of the activity of 'telling lies'. The headteacher (HT) can be heard to make a distinction between what may be called 'normal lying' and the 'abnormal lying' of this child. Thus, with 'so many children . . . it stands out a mile', but the referral is 'a child you just can't tell whether he's lying or not'. Furthermore, it is observable that this category contrast is collaboratively produced. Thus, HT states what can be heard as the first part of the contrast – 'so many children if they are telling you lies you it stands out a mile the lying' – and then offers the contrast or transition marker, 'but' and then 'with Robin'. This hearably incomplete contrast is then completed by its recipient, the educational psychologist, with the candidate categorization 'he's good', which in turn is confirmed and upgraded by HT to 'he's very good'. In this way, the contrast between 'so many' and 'Robin' is developed into a contrast between 'bad liars' and 'good liars', some of whom, like this one, happen also to be 'very good' at this particular activity. In extract (2) a similar category contrast is made between 'all children' and the particular referral in question.

(2) AH/1/LM

1	EP:	Mm hmm yeah I see err does he have any friends in the
2		classroom?
3	FT:	( ) January when I came into the class Alfred
4		was very sort of quiet shy he was always weighing up the
5		situation but I think all children do with a new teacher ˙hhh
6		initially (.) then he started running round the room
7		screaming 'I'm taking no notice' 'I'm not bothered by you' 'I
8		don't care what you say' and if you didn't (.) take notice of
9		him (.) he wanted your attention fair enough all young
10		children do want attention sometimes some more than

11	others but if you didn't notice him he would go and punch
12	there's two children in the class that seem to be picked on
13	more than anyone else and he'd go and punch them or kick
14	them or swear at them.

The category contrast here is one between the typical behaviour of children in general ('all young children') and the behaviour of the referred child in relation to the 'normal' process of adjusting to a new teacher. Whereas all children initially 'weigh up' the situation and then 'settle down', the referral acted unusually in so far as he did not follow this typical pattern. Instead, he became uncooperative and violent. In this, as in the previous extract, the referrals can be seen to be 'marked out' as different, as deviant, by virtue of their 'failure' to display the kinds of activities, attributes, and other predicates bound to the category 'pupil'. The referrals 'stand out' because of this category contrast.

Some Uses of the Stage of Life Device

Many of the membership categories used in making category contrasts belong to what Sacks (1974) calls 'positioned-category devices'. These are membership categorization devices which include membership categories which occupy, or are arranged in, different positions, higher and lower, relative to one another. The basic formula here is as follows: if a person is an X, but he or she behaves like a Y, where X and Y are positioned higher and lower relative to each other as members of a positioned category device, then that person is due either praise or complaint. Of these devices the 'stage of life' membership categorization device is both pervasive and fundamental. It is organized in terms of several different orders of positioned categories. One variety of these contains the membership categories 'baby', 'toddler', 'child', 'adolescent', 'teenager', 'young woman', 'middle aged man', 'old woman'. A second variety contains the 'age terms' such as 'one year old', 'six years old', 'forty years old', for example. A third variety contains the 'age classes' such as 'young', 'old', 'oldest' and so on.

The stage of life device is not only widely used in educationists' discourse about children, it also provides a foundation for a variety of other devices which are 'mapped on to it' (Watson and Wienberg, 1982). These include the 'stage of education', 'stage of emotional development', 'stage of motor development', 'reading age', 'stage of language development', 'stage of physical development', 'stage of sexual development', and so forth. They are 'mapped on to' the stage of life device in the sense that each 'stage' in these devices corresponds to a given age or stage in the stage of life device. Children of particular ages are thus expected to have attained certain levels of speech, reading, motor control, physical development, etc. There are certain 'stages' of physical, social, emotional and psychological development through which children are judged to have or not to have progressed. By a certain age children are expected, given 'normal courses of development' to have attained typical competences, attributes, features, abilities, interests and proclivities for typical activities, and so on. Such normal courses of development offer a readily available standard for comparing children and for evaluating their relative progress. It is in terms of this standard that children may be described as 'underdeveloped', 'behind' and 'backward'.

These 'normal courses of development', which are organized in terms of the stage of life device, operate in a similar fashion to the 'territory of normal appearances' discussed by Sacks (1972a) in connection with the police assessment of moral character. They function, in other words, as a background scheme of interpretation against which the unusual, the abnormal – in short, the 'deviant' – may 'stand out' and be 'marked out'. Children who are seen to remain functioning, in the sense that they perform activities, display attributes and demonstrate levels of competence normally bound to categories of children positioned lower in the stage of life device, may have their competence, progress and development called into question. They may find themselves designated as having some type of problem, 'special need', and/or as 'deviant'.

Examples of the use of positioned category devices which are mapped on to the stage of life device are legion in referral talk. To illustrate the point, three examples will be considered: (i) stage of language development, (ii) maturity and (iii) stage of education. In each case, they provide for category contrast as a method for describing deviance. The first consists of the *stage of language development* device. In the following extract (3), a headteacher of a primary school uses it in accomplishing a category contrast between the referral and other children 'of his age', namely four years old.

(3) (AN/1)

```
 1    HT:   Now, when she brought him in she said er e-e wasn't a good
 2          talker.
 3    EP:   Mm hm.
 4    HT:   And er I think I said was there anything else wrong with
 5          him and er she said no.
 6    EP:   Mm hm.
 7    HT:   And (.) I asked her as usual you know her first name, her
 8          husband's first name.
 9    EP:   Yeah.
10    HT:   So she gave her husband as Paul and she's Pauline.
11    EP:   Mm.
12    HT:   And (.) I accepted this er.
13    EP:   Mm hm.
14    HT:   Quite happily (              ) and er we saw his birth
15          certificate (.) but it wasn't very long before we realized
16          that it was more than just a poor speaker, he-he can't speak
17          very much at all, he-he doesn't know the language, he
18          [doesn't know]=
19    EP:   [Mm hm       ]
```

```
20      HT:     =the names of common objects, no response to various
21              simple instructions such as 'stand up', 'sit down', he's
22              really functioning like an=
23      EP:     =Mm hm=
24      HT:     =eighteen month or two year old baby.
25      EP:     Mm hm
```

Thus, the headteacher reports that a mother had described her child as 'not a good talker'. However, 'it wasn't long', the headteacher continues, before it was 'realized that it was more than just a poor speaker'. The inapplicability of the mother's categorization is then demonstrated via a listing of the child's linguistic deficiencies: he cannot speak very much at all, he does not know the language, and does not respond to simple instructions. Finally, the headteacher formulates the case by categorizing the child's linguistic 'functioning' as that of an 'eighteen-month or two-year-old baby'. The upshot is that the child's language development is hearably designated as a problem. Such recognizability as deviant depends upon a contrast between what is expected in terms of the predicates of the stage of life category to which the child belongs, namely 'four years old', and what is received, namely a level of competence ('functioning') which is typical of the category 'two years old' instead. As a member of the category 'four years old' the child is expected to have certain attributes and to be able to function in ways which are bound to such a category. However, this child is functioning in ways more typical of a different category, namely a two-year-old. Hence, this child, being a four-year-old, may be heard as deviant.

Maturity is another example of a device which may be mapped on to the stage of life. There are two basic categories in this device: 'mature' and 'immature', though they are frequently subjected to various modifiers such as 'very', 'completely', 'rather', and so on, thereby providing gradation levels for making finer distinctions in the terms of the contrast class mature/immature. Furthermore, the categories 'mature' and 'immature' are not particularly informative in the absence of their being tied to the age of the person to whom they are applied because, like age classes, they may be used independently of age. Thus, a twelve-year-old may be described as 'mature' (for his or her age) while a thirty-year-old may be categorized as (relatively) 'immature'. The sense of these categories depends on a knowledge of the age of the person being categorized (and also on the relative age of the person doing the categorization (see Sacks, 1992: 45)). The following extract is an example of the use of categories from the maturity device.

(4)   (WJS/11)

```
1       HT:     You see he's the sort of boy who you will meet on the
2               corridor (.) at breaktime chasing around in an immature
3               sort of way.
```

4	MT:	Mmhmm.
5		(0.4)
6	EP:	Mmhmm.

In this case the sense of 'immature sort of way' as a complaint depends upon, and reflexively invokes, a background knowledge of the child's age (he is a nine-year-old).

It is not only 'immaturity' which can be a problem. 'Maturity' can be a potential source of trouble too. In the following extract the 'stage of life' device is used to describe the pupil as a problem in that she exceeds the 'normal' level of category-bound attributes for a girl of her age. Further, it is said that she mixes with boys older than herself, such a state of affairs giving rise to anxiety as a result of the category-bound features of older boys and younger girls (corrupted innocence, getting into sexual trouble, etc.).

(5) (WJS/5578)

1	EP:	Mhmm.
2	FT:	She's the oldest girl in the school and she's very mature
3		(1.5) and errm she doesn't really mix with other children of
4		her own age group y'see=
5	EP:	=Mm=
6	FT:	=but she just bullies them and they're all very frightened
7		of her.
8	EP:	Mm.
9	FT:	And she mixes with children from Southbend, sixteen year
10		olds, fifteen year olds.
11	EP:	Mm hmm.
12	FT:	And we're a bit concerned about that side of it because it's
13		mainly boys as well.
14	EP:	Mm hmm.

The problem here, then, is not one of deficient competence or performance, it is one of excess. The child exceeds the normal complement of attributes and engages, or at least presents the prospect of engaging, in activities 'beyond her years'. The child is being downgraded not because she is failing to reach some standard but because she is exceeding it. A surfeit can be as noticeable and possibly problematic as a deficiency. The child is described as 'mature', a description which can be heard to pertain to both her physical development and her relations with older boys. Her relative 'maturity' serves as a category contrast with the predicates of other children of her age. In this way, she is 'marked out' as deviant.

A third device which is mapped on to the stage of life device is the *stage of education* device. This device may be invoked in various ways, including references to year of schooling (as in first year, second year, etc.) or type of school attended (as in Infant, Primary, Junior, etc.). In the following extract (6), the child is designated as being 'two years behind'.

(6) (MP/20)

```
1    T1:   I've known remedial children (.) in me other school (.) doin'
2          better work than that (.) look at this
3    SW:   °mmhmm°
4    T1:   All wrong
5          (3.7)
6    T1:   That's his number sense, you look (0.5) there
7    EP:   ⌈Can I actua⌉lly read a page of this lad's (.) I=
8    T1:   ⌊Four right ⌋
9    EP:   =Can can't beat you at somethin' ⌈(              )⌉=
10   T2:                                    ⌊Fair enough ⌋
11   EP:   =Some ⌈written wor⌉k.
12   T1:         ⌊Hhehhh    ⌋
13   T2:   Look at this abysmal figure ⌈(              )⌉
14   T1:                               ⌊English language⌋
15   EP:   Could I ⌈have a look at that?⌉
16   T1:           ⌊the last school term⌋
17         (2.4)
18   T1:   Organization of ideas note (.) that's what
19         err his English teacher was saying, isn't it? (1.1) He's not
20         done very well in anythin' really.
21   EP:   °Mm (.) right°.
22   T1:   ⌈°(              )⌉ to it°.
23   EP:   ⌊Yeah            ⌋
24   T2:   Well, he's not, he's (.) two years behind.
```

'Two years behind' invokes categorical order or 'standard' relative to stage of schooling for a given child's age. Furthermore, 'remedial' children is a category of child defined in terms of the receipt of special educational provision within school, that is remedial help. Incumbency of the category 'remedial' suggests various predicates including being in 'need of help', 'being behind', etc. To say of children they need remedial help is to ascribe incompetence to them; to say they are doing worse than remedial is to mark them out as in need of extraordinary, that is 'outside' help.

Depictions of Seriousness through the Use of Retrospective and Prospective Category Contrasts

Another class of category contrast involves changes in the seriousness of pupil deviance over time. These changes are identified in two ways. Retrospective category contrasts distinguish the present from the past with respect to the kind of problem exhibited by the referral, indicating that the problem is now more serious than it was. Prospective category contrasts project a future state of affairs in which the problem *will* be worse (unless, by implication, something is done about the problem). Extract (7) is an example of the former.

(7) (MP/48)

```
 1    MT:    Well (0.8) as I see it (0.5) er he always has been a nuisance
 2           I mean I hear from other people who've had him you know
 3           from the time when he was in the first and second year that
 4           the way he (.) spoke to teacher in the way he behaved in class.
 5    SW:    Mmhmm.
 6    MT:    You know a continuous disruptive element in the class.
 7    SW:    Mmhmm.
 8    MT:    I've had him now since-s:err (.) last September
 9    SW:    Mhmm-hm-hm.
10    MT:    an-d (0.8) up till: (0.5) ergh Easter (0.6)
11           though-l-his attitude to: teaching he=er to me particularly
12           (we have gathered from what-is-is) attitude to teaching (.)
13           is one of (.) utter (.) non-cooperation and contempt.
14    SW:    Mhmm.
15    MT:    An:d (0.5) but (0.9) this was only in the
16           manner of you know he wasn't prepared to work (0.5)
17           he-e-wasn't as far as I was concerned up till this term.
18    SW:    ⌈Mhmm.⌉
19    MT:    ⌊Um    ⌋ (0.5) actively non-coope⌈rative   y⌉ou know (.)=
20    SW:                                      ⌊mmhmm⌋
21    MT:    =positively disruptive (0.5) and in the last few weeks he
22           has turned to being positively disruptive.
```

Here, then, the teacher contrasts a pupil's history in which he has 'always been a nuisance', continuously disruptive, non-cooperative and contemptuous with a more recent change for the worse. Thus, the pupil has now 'turned to being positively disruptive'. The seriousness of the problem has, in other words, increased to such an extent that it is, by implication, a matter of sufficient concern to warrant referral to the educational psychologist.

The following extract (8) provides a prospective category contrast. Through its use, the teacher indicates that the problem will 'get worse' unless something is done (by implication, educational psychological intervention).

(8) (MP/53)

```
 1    EP:    What's the worst that's happened to him here has he been
 2           temporarily suspended ⌈or⌉ anything like this?
 3    MT:                          ⌊No⌋
 4    MT:    Time he ha:d
 5    EP:    Mhmm.
 6    MT:    Right anytime (.) now (.) cos I: y'know unless something
 7           happens pretty quick that's what's gonna have to happen
```

Where extract (7) reports and projects a change in the seriousness of the problem presented by the pupil in terms of his conduct, and thereby implicates the relevance of an educational psychological assessment of the problem, extract (8) exhibits such a category contrast in terms of the kind of reaction which the school will have to take unless a solution to the problem is found. Such a projected category of reaction constitutes a measure of the seriousness of the problem which implicates educational psychological intervention.

Some Uses of Extreme Case Formulations

Another variety of category contrast which was used in designating deviance was the 'extreme case formulation'. 'Extreme case formulations', according to Pomerantz (1986), comprise 'one practice used in legitimizing claims': 'interactants use extreme case formulations when they anticipate or expect their co-interactants to undermine their claims and when they are in adversarial situations' (Pomerantz, 1986: 222). By formulating descriptions of cases as maximum cases, they forestall the possible objections to their descriptions. Extreme case formulations provide for a sense of the present problem – the referral under consideration for educational psychological intervention – as one which is extreme in contrast to the kinds of problems that the school ordinarily deals with. As such, extreme case formulations can be heard to implicate the seriousness of the problem and thereby its educational psychological relevance. Consider, for example, extract (9):

(9)   (MP/1)

```
1      MT:    Nobody's s-s:poken of this lad as a discipline problem as
2             such: if anything he's rather introverted (0.5) err (1.5) there
3             have been (.) comments which were made to me: when I fir:st
4             became involved which said e-is-his mathematics are
5             atrocious (1.4) his: number concepts seem to be: (.) so poor
6             (.) that (0.7) he shouldn't be in the maths class (.) the
7             teacher didn't know really what to do with the lad (.)
8             because he just couldn't do the things now (.) even at this
9             stage he wasn't disruptive (.) but obviously he was gaining
10            nothing from (0.6) class time.
```

This extract contains the use of three extreme case formulations pertaining to the pupil. The first refers to 'his number concepts' being 'so poor . . . that . . . he shouldn't be in the maths class'. The second consists of a report that 'the teacher didn't know what to do with him'. The third observes that 'he was gaining nothing from class time'. The collective upshot of these formulations is the identification of the child as beyond the limits of normal school provision and hence as requiring some kind of special educational help. Similarly, in extract (10), the referral is depicted as 'beyond remedial help':

(10) (RMSJ/1)

```
1    HT:   I do want him tested I do want to know whether I'm dealing
2          with a dull child.
3    EP:   Uh huh.
4    HT:   And lack of schooling or armm an average child and it's lack
5          of schooling err he's getting ermm remedial help and Mrs
6          Martin is getting nowhere fast with him for all he's er::mm.
7    EP:   Have you contacted the parents?
```

Thus, in this example the child is depicted as being beyond remedial help in so far as the remedial teacher is 'getting nowhere fast with him'. In depicting the child as having problems which are beyond boundaries encompassed by the school's remedial resources, the relevance for the school of educational psychological intervention is made available.

Using Predicates of the Category 'Teacher' to Formulate the Extreme Character of the Problem

The examples considered so far have drawn a category contrast between types of pupil and in so doing have implicated the intervention of educational psychologists by virtue of the recognizable seriousness of the problems presented by the referral. In the following extract this is achieved in terms of the category membership not of the referral but of the teacher.

(11) (MP/49)

```
1    SW:   Mm hmm mmhmm.
2    MT:   Errm (0.5) at the moment I've taken (along his classroom)
3          down in the gym waiting for Jeremy to come down ˙hhh but
4          it's reached such a stage with me: that errm (.) you know I
5          find that the boy's completely uncooperative (1.0) now I've
6          been teaching now for something like twenty five or thirty
7          years (0.5) an never have I had to (0.5) to: call on the help of
8          a year tutor or anybody else to assist me with a child
9          but in this one I must admit that I just don't know what to
10         do to handle him.
```

Here the teacher invokes a category, the 'experienced teacher', of which he is claiming membership. A predicate of this category is standardly being able to handle 'stroppy lads' and other difficult pupils. Hence, under 'normal circumstances', as it were, his category-bound expertise would enable him to manage successfully any problems which such pupils might present. In this case, however, in spite of his incumbency of such a category, the teacher does not know what to do. The clear implication is that the case is one which is beyond the category-bound knowledge of even the experienced teacher; it falls outside the domain of normal practice for such persons and hence can be heard to implicate a need for special educational provision.

In extract (12) the category of 'inexperienced teacher' is used to mark the seriousness of the problem:

(12) (MP/80)

```
1     MT:    Y'see I mean it is going on in other places where some
2            younger teacher or less experienced teacher doesn't want to
3            say: that they can't-that they can't manage Peter Willis.
4     SW:    Mhmm
5     MT:    I mean I don't mind saying it I've handled lots of stroppy
6            lads in my time y'see and I don't mind saying that this one is
7            (0.5) something that I've never experienced before.
8     EP:    Yeah that can be the case ⌈(              )⌉
9     MT:                               ⌊  you   know  ⌋(0.5) but I'm sure
10           there are other teacher⌈s   ⌉ you know
11    EP:                           ⌊yeah⌋
12    MT:    less experienced teachers younger teachers who are going
13           through agonies.
14    EP:    Mm.
```

Thus, while a predicate of the 'experienced teacher' is that particularly difficult and uncooperative pupils can be successfully dealt with (though as this teacher has already said, this is not the case here), for 'inexperienced teachers' this would not be the case; such expertise is not predicated, in the view of this teacher at least, on such a category of teacher. Indeed, faced with such a pupil, such teachers can be expected properly to experience 'agonies'. Given the absence of such competence among this category of teacher, educational psychological intervention clearly 'makes sense'.

Referral Talk, Recipient Design and Membership Categorization

It was indicated earlier that in addition to identifying some categorical resources used in describing children as deviant, an aim of this chapter is to consider how such descriptions are 'recipient-designed'. The issue is how are referrals categorized as to be relevant for educational psychological intervention. As Sacks (1992; cf. Speier, 1971) has pointed out, categorizations are selections from alternatives; there are always alternative choices available to describers of persons. Attention is therefore directed to the procedural or methodical character of category selection and, specifically, to how categories are selected with a view to their interactional implicativeness and the categorical identities of their recipients.

The appropriateness of this formulation of the problem of referral description and recipient design is suggested by its apparent successful deployment in previous studies of the categorization of deviance. Two good examples in this regard are Wieder (1974) in connection with the 'convict code', and Maynard (1984) in connection with plea bargaining; both indicate that descriptions are not just used disinterestedly, but are selected for interactional utility. Two other notable studies which have explored the connections between recipient design are Eglin and Wideman (1986) and Meehan (1989), both with respect to citizen calls to the police. In making such calls people design their talk so as to display their orientation to the task in which they are involved. In Meehan's study, for example, the police had identified 'youth gangs' as 'a problem' and had officially instituted a special 'gang' car for dealing with it. As a result, by using the term 'gangs' when they talked about groups of youths, callers would visibly be cooperating in the interactional business of 'a call to the police' (see Chapter 6 by Zimmerman for a case – the 'riddle call' – in which recipient design goes very wrong).

This view of descriptions of deviance as being recipient-designed would seem to have relevance for the categorization of deviance in referral talk. After all, many of the pupil 'problems' with which teachers have to deal on a daily basis would not be considered 'suitable cases for referral'. Instead, they would be handled 'in house', as it were. It would seem to be one thing to describe a child as deviant and quite another to describe a child whose deviance warrants the intervention of outside agencies and experts such as educational psychologists. Referral deviance, in other words, should be described in such a way as to be recognizably educational psychological in character. If not, then the educational psychologist can quite legitimately respond with something like 'I think that is something you can deal with on your own, you don't need my help'. The issue is: how are descriptions produced and heard as grounds for referral and as grounds for educational psychological intervention?

It would seem, then, at least a priori, that such a distinction would be an oriented-to matter for teachers, such that the educational psychological relevance of the referrals would be exhibited and made available as part and parcel of the description of referrals. When the data are examined in the light of this issue, it is apparent that, with a few exceptions, there is a marked absence of explicit requests for educational psychological intervention. Apart from the request for a test (extract (10)) and, in extract (8), claims that the problems will get worse or the child will have to be suspended unless 'something happens', specific requests for particular forms of intervention are not made. Instead, the teachers describe the contrastive, extreme and serious character of the problem without stating in so many words that they wish for educational psychological intervention to occur. How, then, is this to be squared with the 'hypothesis' that categorization is recipient-designed – that these categorizations have been selected from alternatives with regard to their recipient and organizational implicativeness?

There are several possibilities here. A first is that the categories of deviance described are hearably 'educational' in the sense that they are made manifest in an educational context. They occur, therefore, within a domain of educational psychological expertise and practical action; they comprise categories of problem with respect to which educational psychological action is predicated. A second possibility is that the intervention of an educational psychologist is warranted by the seriousness of the cases described. If so, then the methods of categorization examined earlier can be understood to identify and mark the seriousness of the problems as far as the schoolteachers are concerned and to implicate the intervention of educational psychologists by virtue of that seriousness. In this regard, the categorizations can be understood to invoke the predicated professional expertise of educational psychology. In so far as it is a predicate of educational psychologists to deal with some children – those deemed to have 'special educational' needs and problems – then the categorizations can be heard to implicate intervention. Consequently, even in the absence of explicit requests and justifications for referral, the teachers' descriptions can, nevertheless, be heard to implicate the intervention of the educational psychologist.

Another possibility is that it is not necessary for schools to have to make explicit requests for educational psychological action nor to justify or explain the warrant for referral. This is because a category predicate of teachers, and in particular, school special needs coordinators, is their entitlement to refer when they so judge a child to have reached a stage where referral is warranted. School personnel do not have to state in so many words that they want educational intervention, that the cases are relevant for educational psychology, because the very act of referral itself serves to indicate this. Referral serves to categorize the child as somebody about which something should be done, and specifically done by the educational psychologist. The point is that the pupil is not at first referred, *then* categorized. Rather, the pupil is categorized in the act of referral itself. That is, the fact or act of referral categorizes the child as a bona fide referral. In this sense, the referral and its warrant are 'self-explicating'. It is in the course of the referral meeting that the child is then categorized in detail in terms of the varieties of category contrast discussed earlier. A reason, then, for the absence of explicit justifications and requests is that the referral itself is such a request, just as the justification is part and parcel of the description itself; it displays itself by virtue of the depiction of the seriousness of the case and of how it lies beyond what may be dealt with in the routine ways of deviance management within the school.

A further noticeable feature is the marked absence of formulative work on the part of the teachers, of explicit formulations of what the problem definitively is, with respect to which educational psychological action should now be taken. The educational psychologists would seem, as it were, to be left to formulate the upshot of these various categorizations of deviance, and thereby to produce a diagnosis of some kind which has practical remedial implications. From the transcripts analysed earlier, it is apparently sufficient for teachers to indicate that there is a problem. The descriptions designate how the problems appear to them, what the children are like in the context of the classroom, how they compare with the norm for children of the age in question, and so forth. But they offer neither psychological diagnoses nor candidate solutions. What is offered consists of the 'identifying detail', as it were, but not the 'underlying problems' of which that detail is a document.

This absence of diagnostic formulation, it may be suggested, is part of the recipient-designed character of the teachers' categorizations. That is, not only are the categorizations educationally psychologically relevant in that they deal with 'serious' problems of deviance in school which by implication lie outside the domain encompassed by the predicated obligations and competences of teachers but within the domain of educational psychological expertise, but they also display an orientation to a central asymmetrical dimension of the teacher/educational psychologist relational pair. Thus, it is one thing to describe the problem and indicate (by the various means identified earlier) its seriousness, and another to 'diagnose' the problem. The latter is a 'professional' predicate of the psychologist. It would be inappropriate, therefore, for the school personnel to presume such professional expertise by offering their own diagnoses. Accordingly, the descriptions appear to be designed to allow the educational psychologist to arrive at a formulation or conclusion about the nature of the problem and appropriate ways of reacting to it. In designing their descriptions of the problem in this way, school personnel can therefore be understood to be oriented to the special expertise which is a predicate of the educational psychologist.

Concluding Comments

This chapter has examined the use of various methods of membership categorization in and through which referrals are categorized in the context of referral meetings. The key concept in this analysis has been that of 'category contrast' which, it has been shown, is used in various ways to 'mark' the deviant character of referrals. It has also been shown that such categorizations are recipient-designed in so far as such contrasts implicate educational psychological knowledge, expertise and professional practice. Furthermore, it has been indicated that a feature of such implicativeness is the absence of explicit requests and justifications for educational psychological help. In these ways, then, the categorizations are recipient-designed as much by the absence of what is said as by the presence of particular kinds of utterance. Moreover, such recipient design is replicated in the absence of diagnostic formulations in teachers' categorizations. Instead, a wealth of particular detail is produced whose 'upshot' is left unexplicated and unformulated. This, of course, is the task of the educational psychologist as he or she takes the case forward. Thus, referral talk is not only descriptive, it is sequentially implicative; it calls on the psychologist, not only to 'find out what the problem is' through discussion with school personnel, but also to engage in practical diagnostic and possibly remedial action.

10   Being Ascribed, and Resisting, Membership of an Ethnic Group

Dennis Day

It has often been suggested that much of what it means to be social resides both in our language and in our linguistic communicative practices. Likewise, it has also often been suggested that those studying language need to bear in mind that the language people use in interaction can join them together – or, indeed, keep them apart – in particular social ways. Group categorizations, I will suggest, are both orientations to our sociality and social actions themselves. The identity categories you use in talking to the people around you are tools by which you organize your activities with them, and, at the same time, they are ways in which you constitute them as members of the same, or a different, social group.

The specific sort of group I want to focus on in this chapter is the *ethnic* group. Sometimes people around you can pick out your membership in an ethnic group in contrast to theirs and that may, so to speak, be used against you, casting doubt on your capacities to be a member of the social group pursuing the activity at hand. In my study of linguistic ethnic group categorization at two workplaces in Sweden, I have found that people react against their membership in minority ethnic groups being made relevant for the task at hand. One understanding of this reaction is that they do so in order to alleviate doubt as to their capacities as members of the social group jointly doing what the others are doing. My purpose with this chapter is to describe briefly how I have arrived at this understanding.

An important point of departure for the work presented here has been an attempt to view ethnic identity as a situated accomplishment of interlocutors (Day, 1994; Moerman, 1974). The perspective I take – like other contributors to this book – is not to ask how someone's ethnic background shapes or determines what they say, but, rather, to ask how this ethnicity becomes a resource for them – and others – to use in the business of everyday life. This view, in its turn, stems from Sacks's (e.g., 1974) work on members' social categories, in particular their use in establishing through talk 'who' interlocutors are to be seen and heard as. Further, it is in keeping with Garfinkel's (1967) mandate to distinguish between researchers' resources and the topics they choose to research.

Much previous work on ethnicity and communicative interaction has, as Widdicombe points out in Chapter 12, used ethnicity as a researcher's resource, such that the researcher's vocabulary of ethnic identity is presupposed as relevant for interlocutors. But in the work presented here, ethnic identity is a topic of investigation. Its relevance for interlocutors is an empirical question.

How people categorize each other in everyday face-to-face communicative interaction has been of particular interest within ethnomethodology and conversation analysis. A central element in these fields of study has been the notion of the membership categorization device (MCD) which, as formulated by Harvey Sacks (Sacks, 1974), refers, in particular, to common nouns whose senses rely on social categories, for example, [policeman], [mother], [deviant], and how these and associated social categories might be organized into 'natural' collections sharing family resemblance to each other (hereafter categories will be enclosed by brackets, [ ], to distinguish them from linguistic expressions of a category). Sacks's work has been further developed and applied in empirical studies by, for example, Drew (1978), Hester (1992), Jayyusi (1984), Payne (1976), Watson (1976, 1978, 1983) and, of course, reappears throughout this book.

Of special interest to Sacks, and those who have followed him, has been the following problem: given that a person may be described 'correctly' in a myriad of ways on a given occasion, what are the principles of a 'proper' description. One such principle by which a description becomes proper is through its being heard as relevant by virtue of its falling under an MCD that is relevant to the talk at hand. The types of categorization used by Sacks in his examples, and subsequently studied by his successors, have dealt with what we may call individual social categories. The orientations to people displayed in interactions have concerned them as singular agents, such as policemen, teachers, deviants, etc., usually in 'institutional' interactions. Sacks describes, however, a certain type of device which may remind one of social *groups* (although he doesn't specifically refer to them as such), namely devices which are what he calls 'duplicatively organized':

> If some population has been categorized by use of categories from the same device whose collection has the 'duplicative organization' property (e.g. 'family', 'baseball team', etc.) and a member is presented with a categorized population which can be heard as 'coincumbents' of a case of that device's unit, then hear it that way. (Sacks, 1974: 221)

What I am claiming here is that we can extend this to say that an ethnic characterization of someone is a description of that person as a member of a particular type of social group: namely, of course, an ethnic group. Thus, everyday, or members' social group concepts are of some importance in my analyses.

My characterization, and understanding, of our everyday concepts for social groups is taken from Gilbert (1989) and Jayyusi (1984) who in their turn, I believe, have been inspired by Simmel's notion of a social group as people with a 'consciousness of unity'; Rousseau's 'pool of wills' and Durkheim's 'sui generis' character of social phenomena. Jayyusi has extended Sacks's work in regard to concepts of social groups by what she refers to as 'collectivity categorizations (Jayyusi, 1984).

Jayyusi maintains there are two types of collectivity concept: one where the members are morally organized groups and the other where members are morally and self-organized, the difference being that in the latter people take it that there are certain institutionalized criteria for membership. Jayyusi uses this to distinguish groups such as 'marxists' from what she terms 'organizations', such as the Boy Scouts. But I don't think that institutionalized criteria are *necessary* for membership apart from the conventions needed for some expression, or attribution, of willingness on the part of potential members to share in some action or attribute. Ethnic groups, on the other hand, are those where institutional criteria for membership do appear to be necessary or used, in so far at least as it has been shown that deliberations concerning the criteria for membership in an ethnic group may include (for example) such things as belief in a common origin, political autonomy, a common language, and so on.

However, such criteria vary with the interactive occasion of a linguistic ethnic group categorization (e.g., Barth, 1969; Jayyusi, 1984; Moerman, 1974; Wieder and Platt, 1990). So I believe that the status of some groups as ethnic groups may also be an interactively arrived at matter. This does not imply, however, that the collection of people interlocutors are dealing with is not being oriented to as some form of social group. Rather, what is at issue is essentially how, when, if (and so forth) the group has institutionalized itself. Now let us see how these observations play out in the use made of ethnic identity in the constitution of social groups in the workplace, and in how those groups go about their social activities.

Two Workplace Studies

During 1988 and 1989, and 1992 and 1993, I conducted field studies at two factories in Sweden, Mat AB and Komponenter AB, whose workforces were composed to a large extent of immigrants (the names of the companies, as well as of all informants, are pseudonyms). Field work covered a range of activities, although the data in this chapter will come from recordings of interviews with employees, a video-recording of an arranged 'party-planning' discussion, and recordings of coffee breaks. The data are in Swedish and I will provide glosses, with a rough approximation of some speech features like overlap, in English. I have not attempted to render the Swedish into 'transcription-like' English translations, however, as that would give, I believe, a false impression of authenticity to the translations as examples of spoken language (see also Paoletti's treatment of her Italian data in Chapter 11).

The first study was initiated through contacts at the factory who were disconcerted by problems they had implementing a job-rotation scheme. Top management personnel at the factory felt their problems were a result of workers having built ethnic 'cliques'. Initially my ambition was to show how their problems were communicative in nature, that communication between different ethnic groups had led to misunderstandings which, in their turn, had led to a breakdown in group relations. After some time at the factory, however, I found that such a description of the workplace was only one of many and that 'ethnic group' categorizations – such as a Chinese group, a Polish group, etc. – were often inappropriate and even contested categorizations.

The second workplace I studied was organized quite differently from the first one. Whereas the first workplace reminded one of a typical assembly-line, the second was designed along more innovative 'team-work' lines. I found there that ethnicity was rarely a resource in interactions among members of the work team I studied. This was obviously, however, a 'multiethnic' workplace. In fact, the very first thing the foreman of the work team I studied told me, quite spontaneously, was something like the following which I recall from memory:

> One thing I don't understand is how outsiders, [workers not involved in the work teams organization] say we're 'all white'. Look at us, I'm Finnish but a Swedish citizen, Kaarlo was born in Sweden but is a Finnish citizen, Ahmad is from Ethiopia, Aina's family is Finnish, and Johan and Björn are Swedish.

These observations led me to reconsider the notion of interethnic communication taking the following question as a point of departure: how does one go about identifying communication as interethnic from an interlocutor's perspective? In other words, how can one show that interlocutors are orienting to their communication as something we can gloss as 'interethnic communication'? My attempt to answer this question led to what I have termed ethnification processes (Day, 1994), by which I mean processes through which people distinguish an individual or collection of individuals as a member or members respectively of an ethnic group. A communicative variant of ethnification processes, linguistic ethnic group categorization, will be discussed here. One way of seeing interethnic communication from an interlocutor's perspective, then, is to view it as communication where at least one interlocutor orients to at least one other interlocutor or oneself through direct or indirect linguistic categorization as a member of a differing ethnic group. Interethnic communication in this view is the result of a particular type of social identity work in the course of intentional communicative interaction.

Linguistic Ethnic Group Categorizations

Linguistic ethnic group categorizations, I suggest, ascribe people to a particular sort of social group, namely an ethnic group. I take it that to categorize a person as a member of an ethnic group is to say he or she is ready to share in some action or attribute with other members and there is some particular institutionalized collection of 'owned' characteristics, such as a shared history, common language, etc., which follow from this (for an analysis of cultural resources as 'owned', see Sharrock and Anderson, 1982).

A speaker can categorize a person directly, by referring to him or her with a lexically obvious ethnic group label such as 'Swede'. Alternatively, a speaker may succeed in categorizing someone into a certain linguistic ethnic group not by direct naming, but, more subtly, by some oblique work in his or her description of some *other* person or thing. That description may serve to set up what I will term a case of special relevance. The description is now as it were 'in the air' and will be taken to be relevant to the participants in the group. That is to say, rather formally: if among a group of interlocutors where at least one interlocutor A is describable as a member of X ethnic group and someone ethnically categorizes something or someone other than A as of an X ethnic group type, then X ethnicity can be taken to be of special relevance for A given that neither A nor any other interlocutor has any other special attachment to the thing or person ethnically categorized. I exemplify such a categorization from the 'party planning' activity below.

(1) Party planning

```
58  →  M:     eh entertainment one could have chin chon
59  →         huang ((laughter)) but it's a little
60            hard
61     MA:    mm
62     T:     yeah it is
63     M:     entertainment first and then we can take
64            which food and drink and then entertainment,
65            we'll take it last
66     MA:    ⌈yeah
67     T:     ⌊mm

       M:     eh:(0.5) underhållning (.) man skulle kunna
              ha med chin chon huang (skratt) men det
              är lite svårt.
       MA:    mm:,
       T:     ah!>det är det<
       M:     underhållning (0.2) å först å sen ska vi ta
              vilken mat (.) å drick o sen underhållning. det
              tar vi sist.
       MA:    ⌈ja!
       T:     ⌊mm
```

At lines 58–9, Malia (M) suggests that at the party they have 'chin chon huang' for entertainment. I take this to be Malia's guess at what a Chinese expression might be like. In this way, Malia has initiated an 'identity-rich puzzle' (Schenkein, 1978; see also the discussion of Schenkein's analysis of such puzzles in Chapter 1 of this book). By using a stereotypically 'Chinese-like', but still rather ambiguous, expression, she implicitly nominates anyone with appropriate expertise to clarify, or comment on the proposal – and, among these participants, that person is potentially MA or T. MA passes the turn with a minimal 'mm' while T (Tang) takes it up only slightly less minimally; it is surely hearable that were she to pass further comment on 'chin chon huang', Tang would identify herself as a member of the linguistic category group Malia has thrown into the air. I take Malia's expression 'chin chon huang', then, to be an example of linguistic ethnic group categorization by special relevance. There is a suggestion of what I assume is Chinese entertainment among a group where there is one interlocutor, Tang, who, for others there, can be described as Chinese. Thus, the suggestion is made to be of special relevance for Tang.

Making Linguistic Social Group Categorizations Relevant

In the introduction I suggested that linguistic social group categorizations are relevant, or can be made relevant, to two sorts of things. First, linguistic social group categorizations may be relevant to the social activity that interlocutors are pursuing, and I shall call that *activity relevance* (and for a general elaboration of this view of relevance, see Allwood, 1980). On the other hand, linguistic ethnic group categorizations can also be relevant to the constitution of the social group pursuing the social activity at hand, and I shall call that *group relevance*. In this section I will discuss these two notions of relevance, beginning with activity relevance.

During the course of a piece of activity, somebody might propose a categorization of a 'non-interacting' individual or collection of individuals. The candidate linguistic ethnic group categorization is a partial description of those others' individual characteristics. Linguistic and extra-linguistic context can be viewed in terms of a set of intuitive pragmatic parameters such as purpose, role, preceding discourse, and so forth. For example, an ethnic group categorization may be relevantly tied to the prior utterance, or the role of an interlocutor, and so on. An intricate web of relevance ties might be oriented to by interlocutors for any linguistic ethnic group categorization. That is to say, it is up to the local participants to gauge how it is that the candidate linguistic ethnic group category is relevant to the activity currently at hand. The point I am making is that for someone to bring up that sort of categorization, even of people outside the interaction, can have very specific local relevancies.

To illustrate what I mean, consider the following excerpts from recordings of coffee breaks at Komponenter AB. As social activities at the workplace, coffee breaks can be roughly characterized as affording the possibility of maintaining amicable relations between workers. This is shown in other analyses of this and other coffee-break interactions. Individuals may, of course, have other purposes with the coffee break. However, this does seem to be the major *joint* purpose. The determination of linguistic ethnic group categorizations can be seen as an analysis of their activity relevance. After the excerpts I shall present a suggestion as to how their relevance is tied to the parameters of the social activities of which they are a part.

(2)   Lamb fat

```
 1        T:     what did you say one did?
 2        A:     melt
 3        T:     ah the fat there then
 4        A:     yea drink it up (laughter) then that's
 5               it one (2) one melts it
 6   →    T:     what the hell is this is it something
 7   →           one does in Sweden or abroad or
 8        A:     They do it abroad
 9        T:     I see
10   →    K:     Ethiopia
11        A:     no, the whole wor⌈ld (3) melt it
12        M:                   ⌊in Sweden
13        A:     yes they do (   )

          T:     vad sa du att man gör?
          A:     smälta
          T:     ah fettet där då=
          A:     =ja drycka upp den HAHAAhahahaha sen
                 är det kört (2) smälter man den
          T:     va fan kan det vara för nåt är det nåt
                 man gör i Sverige eller utomlands eller'
          A:     utomlands dom göra
          T:     ahh
          K:     etiopia
          A:     nah det är hela värl⌈den (3) smälta det
          M:                   ⌊i sverige
          A:     naa det finns (   )
```

In this excerpt, Ahmad (A) has just mentioned that if one wants to gain weight, then one can drink liquefied lamb fat. His contribution follows previous talk on the same topic. At line 6 Tommy (T) asks Ahmad if drinking lamb's fat is practised in Sweden or abroad, to which Ahmad responds that it is done abroad. Kaarlo (K) specifies Ahmad's answer by saying that it is done in 'Ethiopia' (line 10). Ahmad takes this as meaning only in Ethiopia and states that it is done all over the world (line 11). Matti then seemingly questions the implication in the assertion by Ahmad that this is done in Sweden (line 12). Ahmad then confirms that this is the case (line 13).

The discussion here as such involves locating a particular practice geographically and culturally. The first distinction raised in this regard is Tommy's question at line 7 if the practice is to be heard as located in Sweden, as a geographical and cultural place, or 'abroad', which we must take culturally and geographically as the negation of 'Sweden', that is as non-'Swedish' and non-'Sweden'. In a weak sense, I believe Tommy's question concerning whether the practice is done in Sweden or abroad could be taken as ethnifying Ahmad, given that such a question might not arise so quickly between two 'Swedes'. At any rate, Tommy's question certainly sets up Kaarlo's further specification of the place where people drink lamb's fat as being Ethiopia. I take it that this is heard by Ahmad as a possible ethnic categorization of him as an Ethiopian. Further, I take this to be a case of special relevance. In distinction to other cases, however, Kaarlo is not 'suggesting' something 'Ethiopian'; rather, he is taken as 'asserting' that something, that is the practice of drinking lamb's fat, is 'Ethiopian'. That this is taken in this way hinges on Ahmad's following contribution where he denies the assertion. That is if he had taken Kaarlo's assertion to be 'Ethiopia is one place of many in the world where this is done', then negating it would be contradictory. What he is negating, then, is that the practice is ethnically Ethiopian.

In the next excerpt we see how participants deal with a 'tease' or 'joke' which plays on the Swedish language. The origin of the play on words is the Swedish expression 'sambo', which means to cohabitate. Thereafter the speakers exploit the morphemic construction of the word ('sam' meaning together and 'bo' to live) to invent new, pseudo-legitimate but jocular words. 'Bo' (to live) is added to a number of similar-sounding prefixes. Thus in 'spermbo', the 'sperm' component (which means sperm) produces the idea that a couple exists only in order to have sex; in 'särbo' ('sär' means separate), the idea is that the couple is still a couple though they do not live together; and in 'sparbo', since 'spar' means to save, the idea is that people live together only because it is cheaper.

(3) The tease

```
 9      D:     one sits out on the balcony
10             (2)
11  →   A:     what does 'sarbo' mean?
12      D:     and enjoys oneself
13             (2)
14      A:     you know
15      M:     what?
16      A:     sarbo
17             (3)
18      D:     sarbo
19      A:     mm
20      J:     sor
21      A:     yeah
22      J:     bo (2) no (1) in what context?
```

23		(2)
24	A:	Those people, like people say, a woman
25		and a man, they for example don't live
26		together, they, they meet occasionally ( )
27		a married couple maybe, they live in
28		different apartments, what's that
29		called?
30	D:	särbo (laughter)
31	A:	it's 'särbo' right?
32	D:	((laughs))
33	J:	⌈and it's
34	M:	⌊and its spermbo too
35	J:	that's what it becomes
36	M:	spermbo
38		(1)
39	A:	not 'sambo'
40	M:	spermbo
41	D:	spermbo ((laughs))
42	A:	is that in Finnish or what?
43	M:	no, in Swedish

	D:	sitter man gärna ute på balkongen
		(2)
	A:	vad betyder sarbo?=
	D:	=friska upp sig
		(2)
	A:	du vet
	M:	va?
	A:	SArbo
		(3)
	D:	SARbo?
	A:	mm
	J:	sor=
	A:	=yea=
	J:	=bo (2) nej (1) vilken sammanhäng?
		(2)
	A:	dom folk (.) det är man säger (.) ens en
		kvinna å en man (.) dom som till exempel
		inte bor ihop (1) dom (1) dom kommer att
		träffas kanske nån gång ( ) gift par
		kanske dom bor i olika lägenheter, vad
		kallas man det?
	D:	särbo ha ha ha ha
	A:	det är särbo va?
	D:	HA HA HA HA ha ha ha
	J:	⌈å det
	M:	⌊spermbo är det
	J:	det är så det blir
	M:	SPErmbo
		(1)

```
A:      inte sambo
M:      SPERMbo
D:      spermbo ha ha ha ha ha ha
A:      det är på finska eller?
M:      nej (.) på svenska
```

As this excerpt begins, D has been talking about sitting outside. Ahmad (A) looks up from the newspaper he is reading and, at line 11, asks the others what the word 'särbo' means. He is taken to be saying the non-word 'sarbo' and, because of this, no one can give him an answer. Matti (M), at line 34, gives his rendition of what 'särbo' means with an analogous neologism 'spermbo', alluding to the fact that people who are 'särbo' may still have intimate relations. Ahmad does not catch the expression 'spermbo'; rather, he hears 'sambo' (a conventional term for cohabitation without marriage). Matti repeats the term 'spermbo', to which Ahmad responds with the questions 'is that in Finnish, or what?' Thereafter – not shown – there are various attempts to clear up the matter of 'särbo' by spelling it, pronouncing it slowly and emphatically, and so on.

If one hears the various attempts to correct and otherwise comment on Ahmad's 'särbo' as concerning a 'foreigner's' Swedish, then this example can be taken to demonstrate an ethnic categorization of Ahmad by means of special relevance. The case of special relevance is set up by an implicit mentioning of Ahmad's Swedish as being 'non-Swedish' or 'foreign', which allows for the inference that the same is true of Ahmad. His question to Matti concerning Finnish is, in its turn, an indirect ethnic categorization of Matti, that is his ability to answer the question hinges on his being 'Finnish'.

Focusing on the pragmatic parameters of the coffee break as a social activity, the following ties of relevance between activity parameters and the linguistic ethnic group categorizations can be suggested. As noted above, the purpose of the activity of the coffee break can be glossed as maintaining amicable relations among colleagues. In the 'lamb fat' excerpt, the categorization can be seen as relevantly tied to such a purpose in the following way: in order to 'normalize' relations among co-workers, the most ethnically distinct co-worker's 'deviant' behaviour should be explained as arising from his or her ethnicity. In 'the tease' excerpt we might see the tie of relevance as follows: in order to maintain good relations among co-workers, the most ethnically distinct co-worker's ethnic background should be joked about. The basis for this type of reasoning would seem to be that amicable relations are brought about by somehow being able to explain or rationalize each other's behaviour.

In telling a joke as well as in 'normalizing relations', interlocutors can be seen in terms of pragmatic or discursive roles. Ahmad can be seen in the role of 'butt' in the 'tease' extract. His distinction, that is, as the target of the tease in this case, is his purported ethnicity. Thus an ethnic categorization can be seen as relevantly tied to his role. In 'lamb fat', Ahmad, again being the most 'distinct' co-worker, is the co-worker whose behaviour is to be explained. His distinction is his ethnicity; thus an ethnic categorization of him is relevantly tied to his role of 'the one to be explained'. Other activity parameters which may be involved in relevance relations include artefacts of the activity and the physical circumstances in which the activity takes place. The linguistic code with which interlocutors communicate can be seen as one such artefact. In the 'tease' extract above, it is the foreign accent of the most ethnically distinct co-worker that may be joked about. Thus a characteristic (the foreign accent) of the artefactual linguistic code helps to make relevant the ethnic membership of an interlocutor. As for physical circumstances we might say that in the 'lamb fat' episode the 'non-Swedish' geographic origin of a practice interprets that practice as an ethnic practice and thus, again, helps to make relevant the ethnic membership of an interlocutor.

Ascription of Membership as a Prerequisite for Group Activity

Linguistic ethnic group categorizations, being descriptions of people as members of a social group, may also be seen as relevant to the prerequisite constitution of the social group jointly pursuing the social activity at hand. From this perspective it is possible to talk of the prerequisites for being a member of a social group in conjunction with the pursuance of a social activity.

A first concern for presumptive members/interactants would be whether a candidate member/interactant can be taken to have committed him- or herself to taking part in the interaction. A second concern would be if he or she can be trusted to pursue the joint purpose of the interaction. A final concern would be the availability to him or her of resources for achieving the joint purpose. I will term these three concerns 'prerequisite conditions' with the understanding that they are prerequisite for participation in a social activity.

The first prerequisite noted above can be seen as dealing with establishing oneself as ready for membership in a social group; the second with having that membership ratified, that is that one will cooperate as a group member; and the third with the availability of resources to use the social activities of that group. In brief, then, we can talk of readiness, trust and resources as explorable dimensions of social groups in relation to social activities. These are, of course, matters which have to be done interactionally – in visible signs and in talk. And, equally, they can all be *resisted*, and in the same way. This is what I shall be showing in the workplace talk below.

Resistance to Ethnic Group Categorizations

On almost every occasion where a speaker offered or asserted an ethnic categorization of an interlocutor, that interlocutor resisted it in some way. I noted five different ways in which resistance was done.

1   One can Dismiss the Relevance of the Category

Consider, for example, Xi's comment (at line 54 in extract (4) below), which might be glossed as her saying that they need not have Chinese food on her account.

(4)   Party planning

```
51    L:      don't we have something that, one can eat
52            that, China or
53    R:      Chinese food is really pretty good
54    X:      haha ( ) it doesn't matter, I'll eat anything
55    R:      ah (that's [what I that)
56    L:                 [yeah, but this concerns everyone
57            doesn't it?

      L:      har vi inte nånting som man kan äta som'(.)
              kina eller
      R:      kinamat är i och för sig bra
      X:      haha ( ) spelar ingen roll jag äter allt
      R:      ah: (det⌈jag som)
      L:               ⌊ja men det gäller alla dom andra
              också va?
```

Lars (L) suggests that they have Chinese food (lines 51–2) at the party, a suggestion which Rita (R) upgrades but neither directly refuses nor accepts. It would appear that it is left for Xi (X) to decide whether what Lars has said is a suggestion which projects an acceptance or refusal. The suggestion may be taken to be of special relevance for Xi by how she responds to it – 'haha, it doesn't matter, I'll eat anything' (line 54). For Lars to suggest 'Chinese food' among this group of interlocutors, where Xi may be taken as 'Chinese', is to make the suggestion specially relevant for her. Her response at line 54 indicates that this was indeed the way it was heard. If this were not the case, then her response that she will eat anything could be heard as a literal, if obtuse, acceptance of the suggestion of Chinese food. Lars, however, does not appear to hear Xi's utterance this way; rather, he hears her response as not wanting Chinese food (line 57). The fact that she says it does not matter can be heard as a denial of the relevance of the ethnic category to which she is being ascribed.

2   One can Minimize the Supposed 'Difference' between Categories

Consider, in extract (5), what we can make of Xi's utterance at line 120 about 'light beer and just soda':

(5) Party planning

```
109   L:      that one has wine and normal drinks too,
110           right, of course like a party
```

111		((writing))
112		that's what we have at least here in
113		Sweden one drinks wine, that's of course
114		what ⌈one wants
115	R:	⌊of course, it's like different that
116		⌈to drink
117	L:	⌊what does one drink in what does one
118		drink
119		((points))
120	X:	⌈don't drink wine but light beer or just (soda)
121	L:	⌊no beer does one drink that
122		((writes))
123	X:	yeah light beer a
124	L:	yea one drinks lightbeer
125		((writes))
126	X:	ah
127		(0.6)
128	L:	that's good now we know what we're going
129		to eat and drink then

L:	att man har vin å dri' vanlig dricka också
	va?=givetvis (0.1) som en fest (.) det har
	((skriver))
	vi' har vi i sverige i alla fall (.) att man
	dricker vin.å de⌈vill man ju ( )
R:	⌊JA VISST det är (som olika)
	som ( ) att⌈DRICKa
L:	⌊ >vad dricker man i:<(.)vad
	dricker
	man
	((peckar))
X:	⌈( ) drickar inte vin men LÄTTöl eller bara (läsk)
L:	⌊nej: ÖL.(.)dricker man det?
	((skriver))
X:	ja lättöl=
L:	= ja lättöl dricker man.
	((skriver))
X:	ah
	(0.6)
L:	ja det är bra.(.) då vet vi vå vi ska äta å
	dricka då?

This example is taken from a sequence of party planning where interlocutors are discussing what to drink at the planned party. There is some
disagreement over what should be drunk. Lars's (L) utterance in lines 117–
18 can be heard as containing a question concerning what people drink in
Xi's (X) country of origin ('what does one drink in . . .' (>vad dricker man
i:<(.)). This implies of course that there is some reason to ask, and makes
'difference' very relevant. Were Xi to agree with the full range of things on

which 'her' category differs from 'his' (i.e., the full range of things drunk in one place and not the other), then the category differential would be acknowledged at its maximum. Her response 'don't drink wine but light beer or just (soda)' can be heard, I think, as a politely mitigated assertion that things are not really so different; certainly they don't drink wine, but they do indeed drink beer, if only light beer. In this way, I propose that Xi resists Lars's ethnic categorization of her, in the sense that she is resisting the full difference he is implying in the behaviour of the two ethnic categories.

3 One can Reconstitute the Category so that one is Excluded

In extract (6), again from the 'party planning' session, consider Clara's refusal of a turn to speak at line 33.

(6) Party planning

1	A:	oh god what'll we do with this
2		((gesture with hands))
3	C:	this is crazy this here
4		((laughter))
5	A:	I ⌈don't understand much I
6	M:	⌊yea it there's the camera
7 →	A:	I don't understand much, have to find a
8		good ⌈Swede or
9	M:	⌊of course
10	A:	they can ⌈talk a lot can't they
11	M:	⌊um
12	C:	that's what I told him too
13	A:	⌈yeah
14	M:	⌊they're filming now
15	C:	they're filming
16	A:	We just
17		(0.2)
18	M:	they'll listen to what we say
19		((laughter))
20	A:	we just talk
21		((laughter))
22	A:	talk like this
23		((gestures))
24	M:	OK a party's not a bad thing
25		but
26		((snickers))
27	A:	not a real party just talk,
28		right
29	M:	yeah yeah yeah
30	C:	we'll plan one yea
31	A:	just plan, who, you start
32		((laughter))

33	→	C:	no you start
34			*((points to A))*
35		A:	no I can't, I gotta go buy some food
36			*((laughter))*

	A:	( ) gud (.) hu r man göra?=med detta,=
		((gester med händerna))
	C:	=( ) de inte klokt de hår.
		((skratt))
	A:	ja::ja ⌈förstå(r) inte mycke:, JA.
	M:	⌊ja de (re ka)(.)där ä kameran,
	A:	ja förstå(r) inte mycke, måste hitta en lite
		bra ⌈svensk eller
	M:	⌊visst.
	A:	dom ka:n ⌈prata mycke: elle hur?
	M:	⌊um:
	C:	va de jag sa te han också
	A:	⌈ja:.
	M:	⌊de-dom fi-filma de göra dom nu
	C:	filmar dom?
	A:	VI: BARA:,
		(0.2)
	M:	dom så ( ) lyssna på ( ) vi säger
		((skratt))
	A:	vi ve'vi bara prata ME:,
		((skratt))
	A:	prata så:,
		((gester))
	M:	okej.(.) det är inte så dumt att göra fest?
		men. (.)
		((fnyser))
	A:	>inte riktigt < fe:st,>bara pratar ELLER
		HUR?<
	M:	ja. jaja.
	C:	vi ska planera en ja.M:
	A:	planera bara (.) vem sk' du börjar.
		((skratt))
	C:	nee, du börja?.
		((pekar ut))
	A:	nej ja kan inte >jag-jag ska handla mat<
		((skratt))

I take this initial assessment at lines 7–8 by Ang (A) of needing someone Swedish and who speaks Swedish to be an indirect ethnic categorization of Clara (C). Clara agrees with the assessment at line 12. At line 33, however, Clara declines Ang's request to talk first. For the next five minutes or so of the interaction (not shown here) Clara is silent, a behaviour for which she is strongly admonished by Ang and Merit (M). My understanding of this is that Ang had expected Clara to take the lead with regard to talking. Her approval of Ang's assessment at lines 7 to 8 lay the grounds for an inference by Ang that Clara would do so. In other words, Ang conceives of Clara as a Swede and that, since Clara agrees that a Swede is needed for the talking, Clara, as the only 'Swede' available, should be the one to do so. Further, it seems that a central feature of the [Swede] category for Ang is [speaks Swedish well]. We might then plausibly see in Clara's response to the request to start talking some resistance to the categorization.

4   One can Ethnify the Ethnifier

Take as an example Ahmad's 'in Finnish' directed to Matti at line 42.

(7) The tease

```
39    A:    not 'sambo'
40    M:    spermbo
41    D:    spermbo ((laughter))
42    A:    is that in Finnish or what?
43    M:    no, in Swedish
44    K:    no
45    D:    ( ) (ssperm)bo
46    L:    you might as well go and buy a sperm
47          container now ( )

      A:    inte sambo
      M:    SPERMbo
      D:    spermbo ha ha ha ha ha ha
      A:    det är på finska eller?
      M:    nej (.) på svenska
      K:    nej
      D:    ( ) (sperm)bo
      L:    det är lika bra du stickar iväg och köper en
            spermattrap nu ( )
```

I take Ahmad's (A) question at line 42 to Matti (M) – whether 'spermbo' is Finnish – as an example of resistance by way of a counter ethnic categorization in reaction to an ethnic categorization of Ahmad by means of special relevance. As I noted earlier, the case of special relevance is set up by an implicit mentioning of Ahmad's Swedish as being 'non-Swedish' or 'foreign' which allows for the inference that the same is true of Ahmad. I do not take Ahmad's question to Matti to be a request for information; rather, it is rhetorical. In my time at Komponenter AB I never heard Matti, or any others, speak Finnish in such circumstances (and only on two occasions otherwise). Thus, Ahmad's question to Matti can be heard as a reminder to Matti that he is not Swedish either.

5   One Can Resist 'Ethnification' by Actively Avoiding It

Take as an example Tang's response to the 'chin chon huang' puzzle we saw earlier, and repeated in extract (8) below.

(8) Party planning

```
58      M:      eh entertainment one could have chin chon
59  →           huang ((laughter)) but it's a little
60              hard
61      MA:     mm
62      T:      yeah it is
63      M:      entertainment first and then we can take
64              which food and drink and then entertainment,
65              we'll take it last
66      MA:     ⌈yeah
67      T:      ⌊mm

        M:      eh:(0.5) underhållning (.) man skulle kunna
                ha med chin chon huang ((skratt)) men det
                är lite svårt.
        MA:     mm:,
        T:      ah!>det är det<
        M:      underhållning (0.2) å först å sen ska vi ta vilk
                en mat (.) å drick o sen underhållning. det
                tar vi sist.
        MA:     ⌈ja!
        T:      ⌊mm
```

As noted above, I take Malia's (M) expression 'chin chon huang', together with its reception by Tang (T), to be another example of ethnic categorization by special relevance. Malia's downgrade of her suggestion to have 'chin chon huang' at line 59 ('but it's a little hard') supplies Tang with the means to resist her ethnic categorization. Rather than going into what 'chin chon huang' might be, she opts to agree with Malia that it would be difficult to implement 'chin chon huang'. I take this as a way to resist ethnification which might be characterized as 'interactive avoidance'. By this I mean that Tang has utilized resources specific to communicative interaction in order to make her resistance a relevant next contribution. She has avoided responding to the previous assessment meant for her, allowed Malia to self-repair through her upgrade, and then responded to that upgrade.

Resistance to Ethnification

To the best of my knowledge there has been no discussion of resistance as I have used the term here in empirical studies of intercultural communication. A general characteristic of this resistance is its 'everyday' nature. It occurs as brief counters to often subtle ethnification processes in ongoing social activities; and, interestingly enough, such counters seem to produce a certain turbulence among participants. On most occasions they seemed to be in some way disruptive to the smooth flow of talk. Table 10.1 collects

TABLE 10.1 *Resistance to ethnic categorization, and subsequent talk*

Extract	Ethnic Categorization Resistance	Subsequent talk
(4)	Xi's 'it doesn't matter, I'll eat anything'	Lars's 'but this concerns everyone doesn't it?'
(6)	Clara's reconstitution of the ethnic category	Clara's minimal participation in the activity until she is admonished.
(7)	Ahmad's rhetorical question which ethnically categorizes Matti	Matti's 'answering' of the question in the negative.
(8)	Tang's interactive avoidance	Malia's upgrade 'but it's a little hard' and closing down of the topic '. . . we can take which food and drink and then entertainment, we'll take it last'

together, and gives something of a gloss on, the disruption visible in some of the extracts above.

Scott (1985, 1990) and de Certeau (1984) have described resistance in ways similar to what I have in mind here. Their focus, however, has not been on the realization of this resistance in face-to-face communication. An understanding of resistance which I believe is suited to the interactions I have analysed would be as follows: resistance is the reaction of active agents who are inextricably, and perhaps non-voluntarily, involved in the social activity which paradoxically exteriorizes them. Resisting this exteriorization means seizing fleeting opportunities within the activity, and using the tools which that activity provides, to do two things: to signal that what their fellow interactants are doing is making choices about them, and to voice an opinion about those choices.

I believe the idea of exteriorization can also be understood in terms of the prerequisite conditions mentioned above. It will be recalled that these requirements consisted of (i) readiness, (ii) trust, and (iii) resources. I do not believe the acts of resistance can be so easily seen as relevantly tied to the parameters of the social activities in which they occur, as was the case for the ethnic categorizations themselves. Rather, I believe they can be seen as relevantly tied to the trust requirement. This is to say that the resistance offered them does not seem to be the type of resistance one would offer if one merely failed to have, or disagreed over, the viability of some activity resource, in this case an ethnic identity of an interlocutor. The interlocutors who resist ethnic categorization are not just resisting the relevance of their purported ethnic identities for the task at hand. Rather, they are resisting the implication that they are not due the trust one needs to be a member of the social group constituted in the social activity. That these interlocutors have clearly been ratified earlier, and that their membership is now being questioned, accounts for the paradoxical situation of being both in and out, or potentially out, of the group.

The participatory status of interlocutors, that is whether one is 'in' or 'out' of, or somewhere in between, an interaction has received considerable treatment from Erving Goffman (e.g., Goffman, 1981). In particular Goffman has focused on how people signal what I have termed their readiness and trust. He has also shown how one may seclude oneself from interaction. Goffman's work takes as its point of departure the individual interlocutor and his or her 'face' and has especially emphasized the non-verbal particularities of social interaction. What I have proposed above concerning interlocutors' readiness and the trust afforded them is consistent with Goffman's notion of face. Extending the analogy, we can say that face for an interlocutor within a given communicative interaction concerns his or her membership within the social group constituted in and by the interaction. There is little to go on in Goffman's work, however, for an explication of my cases of resistance to ethnic categorization. There is little analysis of actual linguistic communication in Goffman's work, thus there is little demonstration of the interactive qualities of interlocutor face. Furthermore, Goffman's focus has most often been on the initiation of joint activity, whereas here I have been interested in its maintenance and in threats of its termination. It is perhaps telling in this regard that Clara and Tang (in extracts (6) and (8) respectively), after being ethnically categorized by others, minimally participated in the ongoing social activities until repair work was done.

The argument that resistance is directed against being exteriorized from a social group can similarly be made with the help of Radcliffe-Brown's analysis of teasing:

> Any serious hostility is prevented by the playful antagonism of teasing, and this in its regular repetition is a constant expression or reminder of that social disjunction which is one of the essential components of the relation, while the social conjunction is maintained by friendliness that takes no offence at insult. (in Kuper, 1977: 231)

In this view, teasing expresses the social disjunction giving rise to teasing and that taking teasing in light-hearted fashion ensures the social conjunction a teasing relationship affords. Thus, in being described as an outsider, one can remain an insider. The problem here for Ahmad and for Tang (taking Malia's 'chin chon huang' as an attempt at humour) seems to be that they have no faith in Radcliffe-Brown's analysis, that is, that the disjunction which is expressed in the teasing is merely 'playful'.

Concluding Comments

My purpose in this chapter was to address what is an important consequence of the power of categorization – that it can be used by one person somehow to disqualify another person from the social group in which they both have a candidate place. As with the rest of the contributors to this book, I took it that such a thing was not to be found in people's retrospective reports, nor in formal complaints, and in secondary data generally; or, at least, not with the same degree of immediacy as in the very acts of speech that took place in live interaction. In looking over episodes from live talk at work, I found that people could point up – directly or subtly – the relevance of a participant's membership of a linguistic ethnic group (Chinese, say, or Ethiopian) in a way that could be heard as being in contrast to the 'local' linguistic ethnic category (Swedish) and thereby casting doubt on their competence or qualification to be a member of the group pursuing the activity at hand. What I think is especially interesting is that the transcripts also reveal that in such circumstances people react against such ascription, and I detailed five ways in which they did so. It is not too much, I think, to call this sort of reaction 'resistance': it is not, of course, the colourful and vivid sense that resistance sometimes means, but in its very quietness and subtlety it is just as heroic. After all, what is being resisted is not simply some casual joke or triviality: what is at issue is the person's place in the activity of the group and their participation in the life it gives.

Handling 'Incoherence' According to the Speaker's On-sight Categorization

Isabella Paoletti

Membership of gender and age categories is – generally – immediately determinable on sight (Jayyusi, 1984: 68). Nevertheless, just because a category is immediately available for use does not guarantee that it *will* be used by the people involved. Other chapters in this book have shown how participants' orientation to particular identities can be evidenced by their use of category labels or by their mobilization of the category-bound features that go along with them. What I want to show here is that on-sight categories can also be made live through the way that people deal with some emergent property of the talk that develops between them, a feature which can be treated either as neutral or as in some way attributable to the speakers' identities. That is what I shall be examining in this chapter, as I focus on how people handle a particularly troublesome feature that is occasionally encountered in talk – incoherence.

The interest in incoherent talk is that it affords – or requires – some uptake or reaction by its hearers; even were they to overlook it, that would be indicative of the sense they make of the talk, or of the speaker who produced it. The aim of this chapter, then, is to look at the identity implications of incoherence, that is, how participants handle talk which seems to consist of seemingly incomplete, inappropriate, and contradictory answers and accounts. I shall be showing how inspection of the talk shows us that identities are indeed mobilized in dealing with this dynamic property of interaction, and that at the heart of the participants' activities is the relation between the on-sight category of 'age' and its attendant implication of incoherence as a sign of senility.

The Talk

I shall be looking at a pair of interviews which come from a corpus of interviews held with women over 50 years old and the people they cared for (Paoletti, 1997b). The study was carried out for the Social and Economic

Department of INRCA (Istituto Nazionale di Ricovero e Cura degli Anziani), Ancona, Italy. The chapter is focused on two interviews I conducted, one with an 81-year-old man being cared for by his son, and, separately, one with a 55-year-old woman looking after her husband. These two interviews are almost useless with regard to their informational content in relation to the institutional aim of the interview (that is, the description of what the caregiver and the person being cared for actually do) because of ambiguities and contradictions in the accounts. But that makes them all the more interesting for my purposes here, is because they provide a point of comparison for the interviewer's handling of the two respondents' incoherence.

I was the interviewer, and, in reading over the transcripts, I was initially struck by the difference in my behaviour in relation to dealing with incoherent accounts in the two interviews: on the one hand, to the cared-for person, I was tolerant, avoiding searching for clarification, but, on the other hand, visibly irritated and pressing for a sensible response from the caregiver. My interest now lies in making sense of those differences.

Interviews here are treated analytically as interactional encounters that can be studied to document various conversational practices, as well as instances of the identity production process (Baker, 1983, 1984; Paoletti, 1997; Silverman, 1993; Watson and Weinberg, 1982). I was confronted with various methodological problems, not least of which is the fact that the participants' very perception of incoherence seemed hard to detect, as they tended to collaborate in making the interaction run smoothly. As Garfinkel points out in relation to one of his breaching experiments: 'In the case of contradictory answers much effort was devoted to reviewing the possible intent of the answer so as to rid the answer of contradiction and meaninglessness, and to rid the answerer of untrustworthiness' (Garfinkel, 1967: 91).

Nevertheless, I want to examine incoherence, so, to some degree, I have the problem of showing what was *not* done conversationally, that is, I want to show that there were points at which an interlocutor (myself) *would have had occasion* to have treated the previous utterance as incoherent – to have sought clarification from the respondent, or challenged their vagueness, or pressed for more detail, and so on – but did not do any of these things. What I propose to do is take the line of the competent cultural member: that is, to identify the sorts of utterances which strike me as incomplete, vague, off-target and so on, and then take the analysis from there. I am at the mercy, of course, of fellow-readers, and they may simply disagree that the talk I focus on is indeed vague, and so on. Non-Italian readers might ask whether, if they use my on-sight classifiability as an Italian, they are competent to agree or disagree with my judgements of Italian talk, even if I give a gloss in English. I acknowledge that there is a standing problem here, as there is perhaps for any like analysis, not excluding several in this book (see, for example, Antaki's discussion of his British speakers' use of the Dickensian fictional character-name 'Fagin', Chapter 5, and

Widdicombe's account of gothics and punks, Chapter 4). But the best thing seems to me to be to proceed, and see what we jointly make of the data.

Constructing the Senile Older Person

In the analysis of the interview that follows, I want to show that 'being senile' is a collaborative construction, achieved by interlocutors in the course of the development of the interview. It is mainly produced by the interviewer's avoidance of asking for clarification when confronted with hearably incoherent answers and accounts.

Previous studies have pointed out how the ageing process is interpreted in a 'natural decrement' perspective (Coupland, Coupland and Giles, 1991: 3). Membership in the category 'old' has negative implications. For example, disclosure of chronological age is reported to be used to account for ill-health (Coupland and Coupland, 1989, 1994). In fact, positive self-images are achieved by older people through distancing from the category (Coupland, Coupland, and Giles, 1991; Paoletti, 1998b), or rejecting it. Such a phenomenon is known as 'denial of ageing' (Bultena and Powers, 1978; Coupland, Coupland and Giles, 1991; Kamler, 1995; Paoletti, 1998b).

Older people's activities and talk are inspected for signs of senescence (Carver and de la Garza, 1984: 72). Younger interactants have been shown to use over-accommodative speech (Coupland, Coupland and Giles, 1991: 36), and, moreover, to project on to their older interlocutors stereotypical images of old age. Particularly noticeable is the case reported by the Couplands and their associates in which an older woman projects two polarized identities when interacting with someone her age and a younger interlocutor. In the first case 'her projected identity is overwhelmingly one of social engagement' (Coupland, Coupland and Grainger, 1991: 195) while, in the second case, 'she aligns to the apathy/loneliness perspective' (Coupland, Coupland and Grainger, 1991: 201) assumed by the younger interlocutor. There is, then, ample social scientific evidence to bolster our intuitions that the category 'old' has some fairly set category attributions.

Paolo, Visibly 'Old'

The first interview I am going to analyse was conducted with an informant I shall refer to as Paolo. He is 81 years old, and has suffered a stroke or, using a medical term we shall see in the transcript, an 'ictus'. As a consequence, he has reduced mobility in his left arm and leg. His pronunciation is not wholly clear, and he mumbles and mutters at times (it is worth saying that understanding Paolo on first hearing was more difficult than it seems on reading the transcript of the interview, which has benefited from repeated hearings). These minor speech impediments were probably also a consequence of the stroke. Paolo lives with his son, Nando, who works in the Pensioner Trade Union. At the beginning of the interview Paolo is talking about his health problems. In this passage we see the first occasion on which Paolo says something unclear, and we also see that the interviewer makes no move to clarify it.

(1) In this and subsequent extracts, the English translation will be given first, followed by the Italian original. Only the lines in the English translation will be numbered. Note also that some transcription notation in the Italian original (e.g., prosody) has not been transferred to the English version. (For the general vexed question of using translated transcripts, see Moerman, 1988; see also Day, this volume.)

I = interviewer; P = Paulo, the respondent
```
1          P:  I had I had a a a is a issis eh eh in in in
2              ( ) well
3     →    I:  in the heart?
4          P:  four four four almost five years ago
5     →    I:  I see
6          P:  um
7          I:  and how old are you?
8          P:  me? I am (0.7) am eightyone
```

```
           P:  Ho avuto ho avuto una un un is un issis eh eh
               nel nel nel ( ) 'nsomma
           I:  nel al cuore?
           P:  quat a quat a quat son già quasi cinque anni
           I:  ho capito
           P:  um
           I:  e quanti anni ha:?
           P:  io? ne ho:: (0.7) no: o:ottantuuno
```

The first turn, 'I had a a a is a issis eh eh in in in ( ) well', includes various repetitions and the sound 'issis' is probably a rendition of the medical term 'ictus'. These turns seem to me to be reasonably characterizable as hearably incoherent. Notice what the interviewer does in the next turn (line 3). The interviewer does not ask for clarification of the problematic word, but attempts cooperatively to complete Paolo's sentence seeking confirmation, 'in the heart?' Paolo appears to continue his turn, referring to the time when the health problem occurred, 'four four four almost five years ago', without taking any notice of the preceding question. The interviewer does not seek any clarification of the problematic word, but instead she expresses understanding, 'I see', and changes topic by asking the question 'how old are you'. It is perhaps not hard to see this question, about age category membership and all the associated features it brings in train as being occasioned by the preceding troubles. It is noticeable that communication difficulties in the early stage of the interaction are immediately followed by a specific age identification move.

In the extract that follows, a central topic of the interview, that is, the description of the cared-for person's daily activities, remains unclear. No move to determine a definite sense of the information is attempted by the interviewer, although the topic is taken up repeatedly.

Contradictory Accounts

In the following extract, Paolo is describing how he spends his day. He claims that he performs various jobs around the house, but, when asked to specify the tasks involved, he starts to speak about his son. No clarification is sought by the interviewer.

(2)

```
 1        I:   and how how do you spend the day how
 2             tell me a bit about your ⌈day
 3        P:                            ⌊eh in
 4             the morning I get up I do what I am
 5             able to do like (0.7) housework
 6             (0.9) your (1.0) some (1.1) um
 7             the things (done) well ⌈(but
 8        I:                          ⌊for
 9             example what do you do what do you
10             do ⌈when
11  →    P:    ⌊he does a bit of cleaning the
12             house the floor em::::::: (2.3) outside
13        I:   and certainly your arm
14             ⌈you don't use it well
15        P:   ⌊well I do what I am able to do


 I        E:: come:: come passa la giornata co
          come: mi racconti un po' la: la
          ⌈sua giornata
          P:   ⌊he al mattino mi alzo:: faccio quello
               che sono capace di fare:: così::
               (0.7) il dovere casalingo:: (0.9)
               tua: (1.0) abbastanza (1.1) um le
               cose (fatte) 'nsomma ⌈ma::
          I:                        ⌊ad ad esempio
               cosa fa cosa fa ⌈quando:
          P:                   ⌊fa un po' di pulizia in
               casa in terra e::: m::n:::n:: (2.3)
               fuori
          I:   a fa anche 'n po' l'orto?
          P:   sì 'n po'mica tanto però perché la la
               que que qui
          I:   e certo la il braccio gli:: non
               ⌈lo usa bene
          P:   ⌊faccio quel che son capace di fare
               insomma
```

Paolo says that in the morning he does the house cleaning, 'eh in the morning I get up I do what I am able to do like (0.7) housework (0.9) your (1.0) some (1.1) um the things (done) well but'. But the interviewer's request for specification in lines 8 to 10 is answered by saying that the cleaning is done by somebody else (referred to as 'he'). I will point out here some grammatical features that are lost in the English translation of the transcript, since they help explain how the shift in reference could have been produced. The interviewer is using the polite form, that is the third-person singular, in Italian 'fa'. Starting to reply Paolo uses 'fa', indicating third-person singular, that is somebody else. Since 'faccio' is first-person singular, mishearing is impossible (notice also that back in extract (1), when the interviewer asked 'how old are you?' she used the polite form, third-person singular, and Paolo showed uncertainty about the object of the query: in fact, he asks, *me*?). The relevant issue here in extract (2) is that the interviewer, when confronted with the problematic reference shift of line 11, does not seek any clarification of what might be a cognitive problem. She continues imperturbably hinting at Paolo's *mobility* problems, 'and certainly your arm you don't use it well'. In so doing she seems to justify Paolo's inability to carry out the housework, therefore implying that somebody else is doing it. Paolo's assessment, 'I do what I am able to do' follows on from this. Shortly after, the topic of the housework is taken up again by Paolo, but the interviewer does not take the opportunity to sort out the ambiguities.

In the next passage the topic of housework is taken up once again, and once again it is not obvious either that the interviewee has formed a clear understanding of the question at issue, nor that the interviewer has sought clarification. In extract (3), Paolo is now describing housework as something that he did in the past:

(3)

```
 1        I:   what did you do before?
 2             (1.2)
 3    →   P:   before I looked after the house and
 4             everything because my wife died
 5             (0.7) (ago) 15 years ago
 6        I:   I see eh
 7        P:   um and there are only the two of us
 8             left (0.7) so
 9             (0.8)
10        I:   and therefore before you were doing
11             everything well in the house
12        P:   yes
13        I:   before
14        P:   yes
15        I:   ⌈before you got sick
16        P:   ⌊I did the house work (I had to do)
17             the shopping well everything
```

```
18        I:   of course
19        P:   and now eh
20   →    I:   and before ummm what was your job
21             em ⌈before retiring
22                ⌊before I was working for the
23             railways

          I:   che faceva prima?
               (1.2)
          P:   prima prima accudivo la casa e tutto
               quanto perché la moglie è morta::
               (0.7) (fa) quindici anni fa
          I:   ho capito eh
          P:   um e siamo rimasti noi due soli
               (0.7) e così
               (0.8)
          I:   e quindi prima pensava a tutto lei
               'nsomma alla casa
          P:   sì
          I:   prima che:
          P:   sì
          I:   ⌈che stesse male
          P:   ⌊facevo le faccende (mi toccava fare)
               le spese tutto quanto 'nsomma
          I:   certo
          P:   e adesso eh
          I:   e prima::: ummm che lavoro faceva
               e::m ⌈di andare in pensione
          P:         ⌊lavoravo in ferrovia
```

The interviewer's question at line 1 might be understandable as being a request for Paolo to expand on just exactly what tasks he did before the stroke, or, as becomes clear in line 20, to ask Paolo 'what he did' in the conventional sense of what job he had. Prior to that specification, Paolo orients to the sense of the question as being about the housework, and this might hearably be treated as a mistake, but the interviewer shows no evidence of doing so: she punctuates his talk with 'I see eh' (line 6) and with a positive, affirmative formulation at lines 10 to 11. It is only by line 20 that a putative repair to Paolo's understanding of the question is offered: 'and before ummm what was your job em before retiring'.

Understanding is an interactional achievement and it is closely related to issues of 'face' (Hamilton, 1994; Heritage, 1988). Pomerantz points out: 'If recipients fail to give a coherent response, his or her behaviour is account-able' (1984: 152). Clarifications are asked, reasons for possible misunder-standings are routinely searched and proposed by questioners. The point I am making is that what is noticeable here is the *absence* of these procedures in the interactional instances reported above. Here incoherence appears to be accounted for with 'conversational incompetence' as a category-bound feature of advanced age. To prod and probe at Paolo would be to imply he was being incoherent and would confirm his on-sight membership of the category 'old'. This is a strongly face-threatening attribution. Hence, avoidance strategies are adopted.

Partially Intelligibility and Incompleteness

In the following passage Paolo produces a partially intelligible sentence, then he makes a vague reference to retiring without specifying further. In neither case does the interviewer ask for clarification.

(4)

```
1          P:   before I was working for the
2               railways
3          I:   ah I see
4          P:   I was here in Ferrara in a in a small
5               town (1.7)(   ) everything
6               came inside there eh yes
7     →    I:   I understand ((whispering)) (1.0)
8               and then you retired and then
9          P:   yes (1.6) I made it in time (    )
10              to retire
11    →    I:   sorry?
12         P:   I just made it in time to retire
13         I:   eh yes nowadays with these reforms
14         P:   eh eh (I did lots)
15              (0.9)
16         I:   of
17         P:   yes
18              (1.2)
19         I:   I see em you were saying so that
20              there aren't aren't eh people who
21              you visit or things you do (outside)
```

```
           P:   prima lavoravo in Ferrovia
           I:   ah ho capito
           P:   ero::: qui a Ferrara in un i::::::::n a
                una piccola città (1.7) ( )
                tutto quanto veniva dentro lì e:: sì
           I:   ho capito ((bisbigliando)) (1.0) e
                poi è andato in pensione e allora:::
           P:   sì (1.6) ho fatto in tempo ( )
                andare    in pensione
           I:   come?
           P:   ho fatto appena appena in tempo di
                andare in pensione
           I:   eh sì con questi tempi con queste
                riforme
```

```
P:  eh eh (ne ho fatte)
    (0.9)
I:  della::
P:  sì
    (1.2)
I:  ho capito e:::m lei diceva:: quindi non
    non non ci sono:: eh:: persone che lei
    va a trovare o cose che fa (fuori
    della casa)
```

Although the material in lines 5 to 6 is incomprehensible, the interviewer shows some sort of expression of understanding (even if in a very low voice) and then changes the subject, asking about retirement. Again (at lines 9–10) a partially intelligible utterance is produced. This time the interviewer asks for clarification. Paolo repeats the sentence. What he says is glossed by the interviewer (line 13) as referring to the present situation in Italy, in which reforms of the pension system are under way. Notice that Paolo should have retired at least 15 years ago, given his age (81), so present reforms could not be in any way relevant to his situation, especially in reference to the expression, 'just in time'.

The false start of the interviewer and the two pauses in lines 15 and 17 express hesitation, or at least an invitation to Paolo to continue, which he does not do. Then she again acknowledges understanding, 'I see', and changes topic: 'you were saying so that there aren't aren't eh people who you visit or things you do (outside)'. Notice the various elongations observable in the Italian transcript that convey hesitation.

Paradoxically, all these episodes of Paolo's incoherence, inappropriate answering, contradictory accounts, vague and incomplete reference, are all followed by interlocutor's turns showing understanding. The phrase 'I see' seems to be marking confusion and misunderstanding, or better, it is used to re-establish communication in order to continue conversation. A new topic is established; in fact, without clarification the current topic could not be pursued.

Clarification Sought and Obtained

The next passage offers an example in which clarification *is* sought and achieved. An inappropriate answer is followed by a restatement of the question and followed by a proper reply.

(5)

```
1    I:  and so what do you do in the
2        afternoon if they don't come to visit
3        you?
4    P:  eh I sit here and we talk of this and
5        that in short about things so
```

```
6      I:   and if nobody comes ⌈to visit you
7      P:                       ⌊aha! I stay
8           here
9      I:   what do you do do you read or
10     P:   if only I could read
```

```
       I:   e quindi che fa il pomeriggio se non
            la vengono a trovare?

       P:   e mi metto seduto qui e parliamo del
            più e del meno delle cose insomma::
            così
       I:   e se non c'è nessuno
            ⌈che la viene a trovare
       P:   ⌊aha! sto qui
       I:   che fa legge o::::
       P:   magari fussi capace de legere⌋
```

In this case, Paolo's inappropriate answer at lines 4 to 5, 'eh I sit here and we talk of this and that well about things so', is followed by the repetition of the question by the interviewer. Notice that the mishearing is not pointed out, the question is simply reformulated. This time a coherent answer is produced: 'aha! I stay here', and the conversation proceeds on the same topic. 'Aha!' seems to be marking Paolo's recognition of the previous misunderstanding (see Heritage, 1984b).

All the observations above, taken together, accumulate to show that 'being senile' is a product of collaboration. It is produced by the interviewer not seeking an on-record, definitive sense of Paolo's responses, *even though what he says is hearably incoherent.* Paolo's on-sight categorizability (as being very old) affords the suspicion of him being incoherent. With such an identity hovering in the wings, to ask for clarification of faulty responses would be visibly face-threatening; so it is avoided by the interviewer.

Vania, Not 'Visibly Old'

In what follows we see the converse of the situation with Paolo. Here, in the interview with Vania, a 55-year-old caregiver, the transcript shows that I persistently pursue something that could count as a clear, on-record answer. My treatment of Vania's occasional inarticulacy is quite unlike my treatment of Paolo. Where Paolo's vagueness and contradiction was allowed to pass, Vania's is not. Her on-sight categorization, though not of a stereotypically 'young' woman – she is 55 years old – is, in the absence of any further evidence, nothing like as powerful a signal of expectable incoherence as was Paolo's.

In our first contact Vania said that she was assisting her husband who had been having various serious health problems. The interviews were mainly designed to elicit detailed descriptions of the caring practices and the effects they had on the caregiver's lifestyle and health, so it seemed that her case would be ideal. But it turned out that her interview yielded no usable information, just as it was impossible to wring recordable detail out of the interview with Paolo. In the long stretch of conversation reported in the following analysis, the description of Vania's present and past caring tasks and of her husband's health problems appears to be vague, sketchy, uncertain, in spite of repeated questions of clarification.

Vania lives with her husband and three grown-up sons. She has had a varied working life. She emigrated to Germany for some years and worked in a factory, then, back in Italy, worked as a self-employed artisan. In recent years she ran a vegetable shop but gave it up when her husband had a heart attack. In the following passage, Vania, asked about the assistance she gives to her husband, replies with a hearably inappropriate, or at least curiously expressed, account: she offers her husband's unwillingness to be present at the interview as an example of his health problems.

(6)   In this and subsequent extracts, I = interviewer; V = Vania

```
 1      I:   Now you were saying that you are
 2           giving some assistance to your
 3           husband aren't you because he hasn't
 4           been well
 5   →  V:   Yes he hasn't been very well now for
 6   →       example I told him look there is this
 7   →       lady coming I say stay here he says
 8   →       now I'm not staying because I'm
 9   →       going away ⌈(       )
10      I:                ⌊no well in fact well it is
11           understandable ((low voice))
12      V:   absolutely eh eh eh
13      I:   and and what did your husband have?
14      V:   he had a heart attack (0.9) eight
15           years ago (0.4)
16      I:   aha
17      V:   after it was OK well it was cured
18           they really found the right treatment
19   →       and (1.0) well the operation wasn't
20   →       even (0.8) necessary
21      I:   sure
22      V:   now he has to take care of his health
23           for the rest of his life

        I:   Ora:: mi diceva fa assistenza un po' a
             suo marito no che è stato poco bene
        V:   Sì e n'è stato tanto bene adè
             presempio io gl'ho detto guarda
             arriva sta signora dico rimane di
             qui dice io adesso non ce sto perché io
```

```
           vado via ⌈( )
I:                ⌊no bé infatti bè era
           logico ((a voce molto bassa))
V:         assolutamente eh eh eh
I:         e e che cosa ha avuto suo marito?
V:         lu ha avuto 'n infarto (0.9)otto anni
           fa (0.4)
I:         aha
V:         dopo::: è andata bene:: 'nsomma s' è
           curato gli hanno azzeccato
           veramente:: la cura e:: (1.0)
           'nsomma 'n c'è voluta nemmeno
           (0.8) l'operazione
I:         certo
V:         adesso se deve curà però: a vita. . .
```

In line 1, the utterance 'Now you were saying' refers to talk before the tape
recorder was switched on, and the yes/no question that follows in lines 2 to
3 is designed to elicit more on the topic of 'being a caregiver'. Vania
develops the topic of her husband's sickness, reporting as an example of his
problems his desire not to be present at the interview. This seems an
inappropriate example that is, at very best, only an indirect and allusive
indication of any medical problem, at least in a physical sense. But the
interviewer accepts the account, so we see no challenge yet.

The interviewer now redirects the conversation, asking for clarification
with a specific question on the health condition of Vania's husband, 'and
what did your husband have?' (line 13). Vania this time replies with a
commonsensically recognizable health problem: 'he had a heart attack
(0.9) eight years ago'. After the interviewer's turn acknowledgement via a
'continuer' (Schegloff, 1982), Vania proceeds with her account. In the first
part of the turn, 'after it was OK well it was cured', she appears to refer to
the heart attack, but in the second part Vania seems to mention a different
health problem, one that will turn out to be described more fully further
on: 'they really found the right treatment and (1.0) well the operation
wasn't necessary'. In fact, an 'operation' is not normally associated with
treatment for a heart attack. She does not mark the passage from one
topic to the other. No components that mark out a prior topic are
recognizable.

Contradictory Answers and Unclear Descriptions

After a brief exchange relating to the husband's needs for a controlled
lifestyle, the interviewer comes back to focusing on the topic of 'caring',
asking a specific question. In the longish passage below Vania asserts that
she is caring for her husband and develops a description of 'being silly' as
her husband's main health problem.

(7)

```
 1        I:   eh (0.4) and so you I mean when do
 2             you assist him?
 3        V:   I always assist him
 4             (0.9)
 5   →    I:   ⌈what do you mean
 6        V:   ⌊more than anything else after two
 7             years ago (1.0) for example
 8             around this time two years ago (0.6)
 9             he had a medical examination (1.7)
10             how do you call it wait eh (2.4) the
11             (low) part how do you call it cyto
12             (0.6) scopy
13        I:   aha
14        V:   and they found a polyp
15        I:   aha
16        V:   well I felt desperate
17        I:   you mean you were thinking of
18             something else
19             (1.1)
20        V:   yes and his brother being dead (1.1)
21             but that was a cancer that one when
22             those come out there is nothing to do
23             (1.5) so then I was working I had a
24             shop I had to stop it and I have to look
25   →       after him (1.2) for example there
26   →       are days when he is quite well and
27   →       days when he is really silly
28             (1.3)
29   →    I:   what do you mean?
30        V:   I don't know why
31             (2.1)
32   →    I:   ⌈what do you mean why
33        V:   ⌊(   ) stupid because either he
34             doesn't understand or he doesn't
35             want to understand (0.7) or he has
36             something on his mind
37             (0.9)
```

```
          I:   è (0.4) quindi lei::::: cioè quand' è che lo
               assiste?
          V:   io l'assisto sempre
               (0.9)
          I:   ⌈cioè
          V:   ⌊più che altro dopo:: due anni fa (1.0)
               presempio e:: di questi tempi due anni
               fa (0.6) gli hanno::: fatto:: un esame
               (1.7) come se chiama aspetti eh (2.4)
               la parte (bassa) come se chiama cisto
```

```
         (0.6) scopia
I:    aha
V:    e gli hanno trovato un polpo
I:    aha
V:    a me:: m' è caduto m'è caduto
      'nsomma: 'l mondo addosso
I:    cioè pensava a qualcos'altro
V:    sì e: essendo il fratello morto (1.1) ma
      quello era un carceroma quello era
      quando escono quelli proprio non c'è
      niente da fa (1.5) allora io dopo::
      lavoravo c'avevo 'l negozio me sò
      ritirata e devo sta attenta a lui (1.2)
      presempio c'è dei giorni che:: stà
      benino dei giorni è proprio stupidino
      (1.3)
I:    Cioè?
V:    non lo sò perché
      (2.1)
I:    ⌈cioè perché
V:    ⌊( ) stupido perché::: o non capisce
      o non vuole capire (0.7) o c' ha
      qualcosa che lu pensa
      (0.9)
```

The interviewer's initial question in lines 1 to 2, 'when do you assist him?', is, given the context of the interview, designed to elicit a catalogue of Vania's current caring practices – a list, perhaps, which would include help at bathtimes, mealtimes, and so on. But what Vania says is rather ambiguous: 'I always assist him' could be referring to the present situation, or might be referring to her whole married life. The interviewer immediately seeks clarification in line 5: 'what do you mean?' – an unusually blunt question, certainly compared to those in the interview with Paolo – and Vania starts talking about the problem her husband had two years before, showing that she interpreted the question in a life-course perspective. Then she describes how his health problems changed her life.

There is more bluntness a little later in the same extract. In lines 25 to 27 Vania produces an account of the nature of her husband's health problems that does not seem pertinent. She says, for example, 'there are days that he is quite well and days when he is really silly'. The phrase 'è proprio stupidino', 'he's being silly', is not commonsensically recognizable as an institutionally legitimate description of sickness, in the physical sense, either in Italian or in English. There is a pause, then the interviewer asks for clarification, again rather bluntly: 'what do you mean?' Vania starts replying, then pauses, 'I don't know why, (2.1)'. This longer pause is followed by the interviewer's repetition of the question, pressing for a reply. Such questions are aimed to furnish the gist of the conversation, that is to formulate it (Garfinkel and Sacks, 1970). Given the closeness of the two questions, the pauses project communication problems.

In the next passage Vania describes effects of treatment that are more recognizable as health problems, but she seems unable to produce an articulated description of them; she just sustains the interviewer's suggestions.

(8)

```
 1        V: the day after and also for a week or
 2           so I had to always be careful because
 3           he (1.1) had a skid in his car
 4           too then I had to (yell) at him
 5           sometimes he scolds me because you
 6           once did that once of course but
 7           there was a reason for it (0.7) me
 8           being close I can see it can't I?
 9     → I: but what does he do that is
10           particularly
11        V: eh I don't know his head I don't I
12           don't in my opinion he has something
13     → I: but has he some moments of mental
14           ⌈absence
15        V: ⌊eh moments yes yes
16     → I: but how does it happen does he faint
17           or ⌈(is it only a mental absence)
18        V:    ⌊no no he doesn't faint it is his
19           head yes just a little bit yes a little
20           bit ⌈(well)
21        I:    ⌊ehe

          V: 'I giorno dopo e anche per 'na
             settimana dovevo sta' sempre
             attento perchè::: lue (1.1)
             sbandava anche con la macchina
             allora dovevo  (gridagli) qualche
             volta me ripiglia lu perché a  tu na
             volta me facevi così na volta egià ma
             c'era 'I motivo (0.7) io stando
             vicino se vede  no?
          I: certo ma che cosa fa particolarmente
             di:
          V: e:: non lo so la testa non non io
             secondo me c'ha qualcosa
          I: ma c'ha dei momenti ⌈di assenza
          V:                      ⌊eh momenti
             sì sì
          I: cioè ma come sviene oppure
             ⌈(solo un'assenza mentale)
          V: ⌊no no non sviene è proprio la testa
```

> sì na mulichina sì 'n pochino
> ⌈('nsomma)
> I: ⌊ehe

Vania specifies some of the serious consequences of the treatment. The interviewer asks her to detail the behaviour, 'but what does he do that is particularly', and then makes a suggestion, 'has he some moments of mental absence'. Vania's strong agreement, achieved through repetition of an item of the previous turn and two acknowledgement tokens, 'eh moments yes yes', does not seem to satisfy the interviewer who seeks further specification: 'how does it happen does he faint or (it is only a mental absence)'. Vania's answer 'no no he doesn't faint it is his head yes just a little bit yes a little bit (well)' is vague as a description of what her husband's problems actually are.

After this Vania starts complaining about the difficulties of communicating with her husband. Up to this point, as I say, it is not clear just exactly what his health problems are, nor is it clear what kind of caring Vania provides, how often, and with what support – in spite of insistent and repeated questioning. The difficulty of making sense of Vania's contribution to the conversation as a fact-finding exercise is made explicit in the next extract, and Vania appears to contradict her earlier statement, asserting that she is not doing any caring work for her husband at present.

(9)

```
1      I:   Um (1.0) but what do you mean what
2   →       what do you have to do for him I
3   →       mean I don't understand (really)  (  )?
4      V:   now for example now I don't do
5           anything anymore for him because at
6           this point I left my job and therefore
7           it's useless to have it back because at
8           50 years old nobody gives you a job

       I:   Um (1.0) cioè ma: che che:: gli deve
            fare cioè non capisco (bene)  (  )?
       V:   io adesso presempio adesso non gli
            faccio più niente perchè:: oramai
            tanto 'l lavoro l'ho lasciato:: e quindi
            'n utile a riprenderlo perché a
            cinquantacinquanni 'l lavoro 'n me lo
            dà nessuno
```

The interviewer does not simply ask for clarification: the *but* in line 1's question signals explicitly a judgement that Vania's answers have been accountably unsatisfactory, and the interviewer goes on to say *I mean I don't understand (really) ( )*. Notice that the interviewer takes a long time to make explicit her difficulties, and she does it in a quite mild form.

Signalling incomprehension is 'face' threatening, both for the doer and the recipient, and may implicitly question competence, cooperation and goodwill of both the interactants. Nevertheless, the interviewer does signal incomprehension, something she never did with Paolo.

At this point (line 4ff.) Vania says 'now for example now I don't do anything anymore for him'. Then, with the conjunction 'because', she introduces material about leaving her job, 'because at this point I left my job and therefore it's useless to have it back because at 50 years old nobody gives you a job'. Now, as Garfinkel and Sacks point out: 'there is a tremendous topical coherence in ordinary conversation' (1970: 354). Topical coherence is not only maintained within turns, but also between turns at talk by different interlocutors (Sacks, 1992, Vol. II: 254). In order to change topic, specific 'topic markers' are generally used. There is no component like this here, and, as in extract (7), topical shift is not signalled. A possible understanding of what Vania is doing is 'distracting'. 'Being a caregiver' is central to the conduct of the interview, so to admit to *not* being a caregiver, to be 'found out', as it were, would question the very status of the interaction and the meaning of the activity she and the interviewer are engaged in. Changing topic to the difficulties of employment for a 50-year-old woman directs the conversation to safer grounds. At the least, there is some ambiguity here, and again we see the interviewer, in the next extract, orient to it and hold Vania accountable for it.

Appealing to Common Sense

In line 1 the interviewer reconnects losing the job with Vania's caring commitments, and keeps pursuing an answer, inquiring after Vania's past experience of caring. A breach in communication is now signalled by Vania when she appeals to common sense.

(10)

```
 1        I:   you mean you left your job when he
 2             had this ⌈problem with the cyst
 3        V:          ⌊yes yes yes yes eh eh
 4        I:   and that and what did you have to do
 5             for him at that time
 6        V:   eh at that time I had to look after him
 7             (1.0) because I don't know well I
 8             had to be also careful taking him out
 9             (2.0) to be with him well (0.9) to
10             make him understand that it wasn't
11             serious well (1.7)
12   →    I:   you mean therefore it was mainly a
13   →         psychological help

14        V:   eh yes yes
```

15 → I: you mean of
16 V: but he doesn't ⌈help
17 I: ⌊but he didn't need for
18   example I don't know he was you had
19   (0.5) to bring his lunch in ⌈bed
20 V: ⌊no
21   well at the beginning when he was a
22   bit sick yes of course
23 I: yes ⌈(after) the operation let's say
24 V: ⌊that's eh normal isn't it?
25 I: but now eh
26 V: no now I let him go out he said he
27   went to look for mushrooms well
28   (1.9)
29 I: but let's say during a period of about
30   one year you had to be always
31   with him

    I: cioè lei ha lasciato il lavoro quando
       c' ha avuto questo
       ⌈problema con la ciste
    V: ⌊sì sì sì sì è è
    I: e quello e: che gli doveva fare in quel
       periodo
    V: e allora io dovevo sta attenta a lui::
       (1.0) perché: non lo so 'nsomma io
       dovevo sta attenta anche a portarlo
       via (2.0) de stargli vicino 'nsomma
       ecco (0.9) de farglie capì che non
       era niente 'nsomma (1.7)
    I: cioè quindi era più che altro un aiuto
       psicologico
    V: è sì sì
    I: cioè di
    V: ma lui non ⌈non aiuta
    I: ⌊(però non aveva bisogno
       ad esempio che ne sò che stava gli
       doveva (0.5) portare da mangiare a
       ⌈letto
    V: ⌊no bè, i primi tempi che è stato un
       po' male sì: certo
    I: sì ⌈(dopo) l'operazione diciamo
    V: ⌊quello è eh normale no?
    I: però adesso e
    V: no adesso l' faccio uscì ha detto che
       andava a cercà:: i funghi bah (1.9)
    I: però diciamo è passato un periodo
       tipo un anno in cui lei gli doveva
       stare sempre vicino

The interviewer keeps looking for a description of what Vania actually did: 'and that and what did you have to do for him at that time'. Vania describes the psychological support she gave her husband, 'taking him out (2.0) to be with him well (0.9) to make him understand that it wasn't serious well'. This does not seem to satisfy the interviewer, who asks for further details suggesting specific, 'more ordinary' caring tasks, 'but he didn't need for example I don't know he was you had (0.5) to bring his lunch in bed'. Vania acknowledges having performed such caring tasks, 'at the beginning when he was a bit sick yes of course', and then appeals to common sense, 'that's eh normal isn't it?' In this way Vania makes the interviewer's press for an account appear unreasonable. In ordinary conversation clarifications can be asked for to a certain extent, after which they are interpreted as a form of non-collaboration. Garfinkel's breaching experiments are a clear example of this. Asking for an explanation for a proverb or platitude is read as provocative and is readily sanctioned (Garfinkel, 1967: 42). Vania's 'that's eh normal isn't it?' can be read as provoked by the interviewer's puzzling request to spell out in detail what is, to Vania, conventionally obvious.

The interviewer re-directs the focus to the present situation, *but now eh*. Vania confirms her husband's good health and re-asserts that he needs no assistance, 'no now I let him go out he said he went to look for mushrooms well'. The interviewer, again with a contradictory *but* proposes a summary of Vania's past caring duty, 'but let's say during a period of about one year you had to be always with him'. Institutionally, the interviewer is there to find out about 'being a carer'; if Vania is not a carer, she must at least have been a carer in the past, otherwise there would be no institutional point to the interaction. Vania's identity as a caregiver orients the conduct of the interview. She is urged by the interviewer to make her being a caregiver witnessable, through producing descriptions of significant practices and pertinent discourses. Failing to provide the required identification undermines the very reason for the encounter.

Concluding Comments

Identification work influences the conduct of the conversation, that is, it orients conversational strategies and moves. As conversation unfolds it shapes different identities for the interlocutors in their here-and-now character (Schenkein, 1978). In the two interviews analysed here, I pointed out that the different ways of handling incoherence were related to age categorization. One speaker, Paolo, was identifiable on-sight as being 'very old', whereas Vania was, at least in contrast, identifiable in a category something like 'not so old as to be incoherent'. Any incoherence she displayed was treated as accountable, prompting requests for clarification and explanation. In the interview with Paolo, on the other hand, clari- fication and explanation were systematically avoided, and Paolo's incoherence was effectively excused by the interviewer displaying understanding of what he was (inarticulately) saying.

The different treatment of incoherence reflects on identification in various ways. In particular, I want to point out the paradox that the interviewer's avoidance of pursuing a coherent response has the effect of *actively constructing Paolo as excusably incoherent* – that is, senile. His accounts are inspected for signs of senescence, and, given his on-sight identity as 'very old', incoherence is expected. Paolo's age carries with it the category-bound feature of being – as it were legitimately – unable to make sense. Not to press him for clarity is to confirm that an inarticulate answer is not only understandable but incorrigible. With Vania, on the other hand, no such on-sight identity can protect her. Indeed, her footing in the interview is not only of a coherent person, but as someone who has special reason to be able to answer the questions, that is, a warranted caregiver. She is requested to stand by that identity and to testify suitably to it by being knowledgeable and fluent.

The paradox of Paolo's situation deserves a final comment. In the course of my interview with him my general intent in the conduct of the conversation was to encourage and bolster his ability to cope. Not seeking clarification was, on the face of it, generously motivated: it avoided pointing out the inadequacy of his answers, and maintained his capacity to converse effectively. But in so doing I was achieving the opposite aim: I was actively contributing to constructing Paolo as senile. If one can generalize, one implication this sort of observation might have is to suggest that personnel working with older people should be trained to be aware of such interactional processes and projections. Older persons will make sense, first of all, if people around them assume that they *can* make sense, and if they resist using the on-sight category of the old as a stereotype which inevitably casts them as being confused.

PART IV

EPILOGUE

12   Identity as an Analysts' and a Participants' Resource

Sue Widdicombe

The view of identity illustrated in this book is that identity is available for use: something that people do which is embedded in some other social activity, and not something they 'are'. This brings into sharp relief the notion that identities are put to local work, and the chapters in this volume attest to the great range of jobs that identities are used for: they may be invoked as footings for the conduct of business, to allocate blame and responsibility, to accuse and defend, to mobilize other identities, and so on. Moreover, the contributors have been concerned in different ways with the question of *how* identities are done, and the answer to this question, they argue, is to be found in a close examination of the details of talk-in-interaction. The important analytic question is not therefore whether someone can be described in a particular way, but to show *that* and *how* this identity is made relevant or ascribed to self or others. The analytic task is to delineate the descriptive devices, the properties of categories in talk, the technical skills of conversation which are employed in the service of mobilizing identities. If there is one defining principle displayed in this kind of analytic approach, it is the ethnomethodological one that identity is to be treated as a resource for the participant rather than the analyst.

This way of treating identity is, in the broader context of the social sciences, very distinctive and there are potential benefits to be derived from treating identity in this way. To appreciate this point, I want to outline various other approaches which have used identity as an analysts' tool. Obviously, an exhaustive review of the literature would be impossible given the limitations of space. I shall therefore restrict my review to some of the ways in which identity has been used as a strategic concept in addressing the relationship between individuals and society, and, related to this, in formulating how selves are socially constituted, and in explaining how social structures or processes affect individuals' lives. I will discuss three broad approaches to these issues: (i) traditional social science models, (ii) more recent constructivist alternatives, and (iii) postmodern perspectives.

Traditional Models of Identity

There are two broad ways in which identity has been used conventionally: (i) as bound to the social classification practices of social scientists, and (ii) to explain a range of social phenomena. As regards the first use, many approaches in sociology and social anthropology seek to describe the constitution of societies in terms of the social structures and institutions which are an integral part of those societies. Identity is a strategic tool in producing such taxonomies of society because it can be used to refer to groups, statuses, roles and, simultaneously, as a description of individuals. That is, in social identity 'the collective and the individual occupy the same [conceptual] space' (Jenkins, 1996: 26). However, identity is more than a descriptive label. It is also used to refer to the content or the defining criteria of the category, such as common experiences or fate, common origin, or common culture, which distinguish it from other categories. Identity is thus a useful tool for dividing up the social world and for saying something about those divisions.

Perhaps the clearest examples of this kind of approach are structuralist-functionalist theories of societies. For example, in sociology, identities such as working class, middle class, upper class, or white collar, blue collar, professional, and so on are treated as corresponding to an independently existing social structure, and researchers aim to specify the criteria which define class (see, for example, Giddens, 1993). In social anthropology, the concept has been used to describe tribes, communities and other collectives, together with defining elements of culture or lifestyle. On a broader scale, there are efforts to define national identities through geographical boundaries, a common language or ethnicity. Some theories simply assume that individuals' identities are ascribed by being assigned, by birth for example, to the categories which make up the social structure, although some identities are obviously acquired (e.g., institutional roles). Other approaches have been concerned to explain how ascribed or acquired identities are not just externally attributed, they are internally 'owned'. The ideas of socialization into and internalization of identities have figured largely in these more explicit attempts to link individual identities and social structure, and to show how individuals come to be constituted through social structures. Two theories in particular are worth mentioning for their explicit formulation of this process: role identity theory and social identity theory.

Role identity theory (Burke, 1980; McCall, 1987; Stryker 1987) views society as made up of roles, and explains how roles are internalized as identities which people enact and try to live up to. Social identity theory (e.g., Tajfel, 1978; Tajfel and Turner, 1979) and its more cognitive derivative, self categorization theory (e.g., Turner et al., 1987) have been discussed in several chapters of this book. They assume that social identities have a social reality by virtue of their relation to social groups and they have psychological reality (Hogg and Abrams, 1988; Oakes, Haslam and Turner, 1994; Turner et al., 1987). Specifically, the notion of internalization is used to claim that the structure of society (and the constitution of social groups) is reflected in the structure of the self. So, it is argued that individuals are born into and are ascribed particular social categories, but over time they develop an awareness of their membership, a preference for 'my group' over 'outgroups', and an emotional attachment to it (Tajfel, 1978). Social category memberships thereby become internalized as aspects of the self-concept and hence identity has a real psychological existence; it is an intrinsic and relatively stable aspect of the self-concept.

Self categorization theory formulates the psychological processes underlying the transformation of individuals into group members who act in terms of a particular identity. Turner et al. (1987) propose that the situational salience of an identity depends on the 'metacontrast' or perceived differences between members of potentially relevant categories and their fit with the consensual category stereotypes. When salient, the argument goes, individuals self-stereotype themselves in terms of these consensual criterial features and behave accordingly. They thereby become depersonalized and by acting as group members bring the group into existence.

I mentioned above that identity is also used as an explanation of social phenomena. In part, this function is derived from assuming a relation between the distribution of resources and identity. In other words, identity is seen as a criterion for the distribution of resources, including power and status. By identifying people in terms of categories like classes, ethnic groups, age groups, gender, and so on, it is thought possible to explain how social structures affect people's lives and to explain social behaviour. In traditional sociological research, for example, class and gender are used as key variables to explain, or at least shed light on, differences in life chances and opportunities, career patterns, and educational achievement, voting patterns, membership of youth subcultures, and so on. By contrast, social identity theory uses identity as a causal variable in explaining how people act to produce the kind of behaviour defined as social or antisocial. For example, Tajfel and Turner (1979) argue that intergroup conflicts develop as a result of social history, but they acquire their force because of the psychologically causal processes of categorization, identification and comparison. According to this view, prejudice and discrimination are caused in part by mental comparisons between 'us' and 'them' which are designed to ensure our superiority (Tajfel and Turner, 1979). Similarly, collective action is regarded as partly a consequence of the cognitive transformation of individuals to bearers of a social identity (e.g., Turner et al., 1987).

Underlying these approaches, whether sociological or social psychological, is a particular concept of identity which can be characterized as essentialist and realist. The concept is essentialist in the sense that identity is taken to be a property of individuals or society; and realist in the sense that it is assumed that there is some kind of correspondence between identity and some aspect of social reality (e.g., the real groups that make up social structures, or nations).

This concept also informs methodological efforts to get at individuals' identity and to use it as a predictive or explanatory variable. It underlies, for example, the way that sociological research often treats identities as demographic facts about people which have predictable consequences. It also informs the production of objective means of ascertaining, say, individuals' class membership, which in survey research can be used as a variable to be correlated with other variables similarly derived. Similarly, social psychological experiments often simply assume that their subjects will have internalized some 'obvious' category: men or women, Scottish or English, students in the Faculties of Science or Social Science, and so on, so all one need do is remind them that they are such people at the start of some experiment, and comfortably assume that they will act as such until its end. Such experiments use identity to make causal predictions about the attitudinal and behavioural consequences of making particular identities salient. A similar essentialist view of identity also informs efforts to get people to assign themselves to categories like class, or to quantify the strength or importance of particular identities via a Social Identification Scale so that identities can be more sensitively correlated with predicted outcomes (Brown et al., 1986; Hinkle et al., 1989). Finally, similar assumptions underlie the studies which aim to elicit the range of identities that make up the self-concept via people's responses to the pen-and-paper question, addressed to themselves, 'who am I?' (the prototype here is the Twenty Statements Test (TST) devised by Kuhn and McPartland, 1954).

Social Classifications and Participants' Orientations

The kinds of questions asked in traditional social science are *what* identities people have, what *criteria* distinguish identities from each other, and what *part* identity plays in the maintenance of society and in enabling the functioning of social structures and institutions. The aim, of course, is to delineate the general principles by which society functions or social behaviour is brought about, and social identities are assumed to have an overarching relevance in this respect.

The focus on identity as a participants' resource in conversation analysis generates very different questions and a very different focus. These different questions tie up directly with the ethnomethodological concern for people's own displays of understandings and conversation analysis' commitment to charting that understanding in talk-in-interaction. Thus a number of contributors argue specifically against treating identities as demographic facts, whose relevance to a stretch of interaction can simply be assumed (see, for example, Edwards, Antaki, Greatbatch and Dingwall). Similarly, the analyses in the chapters by Edwards and McKinlay and Dunnett very explicitly afford a contrast with those theories in psychology which posit an internal mechanism for making identities salient. They show that making an identity salient is demonstrably (and irredeemably) an indexical, local and occasioned matter, shot through with speakers' interests. Thus, instead of asking what identities do people have, conversation analysts focus on *whether*, *when* and *how* identities are used. In other words, their concern is with the occasioned relevance of identities here and now, and how they are consequential for this particular interaction and the local projects of speakers.

In line with this approach, conversation analysts have not been concerned with criteria which define categories. While they have noted that categories and hence identities are conventionally associated with attributes, activities, rights and obligations (see Widdicombe), conversation analysis is more interested in how speakers appeal implicitly or explicitly to this normative knowledge in constructing identities (see Edwards). It takes the view that normative knowledge has to be invoked and can be challenged and transformed, and this suggests that we cannot delineate category attributes or specify in advance which features of a category will be brought to bear on the business of identity on any particular occasion. Hence, we have to treat the status of normative knowledge as a participants' concern and be cautious of it as an analysts' resource (see Antaki and Greatbatch and Dingwall). Treating the status of normative knowledge in this way avoids the kind of difficulties that analysts have faced in trying to find objective and essential criteria which define particular categories. For example, despite the belief in the significance and determining influence of class, the specification of what defines class categories, and how to measure them, is a matter of some debate (see, for example, Giddens, 1993; Marshall et al., 1988). Similar difficulties plague efforts to define nations (see Billig, 1995; Layne, 1994 for a discussion of this problem). These difficulties are compounded by observations of the sheer variability of the meanings or features of categories and hence identities (see, for example, Antaki et al., 1996; Condor, 1989, 1996; Eickelman, 1989) and the way that the same cultural elements can be used by different groups as constitutive of their identity (Yuval-Davis, 1994).

These observations have in turn fuelled the kinds of debate about the ontological status of groups and social categories which has been an issue of dispute in the social sciences since Durkheim (see Greenwood, 1994; Turner et al., 1987; Weber, 1922). Conversation analysis avoids getting embroiled in these issues because it treats reality as a members' phenomenon. In relation to social groups or categories, this means that their status, as real or otherwise, is treated as a members' concern and accomplishment. We have seen, for example, how differences of opinion can be used to fragment gun-owners and hence achieve their status as not a group (McKinlay and Dunnett, see also Chapter 4 for other ways in which speakers avoid a commitment to the in-principle existence of, in this case, the category punk); conversely, similarity in opinion can be used to claim solidarity and achieve group status (Widdicombe). Indeed, just as the ontological status of categories is a much-debated issue among social scientists, studies of more ordinary talk show that categorizations are areas in which debate and negotiation flourish, not least because there is always something at stake in affirming or rejecting group categorizations (this is explicit in Edwards's and McKinlay and Dunnett's chapters, but is also a strong thread in Day's and Widdicombe's).

Finally, conversation analysis's concern with social interaction as a separate domain, only 'loosely coupled' with social structure (Zimmerman), as well as its concern with participants' orientation, also implicates a different view of the workings of social structures and other features of social organization. Indeed, it is worth bearing in mind that in developing ethnomethodology, Garfinkel (1967) was specifically opposing Parsons's (1964) view that institutionalized patterns of social relations – social structures – persist because people internalize cultural norms, which shape both their desires and the courses of action they adopt. Garfinkel argued that Parsons viewed individuals as judgemental and cultural 'dopes' who simply internalize and act in accordance with cultural norms. A focus on the domain of interaction, by contrast, allows insight into the achievements of people in constructing and maintaining their everyday world and thus how social order is possible. Building on this, conversation analysts are concerned with when and how people invoke, manifest, or otherwise make structure live in some given social interaction (see, for example, analyses in Boden and Zimmerman, 1991; and Drew and Heritage, 1992). Their work is guided by the principles that characterizations which connect to what is ordinarily meant by 'social structure' are relevant and consequential for the interaction and the parties are demonstrably oriented to those aspects of who they are (Schegloff, 1991). In addition, the kind of context which is implicated by social structures (e.g., the particular institutional setting) must be shown to be relevant and consequential for the talk.

There are several examples of how these principles are put into practice among the contributors to this book. For example, Greatbatch and Dingwall do not simply assume that some participants in the interactions they analyse are divorce mediators. Instead, they show how these identities are achieved: by invoking discourse identities consistent with this institutional identity; by collaboratively constituting them as neutral facilitators with special rights to manage the organization of turn-taking and the topical focus of talk; through their non-alignment with the disputants, and so on. Moreover, through the selective and asymmetric mobilization of social identities, and by jointly insulating divorce mediators from social identities like gender, age and class, participants display an orientation to conventions of divorce mediation and hence to the institutional context of the interaction. Similarly, Zimmerman examines how identity alignment in the openings and pre-alignment sequences in emergency calls is oriented to establishing the relevant context for the conduct of the business of dispatching emergency services. Hester's chapter too shows how ascriptions of deviance to children displays a sensitivity to their organizational relevance in that they are specifically designed to achieve organizational outcomes. One advantage of conversation analysis, then, is that it converts the sense of the relevance of social structure into analysis which is grounded in details of actual occurrences of conduct in interaction, and hence provides a detailed explication rather than merely a sense of how the world works (Schegloff, 1991).

Social Constructions of Identities

Taking identity seriously as a participants' resource therefore has several advantages in relation to the work it has been required to do by analysts. Nevertheless, across the social sciences, the main criticisms of, and alternatives to, traditional models are found in a variety of constructivist approaches which redefine identity as an analysts' tool, as well as the 'social' and 'the individual' which are thereby integrated. The concept of identity thereby produced is designed in part to deal with variability and flexibility and how even the most obvious identities are negotiable. It is also designed to overcome the kind of dualistic thinking which underlies traditional conceptualizations of the individual–society relationship; in particular, the idea of an independently existing social structure which enters equally independent individuals via internalization or socialization (see Henriques et al., 1984, for a critique). Although they are various, these approaches share in common an emphasis on the multiple ways that social identities are constructed, and how these constructions provide the resources through which individuals' subjectivities and experiences are shaped. Compared with the use of identity for classificatory purposes, or as a causal variable related to other phenomena, this view of identity, it is argued, enables social constructivists to provide a more integrated and dynamic view of individual–social relations. Examples of three broad ways in which this general view is expressed must suffice.

Identities, Groups and Boundaries

The models of identity developed by Barth (1969) and Cohen (1985) in social anthropology, for example, were designed specifically to counter the way that the existence of ethnic groups was traditionally taken for granted, and the tendency in structural-functionalism to over-solidify groups as social facts. Rather than treating social reality or structure as pre-given, they argued that there should be an emphasis on the capacity of humans to define social reality. In addition, rather than cataloguing the history or cultural characteristics of ethnic groups, they proposed that the focus should shift to the processes of ethnic boundary maintenance and group recruitment. In Barth's (1969) view, collective social forms are generated through interaction, and it is here that boundaries and group distinctiveness, as well as relevant criteria of membership, are developed and hence collective identities and individual identities are simultaneously produced. In Barth's model, interaction, like identity, is thus used as a theoretical tool which 'offers a bridge between individuals, their practices and their identities and the macro-level of social forms and collective identities' (Jenkins, 1996: 100).

Cohen's (1985) model of the symbolic construction of communities emphasizes, in addition to the construction of boundaries between 'us' and 'them', the role of symbolism in creating social solidarity. He proposed that the content of identity or community consists of a shared symbolic repertoire by means of which members construct a sense of their similarity in an ongoing historical process. In contrast to structuralist-functionalist models, Cohen argues that communities are not practical, material nor structural; they are cultural or subjective. That is, they rest on people thinking themselves to be part of a community and interacting with others to create the symbolic content or repertoire of identity which then comes to organize members' lives. This view of identity has much in common with Anderson's (1983) widely adopted view of national identity as based not in definable geo-social terms, but as an imagined community; that is, a group of people who feel they belong, together with a constructed heritage and culture.

Resources for Identity Construction

A second kind of social constructivist approach also draws on the idea that identities are symbolic or cultural resources, but it is more concerned with particular identities and how they are constructed through historical, political and cultural processes. These processes are said to construct identities at the collective level, but they also constitute the means by which individuals construct their identities and personal narratives or life histories. Sometimes, the emphasis on identity resources has a political thrust since it is argued that the symbolic or linguistic resources available provide possibilities and constraints on who individuals can be.

For example, a currently popular line of thinking and investigation has been the construction of multiple masculinities (and resources for defining what it means to be a man). Some ethnographic or historical analyses proceed by locating the construction of masculinity in different social institutions or workplaces, and seek to specify the practices, activities and values embedded within them which constitute masculinity (see, for example, Collinson and Hearn, 1996 on multiple masculinities in multiple workplaces; Haywood and Mac an Ghaill, 1996 on the ways that different kinds of values in the education system construct different kinds of teachers' masculinities). Other work has been more concerned with symbolic resources and representations. Canaan (1996), for example, examines the way that the activities of drinking and fighting are used as powerful symbols of masculinity. Featherstone (1991) examines the role played by consumer culture in creating images, representations and ideologies around the body, hence constructing a diverse array of possibilities of what it means to be a man. In social anthropology, and concerning a different kind of identity, Layne (1994) analyses the construction and reciprocal shaping of national and tribal identities in Jordan through the images promoted in political speeches, Royal tours, and by the tourist industry.

Such approaches focus on the availability of resources, generated at a societal level, but assume that in using these resources, people position themselves within society. Some social psychological versions of social constructivism are more explicit, conceptually and empirically, about how the linguistic resources or repertoires available in a culture are used by individuals to construct their self-understanding. In other words, they aim to show how cultural narratives become a set of personalized voices and positions (Wetherell and Maybin, 1996). One of the best examples of this work is Kitzinger's (1987, 1989) on the social construction of lesbianism. She draws on Jeffreys's (1982) historical analysis of how the invention of lesbianism as an identity emerged within the context of political struggles (Jeffreys, 1982; Weeks, 1981), and she provides an informed reading of social scientific and medical texts to make the case that the 'construction of lesbianism as pathology . . . provided, until recently, the major resource upon which lesbians could draw in explaining their "sexual orientation" to themselves and others' (Kitzinger, 1989: 83). Moreover, 'it served to structure lesbians' experience of themselves such that lesbianism was removed from the political arena and relocated in the domain of personal pathology' (ibid.: 84). By contrast, she argues, since the 1970s, liberal humanism has been the dominant cultural narrative. This offers alternative 'texts of identity' which find their expression in accounts which emphasize personal fulfilment, happiness, romance and love.

Identities, Discourses and Power

A similar conceptualization of how individuals are socially produced, via available resources, also informs poststructuralist approaches to the concept of identity and individual–social relations. There are, however, crucial differences in the aims and details of these approaches, partly because of differences in the theoretical tools used which include ideas of post-structuralist thinkers like Foucault and Althusser (whose influence I will concentrate upon here). These approaches accord a more central role to discourse as the dominant organizing factor and the means through which identities are produced (Burkitt, 1991). The term discourse also tends to have a broader meaning than the talk, texts, or linguistic repertoires which feature in some of the social constructivist perspectives. That is, discourses are variously interpreted as 'delimited tissues of meaning' (Parker, 1992: 6), as the instantiation of power-knowledge, or as ideological. This view in turn relates to a concern with broader 'ideological' processes and how they work to produce particular kinds of subjectivities. It also relates to a central aim of poststructuralism which has been to use a reformulated concept of identity to displace the kind of unitary, isolated subject assumed by the traditional approaches discussed earlier, and to rethink the onto-logical status of the self (or 'the subject'). Finally, these approaches use Foucault's claim that knowledge is socially constructed and intimately related to power to argue that the truth-seeking aims of traditional social science should be replaced with political aims of uncovering the operation of power and liberating the oppressed.

These aims are realized in part through the concept of identity as 'posi-tioning' in socially and culturally available discourses. Thus, Hall (1996) suggests that identity may be regarded as the meeting point of discourses and practices which 'call us into place' as the social subjects of particular discourses. It is argued that this spatial metaphor entails a shift, from questions of 'who I am' to notions of 'where I am', and that this is a more useful concept for analysts because it demands that we attend to the creation and production of those positions rather than treating them as given (Bondi, 1993). The idea is that discourses, and related discursive practices, form the raw materials and manufacturing processes through which people are produced. Hence selves and identities are regarded as the product of prevailing discourses which are tied to social arrangements and practices; the positions we adopt tie us into those social practices while providing the content of our subjectivity.

The notion of positioning and how it constructs persons has its roots in Althusser. His central thesis was that ideology 'interpellates' or 'hails' individuals into particular positions so that they come to have the kinds of identity which are necessary for social practices. More specifically, Althusser (1971) argued that ideologies (and hence discourses) have a concrete life within institutions embodied in 'ideological state apparatuses' (such as the media, churches, schools, trade unions). In all these places, people are subjected and trained to recognize themselves in particular ways, and they are thereby produced as particular kinds of being predisposed to certain kinds of activity which fit with the demands of society. However, Althusser also argued that as we live out the require-ments of the prevailing ideologies we are under the illusion that we have freely chosen our way of life.

Foucault's work is also used to warrant the constitutive role of dis-courses in identity as well as a more political agenda for research. In his early work (1970, 1972) he was concerned with the role of the human sciences in defining reality or creating 'regimes of truth' which are embodied in discourses, and which achieve the subjection of the population into particular ways of thinking about themselves. In his later 'genealogical' work, Foucault (1977, 1981) developed these ideas by discussing various 'modes of objectification' and disciplinary technologies through which contemporary forms of subjectivity have been constituted. These included 'dividing practices' of separating certain categories of people from others, physically and socially, together with the scientific and social scientific 'modes of inquiry' which created knowledge about these categories of people. Moreover, the categorizing procedures of the social sciences have a role in the bureaucratic practices of government: they are one of the ways in which people are constituted as objects of government; they can be used as a way of intervening in people's lives and thus as a means of social control (Jenkins, 1996). Therefore, social identities 'exist and are acquired, claimed and allocated within power relations' (Jenkins, 1996: 25). So, the exercise of power, the production of knowledge, and institutional practices work together to produce multiple, overlapping and contradictory discourses which in turn create different kinds of subjectivities. Some subject positions are long-term, others temporary and fleeting; therefore the self, which depends on the changing positions we take up or resist, is in constant flux.

These ideas have been used to inform a theoretical and analytic approach to identity which foregrounds the relation between power and discourse to develop an explicitly political agenda for research (e.g., Gavey, 1989; Hollway, 1989). Specifically, it is argued that it is through discourse that material power is exercised and power relations are established and perpetuated (Gavey, 1989). Since identity and subjectivity are constituted through a person's positions in different discourses, which are related to different positions of power, they are by implication thoroughly political. Thus it is argued that to understand identity and subjectivity, we need first to identify the relevant discourses and the positions they make available. To do so, texts (i.e., anything with meaning) are examined to discover the discourses operating within them. To be useful, however, analysts are then told to examine the power relations that are facilitated, and the historical and structural conditions that give rise to those particular discourses, and their ideological effects (Parker, 1992; Wilkinson, 1991; see also Banister et al., 1994: Chapter 6). Within this approach, feminist poststructuralist analyses have given special emphasis to women's positions and other categories of oppression; black women, working-class women, and lesbians. The aim is to bring about women's liberation, to change oppressive practices, or to change gender relations by disrupting and displacing dominant (oppressive) knowledge or discourses (Gavey, 1989; see also Burman, 1990).

Analysts' and Participants' Projects

Social constructivist alternatives share in common with conversation analysis an emphasis on construction and variability as well as an anti-essentialist and anti-realist view of identity; that is to say, identity is not presumed to be a relatively fixed property of people or societies, nor is it assumed that identity terms are simply reflections of social and psychological reality. There is, moreover, a certain parallel in the way that analysts, like participants, mould identity to fit the work required of it. Nevertheless, there is a vast difference between the local projects in which speakers are engaged and the broader theoretical and sometimes political projects of social constructivists. This is reflected in the very different ways that the construction of identities is dealt with, conceptually and analytically. The aim for social constructivism is not to see what people do with identity, nor to see how identities are mobilized in immediate local contexts, but to provide general models and principles of the interrelationships between individuals and social forms, or to delineate the symbolic or linguistic constitution of cultural and hence individuals' identities.

Related to this is often a concern to replace the unitary self with the idea of a 'fragmented self' who is always in flux. So, it is argued that selves are constructed through the multiple discourses or narratives within which they are momentarily positioned. This solution to the problem of self, which is set against traditional assumptions of selfhood, has not however entirely satisfied its proponents. Some worry about the implications of this solution: are we merely constructed through discourses or other resources? And, if so, what does the positioning? For example, Heath (1981) argues that there must be something with the capacity to perform before it has been constituted within discourse as a subject, so we are forced to presuppose an already constituted subject. This, in turn threatens the aim of using identity to overcome the problems of assuming an underlying core self. Similarly, Hall (1996) argues that we need an account of the mechanisms through which subjects identify with positions, and how individuals 'perform' them in different ways. Hollway (1989) and Henriques et al. (1984) argue that without a theory – most promisingly a psychoanalytic theory – of a 'psychological subject' or 'a person in relation to discourses' (Hollway, 1989: 47), there is no way of explaining how discursive positions are held together, nor of accounting for the 'predictability of people's actions, as they repeatedly position themselves within particular discourses' (ibid.: 47; see also Butler, 1990, 1993). Nor, indeed, as Hall observes, will one know how a person might embody a discourse at one time and resist it at another (Hall 1996).

Like social constructivist approaches, conversation analysts are keen to point out that they make no intentionalist assumptions; they do not, in other words, assume an underlying self who brings about the actions accomplished in interaction. Nevertheless, the emphasis on interaction would seem to have several advantages in relation to the problems of the ontological status of self, and of how to produce a social vision of selfhood without denying human agency. A first point is that conversation analysis treats the reality of self as a members' phenomenon; from this point of view selves can be real by virtue of their functioning in people's actions and joint activities (see Shotter, 1993). Secondly, it has been observed throughout this book that identities are the products of joint actions and the intersubjective organization of verbal interaction: that is, their production is contingent on publicly displayed understanding. The focus of these chapters, for example, has been on what people are doing together in talk, on details of how identities are mobilized and co-produced. Conversation analysis thus implicates a thoroughly social view of selves embedded in social action and interaction. Moreover, conversation analysis provides in rich technical detail how identities are mobilized in actual instances of interaction. In this way, conversation analysis avoids the problem of 'how subjects are positioned' or come to be incumbents of particular identities without the need for a theory of self. That is, instead of worrying about what kind of concept of self we need to explain how people are able to do things, conversation analysis focuses on the things they do. Agency, in the sense of an action orientation is thus intrinsic to the analysis without locating it in self-conscious intentionality, cognitive process, or in abstract discourses.

A further use of identity found in some varieties of social constructivism is to help achieve analysts' political aims. Whereas traditional approaches regard identity as a criterion for the distribution of resources, and hence political, social constructivism is concerned with how power is inherent in the availability of resources for identity construction. Moreover, there seems to be a sense that issues of political concern and power can only be revealed in an analytic stance that adopts a broad, ideological focus on discourses as texts (e.g., Parker, 1992). By contrast, conversation analysts argue that asymmetries in status and the exercise of institutional power, for example, infuse social life at its most basic level of interaction; it is through their communicative competencies that people exhibit their orientation to the relevance of inequalities in actual episodes in their lives. So conversation analysis addresses the traditional concern with power at the level of the turn-by-turn sequential unfolding of interaction, by showing its instantiation in interaction: in, for example, pre-allocated turn-taking systems, or, to use some examples from this book, the details of how speakers resist the ascription of identities such as punk or carer (Widdicombe, Paoletti), or the relevance of ethnic identities (Day), or they display an orientation to the institutionalized rights of divorce mediators to 'police' the interaction (Greatbatch and Dingwall). Similarly, the powerful role of institutions in controlling what is defined as deviance is shown to be accomplished at a tangible level of interaction, specifically through teachers' descriptive practices (Hester). By focusing on the instantiation or embodiment of social structure in particular contexts and on particular occasions, conversation analyses 'demystify' and hence enhance our understanding of social structure and power.

Finally, conversation analysis's emphasis on identity as a participants' resource is free from the kinds of complaint which have accompanied its use as an analytic resource, in terms of which the products of research are interpreted. For example, one complaint levelled against ethnographic studies is that analysts' categories always stand as the framework within which activities, values, or other phenomena are interpreted (see, for example, Hammersley, 1990). Another is that the role of the interpreter is often ignored. The concern is that the analytic categories impose certain limitations on ways of understanding. (Though it should also be noted that efforts to identify narratives or repertoires fare better in this respect, since an effort is made to ground identities more explicitly in what people say.) The use of identity as an analysts' category has also been associated with a tendency to reify, albeit multiple, identities by first assuming a particular identity, and asking how it comes about, or trying to delineate different kinds of cultural identity within a particular site (e.g., school). This seems to compromise the constructivist thrust of the work.

Similar complaints have been levelled at the kind of discourse analysis practised by poststructuralists: for example, that its practitioners are reifying discourses and sometimes doing little more than labelling common-sense topics as discourses (Potter et al., 1990). A tendency towards ascriptivism has also been noted: that is, imputing a discourse to texts without explaining the basis for that imputation (Widdicombe and Wooffitt, 1995). A related point is that the 'texts' with which analysts often work are derived from interaction. Talk, as conversation analysis clearly shows, is designed for the interactional business at hand, and interactional considerations 'have an impact on the very composition of the utterances people produce; utterances which in turn become the "text" for discourse analysts to analyse' (Widdicombe and Wooffitt, 1995: 64). To treat talk as text, however, invites the analyst to overlook the situated relevance and production of communicative actions; instead, the details of what are said are simply glossed as illustrative of pre-defined discourses (Widdicombe, 1995; Widdicombe and Wooffitt, 1995).

Identities in the Postmodern Age

Postmodernists have used identity as a key tool in specifying the impact in people's lives of the changes and processes which have propelled us into postmodernity. For example, it is argued that the postmodern era is marked by a growing 'globalization' which is related to a matrix of economic, cultural and psychological changes (Kvale, 1992; Lash, 1990). Communication technologies like satellite television, electronic mail and the World Wide Web make it possible to encounter world-wide events and peoples and to experience multiple realities. On this basis, theorists argue that some identities, like nationality, are no longer relevant; instead, multiple narratives and new identities are emerging (Bauman, 1996). Some of these are related to globalization and the idea that we live in a 'global village' with trademarked corporate symbols like Coca-Cola and Levi jeans. (Although it should also be noted that commentators have also pointed to 'events in the world' which seem to suggest that nationalism is alive and well: the resurgence of nationalism and fundamentalism, ethnic cleansing, and the tightening up of immigration controls (e.g., Burman, 1994), as well as banal statements, little words, assumptions which pervade our everyday lives (Billig, 1995).) It is also argued that technological change has granted quasi-human agency to previously purely mechanical objects, and made humans themselves somehow more than human; so there is an interest in a theory of identities which dispenses with the human/non-human boundary (Michael, 1996).

Another feature of postmodernity is multiculturalism brought about by processes of colonial migration and immigration which have challenged the idea of a homogeneous culture and have produced cultural diversity (Bhabha, 1996). This has in turn produced a plethora of 'hybrid' or in-between identities and border identities. In addition, the postmodern emphasis on consumption rather than production has been used to point to the ways that consumers can create their own identities through their changing patterns of consumption (Billig, 1995: 132). In a more general sense it is argued that one effect of the uncertainty of the postmodern age, and changes in the nature of social relations (through divorce, premarital sexual relations, the movement of people), is that people experience a fear of commitment. Therefore, the postmodern problem of identity is said to be how to avoid fixation (Bauman, 1996).

The postmodern perspective on identities also has a political thrust in that, like the poststructuralists, identities are regarded as sites of political struggle. For example, it is argued that local, ethnic and gender identities have become sites for postmodern politics (Grossberg, 1996; Roosens, 1989) as those hitherto excluded from the power to make definitions are claiming the right to re-imagining the community (Billig, 1995), and to construct their own representations (Giroux, 1993). 'Life politics', rather than social structure and the bureaucratic mode of managing social processes and coordinating action, are said to be the life strategies that are currently consequential for shaping the identities of postmodern people (Bauman, 1996).

This, then, provides a different perspective on the relation between society and individuals. But one of the concerns expressed by com-mentators in relation to the postmodern thesis of identity concerns the fit between theory and the 'reality' of the individuals' lives it claims to be describing. For example, one complaint is that the thesis of postmodernity makes important psychological assumptions about the way identity is shaped, yet few analysts get around to talking to ordinary people to see how so-called subjects of postmodernity actually think and feel (Brunt, 1992; and Morley, 1992, both cited in Billig, 1995: 134; see also Billig, 1997 on the dearth of detailed ethnography in cultural studies). Poststructuralist and social constructivist work has not escaped these criticisms. Hearn (1996) argues that most social constructivist and poststructuralist versions fail to address the question of how the 'qualities' of masculinity relate to what men actually do. Cohen (1994) makes the point that delineating the symbolic and cultural resources for identity construction does not show

how individuals use these forms creatively to characterize their selves, to make sense of their world and how, in so doing, they are active in the creation of society (Rapport, 1993).

There is an important difference between the way the contributors to this book have (in their various ways) gone about things and the implications of these criticisms. It is this. Whereas critics seem to be primarily concerned with empirical investigations of identity from the 'ground up' to see how they fit with observations about the social construction of identities, or the postmodern state of identities, conversation analysts are not concerned with performing some kind of test of the goodness of fit. Instead, the point is that this work is of value in itself. What we hope to have done through this book is to show that the analysis of identities in talk is indeed a fruitful way to proceed.

Concluding Comments

In this chapter, I have traced through some of the ways in which identity has been used to conceptualize the relationship between individuals and society. I have noted the ways in which the concept has been variously redefined to fit with the broader theoretical concerns, aims and assumptions of theorists. In the hands of analysts, then, identity is moulded to do important conceptual work; it carries a heavy theoretical burden. I have also noted some of the conceptual and analytic problems encountered in the course of that work, and have discussed the way that an ethnomethodologically or conversation analysis-minded approach would deal with (or just bypass) some of those dangers. Moreover, I hope to have shown that taking seriously participants' orientation to issues of identity does not preclude, and may even enhance, an understanding of the relation between self and social structure, power, and the active role people play in constructing identities and creating social order.

References

Allwood, J. (1980) 'On the analysis of communicative action', in M. Brenner (ed.), *The Structure of Action*. Oxford: Basil Blackwell.

Althusser, L. (1971) *Lenin and Philosophy and Other Essays*. London: New Left Books.

Anderson, B. (1983) *Imagined Communities*. London: Verso.

Antaki, C. (1994) *Explaining and Arguing: The Social Organization of Accounts*. London: Sage.

Antaki, C., Condor, S. and Levine, M. (1996) 'Social identities in talk: speakers' own orientations', *British Journal of Social Psychology*, 35: 473–92.

Atkinson, J.M. (1984) *Our Masters' Voices: The Language and Body Language of Politics*. London: Methuen.

Atkinson, J.M. and Drew, P. (1979) *Order in Court: The Organization of Verbal Interaction in Judicial Settings*. London: Macmillan.

Atkinson, J.M. and Heritage, J. (eds) (1984) *Structures of Social Action: Studies in Conversation Analysis*. Cambridge: Cambridge University Press.

Baker, C. (1983) 'A "second look" at interviews with adolescents', *Journal of Youth and Adolescence*, 12: 501–19.

Baker, C. (1984) 'The "search for adultness": membership work in adolescent–adult talk', *Human Studies*, 7: 301–23.

Banister, P., Burman, E., Parker, I., Taylor, M. and Tindall, D. (1994) *Qualitative Methods in Psychology: A Research Guide*. Buckingham: Open University Press.

Barth, F. (1969) *Ethnic Groups and Boundaries: The Social Organization of Culture Difference*. Oslo: Oslo University Press.

Bauman, Z. (1996) 'From pilgrim to tourist – or a short history of identity', in S. Hall and P. du Gay (eds), *Questions of Cultural Identity*. London: Sage.

Bergmann, J.R. (1987) *Klatsch: Zur Socialform der disketen Indiskretion*. Berlin: de Gruyter.

Bhabha, H.K. (1996) 'Culture's in-between', in S. Hall and P. du Gay (eds), *Questions of Cultural Identity*. London: Sage.

Bhavnani, K.-K. and Phoenix, A. (1994) 'Shifting identities shifting racisms: an introduction', in K.-K. Bhavnani and A. Phoenix (eds), *Shifting Identities Shifting Racisms: A Feminism and Psychology Reader*. London: Sage.

Billig, M. (1985) 'Prejudice, categorisation and particularisation: from a perceptual to a rhetorical approach', *European Journal of Social Psychology*, 15: 79–103.

Billig, M. (1987) *Arguing and Thinking: A Rhetorical Approach to Social Psychology*. Cambridge: Cambridge University Press.

Billig, M. (1995) *Banal Nationalism*. London: Sage.

Billig, M. (1996) 'Remembering the background of social identity theory', in W.P. Robinson (ed.), *Social Groups and Identities: Festschrift for Henri Tajfel*. London: Butterworth-Heinemann.

Billig, M. (1997) 'From codes to utterances: cultural studies, discourse and psychology', in M. Ferguson and P. Golding (eds), *Cultural Studies in Question*. London: Sage.

Bilmes, J. (1992) 'Mishearings', in G. Watson and R.M. Seiler (eds), *Text in Context*. Newbury Park, CA: Sage.

Boden, D. and Zimmerman, D.H. (eds) (1991) *Talk and Social Structure: Studies in Ethnomethodology and Conversation Analysis*. Oxford: Polity Press.

Bondi, L. (1993) 'Locating identity politics', in M. Kett and S. Pile (eds), *Place and the Politics of Identity*. London: Routledge.

Brown, R.J., Condor, S., Mathews, A., Wade, G. and Williams, J.A. (1986) 'Explaining intergroup differentiation in an industrial organisation', *Journal of Occupational Psychology*, 59: 273–86.

Bruner, J.S. (1957) 'On perceptual readiness', *Psychological Review*, 64: 123–52.

Bruner, J.S. (1990) *Acts of Meaning*. Cambridge, MA: Harvard University Press.

Brunt, R. (1992) 'Engaging with the popular: audiences for mass culture and what to say about them', in L. Grossberg, C. Nelson and R. Treichler (eds), *Cultural Studies*. London: Routledge.

Bultena, G.L. and Powers, E.A. (1978) 'Denial of ageing: age identification and reference group orientation', *Journal of Gerontology*, 33: 748–54.

Burke, P. (1980) 'The self: measurement requirements from an interactionist perspective', *Social Psychology Quarterly*, 44: 18–29.

Burkitt, I. (1991) *Social Selves: Theories of the Social Formation of Personality*. London: Sage.

Burman, E. (1990) 'Introduction', in E. Burman (ed.), *Feminists and Psychological Practice*. London: Sage.

Burman, E. (1994) 'Experience, identities and alliances: Jewish feminism and feminist psychology', in K.-K. Bhavnani and A. Phoenix (eds), *Shifting Identities Shifting Racisms: A Feminism and Psychology Reader*. London: Sage.

Burman, E. and Parker, I. (eds) (1993) *Discourse Analytic Research*. London: Routledge.

Butler, J. (1990) *Gender Trouble*. London: Routledge.

Butler, J. (1993) *Bodies that Matter*. London: Routledge.

Buttny, R. (1993) *Social Accountability in Communication*. London: Sage.

Button, G., Coulter, J., Lee, J. and Sharrock, W. (1995) *Computers, Minds and Conduct*. Oxford: Polity Press.

Canaan, J.E. (1996) '"One thing leads to another": drinking, fighting and working-class masculinities', in M. Mac an Ghaill (ed.), *Understanding Masculinities: Social Relations and Cultural Arenas*. Buckingham: Open University Press.

Carver, C.S. and de la Garza, N.H. (1984) 'Schema-guided information search in stereotyping of the elderly', *Journal of Applied Social Psychology*, 14: 69–81.

Clayman, S.E. (1988) 'Displaying neutrality in television news interviews', *Social Problems*, 35: 474–92.

Clayman, S.E. (1992) 'Footing in the achievement of neutrality: the case of news interview discourse', in P. Drew and J. Heritage (eds), *Talk at Work: Interaction in Institutional Settings*. Cambridge: Cambridge University Press.

Cohen, A.P. (1985) *The Symbolic Construction of Community*. London: Tavistock.

Cohen, A.P. (1994) *Self Consciousness: An Alternative Anthropology of Identity*. London: Routledge.

Coleman, J.C. and Hendry, L. (1990) *The Nature of Adolescence* (2nd edn). London: Routledge.

Collinson, D. and Hearn, J. (1996) '"Men" at "work": multiple masculinities/ multiple workplaces', in M. Mac an Ghaill (ed.), *Understanding Masculinities: Social Relations and Cultural Arenas*. Buckingham: Open University Press.

Condor, S. (1988) '"Race stereotypes" and racist discourse', *Text*, 8: 69–90.

Condor, S. (1989) '"Biting into the future": social change and the social identity of women', in S. Skevington and D. Baker (eds), *The Social Identity of Women*. London: Sage.

Condor, S. (1996) 'Social identity and time', in W.P. Robinson (ed.), *Social Groups and Identities*. London: Heinemann.

Coulter, J. (1990) *Mind in Action*. Oxford: Polity Press.

Coupland, J. and Coupland, N. (1994) '"Old age doesn't come alone": discursive representations of health-in-aging in geriatric medicine', *International Journal of Aging and Human Development*, 39: 81–95.

Coupland, N. and Coupland, J. (1989) 'Age identity and elderly disclosure of chronological age', *York Papers in Linguistics*, 13: 77–88.

Coupland, N., Coupland, J. and Giles, H. (1991) *Language, Society and the Elderly*. Oxford and Cambridge, MA: Blackwell.

Coupland, N., Coupland, J. and Grainger, K. (1991) 'Intergenerational discourse: contextual versions of ageing and elderliness', *Ageing and Society*, 11: 189–208.

Day, D. (1994) 'Tang's dilemma and other problems: ethnification processes at some multicultural workplaces', *Pragmatics*, 4: 315–36.

de Certeau, M. (1984) *The Practice of Everyday Life*. Berkeley, CA: University of California Press.

Derrida, J. (1981) *Positions*. Chicago: University of Chicago Press.

Drew, P. (1978) 'Accusations: the occasioned use of members' knowledge of "religous geography" in describing events', *Sociology*, 12: 1–22.

Drew, P. (1987) 'Po-faced receipts of teases', *Linguistics*, 25: 219–53.

Drew, P. (1992) 'Contested evidence in courtroom cross-examination: the case of a trial for rape', in P. Drew and J. Heritage (eds), *Talk at Work: Interaction in Institutional Settings*. Cambridge: Cambridge University Press.

Drew, P. and Heritage, J. (1992) *Talk at Work: Interaction in Institutional Settings*. Cambridge: Cambridge University Press.

Drew, P. and Holt, E.J. (1988) 'Complainable matters: the use of idiomatic expressions in making complaints', *Social Problems*, 35: 398–417.

Edwards, D. (1991) 'Categories are for talking: on the cognitive and discursive bases of categorisation', *Theory and Psychology*, 1: 515–42.

Edwards, D. (1994a) 'Script formulations: an analysis of event descriptions in conversation', *Journal of Language and Social Psychology*, 13: 211–47.

Edwards, D. (1994b) 'Imitation and artifice in apes, humans, and machines', *American Behavioral Scientist*, 37: 754–71.

Edwards, D. (1995a) 'Sacks and psychology', *Theory and Psychology*, 5: 579–97.

Edwards, D. (1995b) 'Two to tango: script formulations, dispositions, and rhetorical symmetry in relationship troubles talk', *Research on Language and Social Interaction*, 28: 319–50.

Edwards, D. (1997) *Discourse and Cognition*. London: Sage.

Edwards, D. and Potter, J. (1992) *Discursive Psychology*. London: Sage.

Eglin, P. and Hester, S. (1992) 'Category, predicate and task: the pragmatics of practical action', *Semiotica*, 88: 243–68.

Eglin, P. and Wideman, D. (1986) 'Inequality in professional service encounters: verbal strategies of control versus task performance in calls to the police', *Zeitschrift für Soziologie*, 15: 341–62.

Eickelman, D.F. (1989) *The Middle East: An Anthropological Approach* (2nd edn). Englewood Cliffs, NJ: Prentice-Hall.

Featherstone, M. (1991) *Consumer Culture and Postmodernism*. London: Sage.

Foucault, M. (1970) *The Order of Things: An Archaeology of the Human Sciences*. New York: Vintage/Random House.

Foucault, M. (1972) *The Archaeology of Knowledge*. London: Tavistock.

Foucault, M. (1977) *Discipline and Punish: The Birth of the Prison* (trans. A.M. Sheridan). Harmondsworth: Penguin.

Foucault, M. (1981) *The History of Sexuality, Volume 1: An Introduction* (trans. Robert Hurley). New York: Vintage/Random House.

Garcia, A. (1998) 'The relevance of interactional and institutional contexts for the study of gender difference: a demonstrative case study', *Symbolic Interaction*, 21: 35–58.

Garfinkel, H. (1967) *Studies in Ethnomethodology*. Englewood Cliffs, NJ: Prentice-Hall.

Garfinkel, H. and Sacks, H. (1970) 'On formal structures of practical actions', in J.C. McKinney and E.A. Tiryakian (eds), *Theoretical Sociology: Perspectives and Developments*. New York: Appleton-Century-Crofts.

Gavey, N. (1989) 'Feminist poststructuralism and discourse analysis: contributions to feminist psychology', *Psychology of Women Quarterly*, 13: 459–75.

Gibbs, R.W. (1994) *The Poetics of Mind: Figurative Thought, Language, and Understanding*. Cambridge: Cambridge University Press.

Giddens, A. (1993) *Sociology* (2nd edn). Cambridge: Polity Press.

Gilbert, M. (1989) *On Social Facts*. London: Routledge.

Giroux, H.A. (1993) 'Living dangerously – identity politics and the new cultural racism', *Cultural Studies*, 7: 1–28.

Goffman, E. (1981) *Forms of Talk*. Philadelphia: University of Pennsylvania Press.

Goffman, E. (1983) 'The interaction order', *American Sociological Review*, 48: 1–17.

Goodwin, C. (1984) 'Notes on story structure and the organization of participation', in J.M. Atkinson and J. Heritage (eds), *Structures of Social Action: Studies in Conversation Analysis*. Cambridge: Cambridge University Press.

Goodwin, C. (1987) 'Forgetfulness as an interactive resource', *Social Psychology Quarterly*, 50: 115–30.

Goodwin, C. (1996) 'Transparent vision', in E. Ochs, E.A. Schegloff and S.A. Thompson (eds), *Interaction and Grammar*. Cambridge: Cambridge University Press.

Greatbatch, D. and Dingwall, R. (1989) 'Selective facilitation: some preliminary observations on a strategy used by divorce mediators', *Law and Society Review*, 23: 613–41.

Greatbatch, D. and Dingwall, R. (1997) 'Argumentative talk in divorce mediation sessions', *American Sociological Review*, 62: 151–70.

Greenwood, J.D. (1994) *Realism, Identity and Emotion: Reclaiming Social Psychology*. London: Sage.

Grossberg, L. (1996) 'Identity and cultural studies – is that all there is?' in S. Hall and P. du Gay (eds), *Questions of Cultural Identity*. London: Sage.

Hall, S. (1996) 'Introduction: who needs "identity"?' in S. Hall and P. du Gay (eds), *Questions of Cultural Identity*. London: Sage.

Hamilton, H.E. (1994) *Conversations with an Alzheimer's Patient*. Cambridge: Cambridge University Press.

Hammersley, M. (1990) 'What's wrong with ethnography? The myth of theoretical description', *Sociology*, 24: 597–615.

Haywood, C. and Mac an Ghaill, M. (1996) 'Schooling masculinities', in M. Mac an Ghaill (ed.), *Understanding Masculinities: Social Relations and Cultural Arenas*. Buckingham: Open University Press.

Hearn, J. (1996) 'Is masculinity dead? A critique of the concept of masculinity/masculinities', in M. Mac an Ghaill (ed.), *Understanding Masculinities: Social Relations and Cultural Arenas*. Buckingham: Open University Press.

Heath, C. (1992) 'Gestures discreet tasks: multiple relevancies in visual conduct and in the contextualization of language', in P. Auer and A. di Luziio (eds), *The Contextualization of Language*. Amsterdam: John Benjamins.

Heath, S. (1981) *Questions of Cinema*. Basingstoke: Macmillan.

Henriques, J., Hollway, W., Urwin, C., Venn, C. and Walkerdine, V. (1984) *Changing the Subject: Psychology, Social Relations and Subjectivity*. London: Methuen.

Heritage, J. (1984a) *Garfinkel and Ethnomethodology*. Oxford: Polity Press.

Heritage, J. (1984b) 'A change of state token and aspects of its sequential placement', in J.M. Atkinson and J. Heritage (eds), *Structures of Social Action: Studies in Conversation Analysis.* Cambridge: Cambridge University Press.

Heritage, J. (1985) 'Analyzing news interviewers: aspects of the production of talk for an "overhearing" audience', in T. van Dijk (ed.), *Handbook of Discourse Analysis* (vol. III). London: Academic Press.

Heritage, J. (1988) 'Explanation as accounts: a conversational analytic perspective', in C. Antaki (ed.), *Analysing Everyday Explanations.* London: Sage.

Heritage, J. and Greatbatch, D. (1991) 'On the institutional character of institutional talk: the case of news interviews', in D. Boden and D.H. Zimmerman (eds), *Talk and Social Structure: Studies in Ethnomethodology and Conversation Analysis.* Oxford: Polity Press.

Heritage, J. and Sefi, S. (1992) 'Dilemmas of advice: aspects of the delivery and reception of advice in interactions between health visitors and first-time mothers', in P. Drew and J.C. Heritage (eds), *Talk at Work: Interaction in Institutional Settings.* Cambridge: Cambridge University Press.

Heritage, J. and Watson, D.R. (1979) 'Formulations as conversational objects', in G. Psathas (ed.), *Everyday Language: Studies in Ethnomethodology.* New York: Irvington Press.

Hester, S. (1990) 'The social facts of deviance in school: a study of mundane reason', *British Journal of Sociology,* 42: 443–63.

Hester, S. (1992) 'Recognizing references to deviance in referral talk', in G. Watson and R. Seiler (eds), *Text in Context: Contributions to Ethnomethodology.* Newbury Park, CA: Sage.

Hester, S. and Eglin, P. (eds) (1997a) *Culture in Action: Studies in Membership Categorization Analysis.* Lanham, MD: International Institute for Ethnomethodology and Conversation Analysis and University Press of America.

Hester, S. and Eglin, P. (1997b) 'The reflexive constitution of category, predicate and context in two settings', in S. Hester and P. Eglin (eds), *Culture in Action: Studies in Membership Categorization Analysis.* Lanham, MD: International Institute for Ethnomethodology and Conversation Analysis and University Press of America.

Hinkle, S., Taylor, L.A. and Fox-Cardamone, D.L. (1989) 'Intragroup identification and intergroup differentiation: a multicomponent approach', *British Journal of Social Psychology,* 28: 305–17.

Hogg, M.A. and Abrams, D. (1988) *Social Identifications: A Social Psychology of Intergroup Relations and Group Processes.* London: Routledge.

Hogg, M.A., Terry, D.J. and White, K.M. (1995) 'A tale of two theories: critical comparison of identity theory and social identity theory', *Social Psychology Quarterly,* 58: 255–69.

Hoggart, S. and Hutchinson, M. (1995) *Bizarre Beliefs.* London: Richard Cohen Books.

Hollway, W. (1989) *Subjectivity and Method in Psychology: Gender, Meaning and Science.* London: Sage.

Jayyusi, L. (1984) *Categories and the Moral Order.* London: Routledge.

Jefferson, G. (1978) 'Sequential aspects of storytelling in conversation', in J. Schenkein (ed.), *Studies in the Organization of Conversational Interaction.* New York: Academic Press.

Jefferson, G. (1983) 'Notes on some orderlinesses of overlap onset', in V. D'Urso and P. Leonardi (eds), *Discourse Analysis and Natural Rhetoric.* Padua: Cleup Editore.

Jefferson, G. (1984) 'On the organization of laughter in talk about troubles', in J.M. Atkinson and J. Heritage (eds), *Structures of Social Action: Studies in Conversation Analysis.* Cambridge: Cambridge University Press.

Jefferson, G. (1991) 'List construction as a task and resource', in G. Psathas and R. Frankel (eds), *Interactional Competence.* Hillsdale, NJ: Lawrence Erlbaum.

Jefferson, G. and Lee, J.R.L. (1992) 'The rejection of advice: managing the problematic convergence of a "troubles teller" and a "service encounter"', in P. Drew and J. Heritage (eds), *Talk at Work: Interaction in Institutional Settings*. Cambridge: Cambridge University Press.

Jeffreys, S. (1982) '"Free from all uninvited touch of man": Women's campaigns around sexuality, 1880–1914', *Women's Studies International Forum*, 5: 629–45.

Jenkins, R. (1996) *Social Identity*. London: Routledge.

Kamler, B. (1995) 'From autobiography to collective biography: writing workshop practice with women 60–80'. Paper presented to America Educational Research Association Annual Meeting, San Francisco, California.

Kitzinger, C. (1987) *The Social Construction of Lesbianism*. London: Sage.

Kitzinger, C. (1989) 'The regulation of lesbian identities: liberal humanism as an ideology of social control', in J. Shotter and K.J. Gergen (eds), *Texts of Identity*. London: Sage.

Kuhn, M.H. and McPartland, T.S. (1954) 'An empirical investigation of self-attitudes', *American Sociological Review*, 19: 68–76.

Kuper, A. (ed.) (1977) *The Social Anthropology of Radcliffe-Brown*. London: Routledge & Kegan Paul.

Kvale, S. (1992) 'Postmodern psychology: a contradiction in terms?', in S. Kvale (ed.), *Psychology and Postmodernism*. London: Sage.

Laclau, E. (1990) *New Reflections on the Revolution of Our Time*. London: Verso.

Lakoff, G. (1987) *Women, Fire and Dangerous Things: What Categories Reveal about the Mind*. Chicago: University of Chicago Press.

Lash, S. (1990) *The Sociology of Postmodernism*. London: Routledge.

Lather, P. (1992) 'Postmodernism and the human sciences', in S. Kvale (ed.), *Psychology and Postmodernism*. London: Sage.

Lawrence, S.G. (1996) 'Normalizing stigmatized practices: achieving co-membership by "doing being ordinary"', *Research on Language and Social Interaction*, 29: 181–218.

Layne, L.L. (1994) *Home and Homeland: The Dialogics of Tribal and National Identities in Jordan*. Princeton, NJ: Princeton University Press.

Lee, D. (1987) 'The semantics of *just*', *Journal of Pragmatics*, 11: 377–98.

Lerner, G. (1992) 'Assisted story telling: deploying shared knowledge as a practical matter', *Qualitative Sociology*, 15: 247–71.

Lerner, G. (1993) 'Collectivities in action: establishing the relevance of cojoined participation in conversation', *Text*, 13: 213–45.

MacBeth, D. (1990) 'Classroom order as practical action: the making and unmaking of a quiet reproach', *British Journal of Sociology of Education*, 11: 189–214.

MacBeth, D. (1991) 'Teacher authority as practical action', *Linguistics and Education*, 3: 281–313.

Marshall, G., Rose, D., Newby, H. and Vogler, C. (1988) *Social Class in Modern Britain*. London: Unwin Hyman.

Matza, D. (1969) *Becoming Deviant*. Englewood Cliffs, NJ: Prentice-Hall.

Maynard, D. (1984) *Inside Plea Bargaining: The Language of Negotiation*. New York: Plenum.

Maynard, D.W. and Zimmerman, D.H. (1984) 'Topical talk, ritual, and the social organization of relationships', *Social Psychology Quarterly*, 47: 301–16.

McCall, G.J. (1987) 'The structure, content, and dynamics of self: continuities in the study of role-identities', in K. Yardley and T. Honess (eds), *Self and Identity: Psychosocial Perspectives*. Chichester: John Wiley.

McMahon, A. (1993) 'Male readings of feminist theory: the psychologization of sexual politics in the masculinity literature', *Theory and Society*, 22: 675–96.

Meehan, A.J. (1989) 'Assessing the "police-worthiness" of citizens' complaints to the police: accountability and the negotiation of "facts"', in D.T. Helm, W.T.

Anderson, A.J. Meehan and A.W. Rawls (eds), *The Interactional Order: New Directions in the Study of Social Order*. New York: Irvington Press.

Mehan, H. (1983) 'The role of language and language of role in education decision making', *Language in Society*, 12: 187–211.

Mehan, H., Heertweck, A. and Neihis, J.L. (1986) *Handicapping the Handicapped: Decision Making in Students' Educational Careers*. Stanford, CA: Stanford University Press.

Michael, M. (1996) *Constructing Identities*. London: Sage.

Moerman, M. (1974) 'Accomplishing ethnicity', in R. Turner (ed.) *Ethnomethodology*. Harmondsworth: Penguin. First published in J. Helm (ed.) (1968), *Essays in the Problem of Tribe*. Washington: University of Washington Press.

Moerman, M. (1988) *Talking Culture: Ethnography and Conversation Analysis*. Philadelphia: University of Pennsylvania Press.

Morley, D. (1992) *Television, Audiences and Cultural Studies*. London: Routledge.

Oakes, P.J., Haslam, S.A. and Turner, J.C. (1994) *Stereotyping and Social Reality*. Oxford: Blackwell.

Oakes, P.J., Turner, J.C. and Haslam, S.A. (1991) 'Perceiving people as group members: the role of fit in the salience of social categorisations', *British Journal of Social Psychology*, 30: 125–44.

Paoletti, I. (1997) 'La produzione dell'identità nell'intervista con anziane', in A. Macarino (ed.), *Analisi della conversazione e prospettive di ricerca in etnometodologia*. Urbino: Edizioni Quattroventi.

Paoletti, I. (1998a) 'A half life: women caregivers of older disabled relatives', *Journal of Women and Aging*, 11 (forthcoming).

Paoletti, I. (1998b) *Being an Older Woman: A Study in the Social Production of Identity*. Hillsdale, NJ: Lawrence Erlbaum.

Parker, I. (1992) *Discourse Dynamics: Critical Analysis for Social and Individual Psychology*. London: Routledge.

Parsons, T. (1964) *Social Structure and Personality*. New York: Free Press.

Payne, G. (1976) 'Making a lesson happen', in M. Hammersley and P. Woods (eds), *The Process of Schooling*. London and Henley: Routledge & Kegan Paul and the Open University Press.

Payne, G. (1982) 'Dealing with a latecomer', in E. Cuff and G. Payne (eds), *Doing Teaching: The Practical Management of Classrooms*. London: Batsford.

Pomerantz, A. (1984) 'Agreeing and disagreeing with assessments: some features of preferred/dispreferred turn shapes', in M.J. Atkinson and J. Heritage (eds), *Structures of Social Action: Studies in Conversational Analysis*. Cambridge: Cambridge University Press.

Pomerantz, A. (1986) 'Extreme case formulations: a way of legitimizing claims', *Human Studies*, 9: 219–29.

Potter, J. (1987) 'Reading repertoires: a preliminary study of some techniques that scientists use to construct readings', *Science and Technology Studies*, 5: 112–21.

Potter, J. (1988) 'Cutting cakes: a study of psychologists' social categorizations', *Philosophical Psychology*, 1: 17–33.

Potter, J. (1996) *Representing Reality: Discourse, Rhetoric, and Social Construction*. London: Sage.

Potter, J. and Reicher, S. (1987) 'Discourses of community and conflict: the organization of social categories in accounts of a "riot"', *British Journal of Social Psychology*, 26: 25–40.

Potter, J. and Wetherell, M. (1987) *Discourse and Social Psychology: Beyond Attitudes and Behaviour*. London: Sage.

Potter, J. and Wetherell, M. (1988a) 'The politics of hypocrisy: notes on the discrediting of apartheid's opponents', *The British Psychological Society Social Psychology Section Newsletter*, 19: 30–42.

Potter, J. and Wetherell, M. (1988b) 'Accomplishing attitudes: fact and evaluation in racist discourse', *Text*, 8: 51–68.

Potter, J., Wetherell, M., Gill, R. and Edwards, D. (1990) 'Discourse: noun, verb or social practice?', *Philosophical Psychology*, 3: 205–17.

Rapport, N.J. (1993) *Diverse Worldviews in an English Village*. Edinburgh: Edinburgh University Press.

Ridgeway, C.L. (1997) 'Interaction and the conservation of gender inequality: considering employment', *American Sociological Review*, 62: 218–35.

Roosens, E.E. (1989) *Creating Ethnicity*. London: Sage.

Rosch, E. (1978) 'Principles of categorization', in E. Rosch and B. Lloyd (eds), *Cognition and Categorization*. Hillsdale, NJ: Lawrence Erlbaum.

Sacks, H. (1972a) 'Notes on police assessment of moral character', in D. Sudnow (ed.), *Studies in Social Interaction*. New York: Free Press.

Sacks, H. (1972b) 'An initial investigation of the usability of conversational data for doing sociology', in D. Sudnow (ed.), *Studies in Social Interaction*. New York: Free Press.

Sacks, H. (1974) 'On the analysability of stories by children', in R. Turner (ed.), *Ethnomethodology*. Harmondsworth: Penguin.

Sacks, H. (1979) 'Hotrodder: a revolutionary category', in G. Psathas (ed.), *Everyday Language: Studies in Ethnomethodology*. New York: Irvington Press.

Sacks, H. (1992) *Lectures on Conversation* (ed. G. Jefferson, 2 vols). Oxford and Cambridge, MA: Blackwell.

Said, E. (1978) *Orientalism*. Harmondsworth: Penguin.

Schegloff, E.A. (1968) 'Sequencing in conversational openings', *American Anthropologist*, 70: 1075–95.

Schegloff, E.A. (1979) 'Identification and recognition in telephone openings', in G. Psathas (ed.), *Everyday Language: Studies in Ethnomethodology*. New York: Irvington Press.

Schegloff, E.A. (1982) 'Discourse as an interactional achievement: some uses of uh huh, and other things that come between sentences', in D. Tannen (ed.), *Analyzing Discourse, Text and Talk*. Washington, DC: Georgetown University Press.

Schegloff, E.A. (1984) 'On some questions and ambiguities in conversation', in J.M. Atkinson and J. Heritage (eds), *Structures of Social Action: Studies in Conversation Analysis*. Cambridge: Cambridge University Press.

Schegloff, E.A. (1987) 'Between micro and macro: contexts and other connections', in J. Alexander (ed.), *The Micro–Macro Link*. Berkeley, CA: University of California Press.

Schegloff, E.A. (1991) 'Reflections on talk and social structure', in D. Boden and D.H. Zimmerman (eds), *Talk and Social Structure: Studies in Ethnomethodology and Conversation Analysis*. Oxford: Polity Press.

Schegloff, E.A. (1992a) 'On talk and its institutional occasions', in P. Drew and J. Heritage (eds), *Talk at Work: Interaction in Institutional Settings*. Cambridge: Cambridge University Press.

Schegloff, E.A. (1992b) 'In another context', in A. Duranti and C. Goodwin (eds). *Rethinking Context: Language as an Interactive Phenomenon*. Cambridge: Cambridge University Press.

Schegloff, E.A. (1996) 'Turn organization: one intersection of grammar and interaction', in E. Ochs, E.A. Schegloff and S.A. Thompson (eds), *Interaction and Grammar*. Cambridge: Cambridge University Press.

Schegloff, E.A. (1997) 'Whose text? Whose context?', *Discourse and Society*, 8: 165–87.

Schenkein, J. (1978) 'Identity negotiation in conversation', in J. Schenkein (ed.), *Studies in the Organization of Conversational Interaction*. New York: Academic Press.

Schiffrin, D. (1977) 'Opening encounters', *American Sociological Review*, 44: 679–91.

Scott, J.C. (1985) *Weapons of the Weak: Everyday Forms of Peasant Resistance*. New Haven, CT: Yale University Press.

Scott, J.C. (1990) *Domination and the Arts of Resistance: Hidden Transcripts*. New Haven, CT: Yale University Press.

Sharrock, W.W. (1974) 'On owning knowledge', in R. Turner (ed.), *Ethnomethodology: Selected Readings*. Harmondsworth: Penguin.

Sharrock, W.W. and Anderson, R.J. (1982) 'On the demise of the native: some observations on and a proposal for ethnography', *Human Studies*, 5: 119–35.

Shotter, J. (1993) *Cultural Politics of Everyday Life*. Buckingham: Open University Press.

Silverman, D. (1993) *Interpreting Qualitative Data*. London: Sage.

Spears, R. (1997) 'Introduction', in T. Ibáñez and L. Iñiguez (eds), *Critical Social Psychology*. London: Sage.

Speier, M. (1971) 'The everyday world of the child', in J. Douglas (ed.), *Understanding Everyday Life*. London: Routledge & Kegan Paul.

Stryker, S. (1987) 'Identity theory: developments and extensions', in K. Yardley and T. Honess (eds), *Self and Identity: Psychosocial Perspectives*. Chichester: John Wiley.

Tajfel, H. (ed.) (1978) *Differentiation between Social Groups: Studies in Social Psychology*. London: Academic Press.

Tajfel, H. (1980) 'The "new look" and social differentiations: a semi-Brunerian perspective', in D.R. Olson (ed.), *The Social Foundations of Language and Thought: Essays in Honor of Jerome S. Bruner*. New York: Norton.

Tajfel, H. (1981) *Human Groups and Social Categories: Studies in Social Psychology*. Cambridge: Cambridge University Press.

Tajfel, H. (1982a) *Social Identity and Intergroup Relations*. Cambridge: Cambridge University Press.

Tajfel, H. (1982b) 'Social psychology of intergroup relations', *Annual Review of Psychology*, 33: 1–30.

Tajfel, H. and Turner, J.C. (1979) 'An integrative theory of intergroup conflict', in W.C. Austin and S. Worchel (eds), *The Social Psychology of Intergroup Relations*. Monterey, CA: Brooks/Cole.

Tajfel, H. and Turner, J.C. (1985) 'The social identity theory of intergroup behaviour', in S. Worchel and W.G. Austin (eds), *Psychology of Intergroup Relations*. Chicago: Nelson-Hall.

Turner, J.C. (1987) 'A self-categorization theory', in J.C. Turner, M.A. Hogg, P.J. Oakes, S.D. Reicher and M.S. Wetherell (eds), *Rediscovering the Social Group: A Self-Categorization Theory*. Oxford: Basil Blackwell.

Turner, J.C., Hogg, M.A., Oakes, P.J., Reicher, S.D. and Wetherell, M.S. (1987) *Rediscovering the Social Group: A Self-Categorization Theory*. Oxford: Basil Blackwell.

Watson, D.R. (1976) 'Some conceptual issues in the social identifications of "victims" and "offenders"', in E.C. Viano (ed.). *Victims and Society*. Washington, DC: Visage.

Watson, D.R. (1978) 'Categorisation, authorisation and blame-negotiation in conversation', *Sociology*, 12: 105–13.

Watson, D.R. (1983) 'The presentation of "victim" and "motive" in discourse: the case of police interrogations and interviews', *Victimology: An International Journal*, 8: 31–52.

Watson, D.R. (1990) 'Some features of the elicitation of confessions in murder interrogations', in G. Psathas (ed.), *Interactional Competence*. Lanham, MD: University Press of America.

Watson, D.R. (1997) 'Some general reflections on "categorization" and "sequence" in the analysis of conversation', in S. Hester and P. Eglin (eds), *Culture in Action: Studies in Membership Categorization Analysis*. Lanham, MD and London: International Institute for Ethnomethodology and University Press of America.

Watson, D.R. and Weinberg, T.S. (1982) 'Interviews and the interactional construction of accounts of homosexual identity', *Social Analysis*, 11: 56–78.

Watson, G. (1992) 'Introduction', in G. Watson and R.M. Seiler (eds), *Text in Context: Contributions to Ethnomethodology*. Newbury Park, CA: Sage.

Weber, M. (1922) *Economy and Society* (vols I and II: ed. H.G. Roth and C. Wittich). Berkeley, CA: University of California Press.

Weeks, J. (1981) *Sex, Politics and Society: The Regulation of Sexuality since 1800*. London: Longman.

Wetherell, M. (1996) 'Constructing social identities: the individual/social binary in Henri Tajfel's social psychology', in W.P. Robinson (ed.), *Social Groups and Identities: Festschrift for Henri Tajfel*. London: Butterworth-Heinemann.

Wetherell, M. and Maybin, J. (1996) 'The distributed self: a social constructionist perspective', in R. Stevens (ed.), *Understanding the Self*. London: Sage.

Wetherell, M. and Potter, J. (1989) 'Narrative characters and accounting for violence', in J. Shotter and K.J. Gergen (eds), *Texts of Identity*. Hemel Hempstead: Harvester Wheatsheaf.

Wetherell, M. and Potter, J. (1992) *Mapping the Language of Racism: Discourse and the Legitimation of Exploitation*. Hemel Hempstead: Harvester Wheatsheaf.

Whalen, J., Zimmerman, D.H. and Whalen, M.R. (1988) 'When words fail: a single case analysis', *Social Problems*, 35: 335–62.

Whalen, M.R. (1990) 'Ordinary talk in extraordinary situations: the social organization of interrogation in calls for help'. Unpublished PhD dissertation, University of California, Santa Barbara.

Whalen, M.R. and Zimmerman, D.H. (1990) 'Describing trouble: epistemology in citizen calls to the police', *Language in Society*, 19: 465–92.

Widdicombe, S. (1993) 'Autobiography and change: rhetoric and authenticity of "gothic" style', in E. Burman and I. Parker (eds), *Discourse Analytic Research: Repertoires and Readings of Texts in Action*. London: Routledge.

Widdicombe, S. (1995) 'Identity, politics and talk: a case for the mundane and the everyday', in S. Wilkinson and C. Kitzinger (eds), *Feminism and Discourse: Psychological Perspectives*. London: Sage.

Widdicombe, S. and Wooffitt, R. (1990) '"Being" versus "doing" punk: on achieving authenticity as a member', *Journal of Language and Social Psychology*, 9: 257–77.

Widdicombe, S. and Wooffitt, R. (1995) *The Language of Youth Subcultures: Social Identity in Action*. Hemel Hempstead: Harvester Wheatsheaf.

Wieder, D.L. (1974) *Language and Social Reality: The Case of Telling the Convict Code*. The Hague: Mouton.

Wieder, D.L. (1988) 'From resource to topic: some aims of conversation analysis', in J. Anderson (ed.), *Communication Yearbook 11*. London: Sage.

Wieder, D.L. and Platt, S. (1990) 'On being a recognizable indian', in D. Carbaugh (ed.), *Cultural Communication and Intercultural Contact*. Hillsdale, NJ: Lawrence Erlbaum.

Wilkinson, S. (1991) 'Feminism and psychology: from critique to reconstruction', *Feminism and Psychology*, 1: 5–18.

Willis, P. (1977) *Learning to Labour*. Farnborough: Saxon House.

Wilson, I. (1987) *The After Death Experience*. London: Sidgwick & Jackson.

Wilson, T.P. (1991) 'Social structure and the sequential organization of interaction', in D. Boden and D.H. Zimmerman (eds), *Talk and Social Structure: Studies in Ethnomethodology and Conversation Analysis*. Oxford: Polity Press.

Wooffitt, R. (1992) *Telling Tales of the Unexpected: The Organization of Factual Discourse*. Hemel Hempstead: Harvester Wheatsheaf.

Wooffitt, R., Fraser, N., Gilbert, G.N. and McGlashan, S. (1997) *Humans, Computers and Wizards: Analysing Human (Simulated) Computer Interaction*. London: Routledge.

Wowk, M.T. (1984) 'Blame allocation, sex and gender in a murder interrogation', *Women's Studies International Forum*, 7: 75–82.

Yuval-Davies, N. (1994) 'Women, ethnicity and empowerment', in K.-K. Bhavnani and A. Phoenix (eds), *Shifting Identities Shifting Racisms: A Feminism and Psychology Reader*. London: Sage.

Zimmerman, D.H. (1984) 'Talk and its occasion: the case of calling the police', in D. Schiffrin (ed.), *Meaning, Form, and Use in Context: Linguistic Applications*. Washington, DC: Georgetown University Roundtable on Language and Linguistics.

Zimmerman, D.H. (1990) 'Prendre position [Accomplishing footing]', in *Le parler frais d'Erving Goffman*. Paris: Les Editions de Minuit.

Zimmerman, D.H. (1992a) 'Achieving context: openings in emergency calls', in G. Watson and R.M. Seiler, (eds), *Text in Context: Contributions to Ethnomethodology*. Newbury Park, CA: Sage.

Zimmerman, D.H. (1992b) 'The interactional organization of calls for emergency assistance', in P. Drew and J. Heritage (eds), *Talk at Work: Interaction in Institutional Settings*. Cambridge: Cambridge University Press.

Zubaida, S. (1993) *Islam, the People and the State: Political Ideas and Movements in the Middle East* (2nd edn). London: I.B. Taurus.

Index